Lives of the Queens of England, from the Norman Conquest, Volume 1

Agnes Strickland

LIVES

OF THE

QUEENS OF ENGLAND,

FROM

THE NORMAN CONQUEST;

WITH

ANECDOTES OF THEIR COURTS,

NOW FIRST PUBLISHED FROM

OFFICIAL RECORDS AND OTHER AUTHENTIC DOCUMENTS, PRIVATE AS WELL AS PUBLIC.

NEW EDITION, WITH CORRECTIONS AND ADDITIONS.

BY

AGNES STRICKLAND.

||

The treasures of antiquity laid up
In old historic rolls, I opened.

BEAUMONT.

VOL. I.

PHILADELPHIA:
LEA AND BLANCHARD.
1848.

TO

HER MOST EXCELLENT MAJESTY,

Our Sovereign Lady Queen Victoria,

THE LIVES OF THE QUEENS OF ENGLAND

ARE BY GRACIOUS PERMISSION INSCRIBED,

WITH FEELINGS OF PROFOUND RESPECT AND LOYAL AFFECTION,

BY HER MAJESTY'S FAITHFUL SUBJECT

AND DEVOTED SERVANT

AGNES STRICKLAND.

(3)

CONTENTS

OF THE

FIRST VOLUME.

~~~~~~~~~~

1*

PREFACE

TO

THE FIRST EDITION.

~~~~~~~

An announcement of this work, the first volume of which is now submitted to the public, appeared in the Literary Gazette of August 26, 1837, and other leading periodicals of the day, under its original title of "Historical Memoirs of the Queens of England." I had *previously* had the honour of communicating to her majesty, queen Victoria, that for some years I had been engaged in preparing for publication, the personal history of those royal ladies, from many of whom her own illustrious descent is derived; and I was favoured with a most gracious permission from her majesty, to dedicate the work to herself.

A long and dangerous illness delayed the publication of the first series. Meantime, the title I had chosen was appropriated by another writer, and, under that very title, memoirs have been published of *some* of the queens whose biographies, in regular and unbroken succession, are comprised in the present series of the "Lives of the Queens of England."

Biography, however, especially when historically treated, is a widely extended field, to which all labourers are freely welcomed, in this intelligent age of inquiry. Such opposite views, indeed, are taken of the same events and characters, by persons of differently constituted minds, that the cause of truth is sure to be benefited, when the research of several writers is directed to the same subjects.

"Facts, not opinions," should be the motto of every candid historian; and it is a sacred duty to assert nothing lightly, or without good evidence, of those who can no longer answer for themselves. I have borne in mind the charge which prefaces the juryman's oath,—it runs as follows:—"You shall truly and justly try this cause; you shall present no one from malice; you shall excuse no one from favour," &c. &c.

Feeling myself thus charged, by each and every one of the buried queens of England, whose actions, *from the cradle to the tomb*, I was about to lay before the public, I considered the responsibility of the task, rather than the necessity of expediting the publication of the work. The number of authorities required, some of which could not be obtained in England, and the deep research among the Norman, Provençal, French, and monastic Latin chroniclers, that was indispensably necessary, made it impossible to hurry out a work which I hoped to render permanently useful.

As it has been one of my principal objects to render the Lives of our Queens a work of general interest to every class of readers, I have modernized the orthography of extracts from ancient authors, and endeavoured as much as possible to avoid prolix and minute details, on matters more suited to the researches of the antiquary than to volumes which, I would fain hope, may find a place in domestic libraries, as well as public literary institutions.

The Introduction contains brief notices of our ancient British and Saxon queens. Their records are, indeed, too scanty to admit of any other arrangement. Yet a work professing to be the history of the female royalty of our country, would have been incomplete without some mention of those princesses.

The plan of chronological arrangement adopted in this work presented, at first sight, great difficulties in writing the lives of queens who survived their royal husbands, and were involved, as queen-dowagers, with the annals of succeeding queen-consorts. Sometimes there have been two dowager-queens of England contemporaries, or two dowager-queens and a queen-consort, as in the reign of John, when Eleanora, the widow of Henry II., Berengaria, the widow of Richard I., and Isabella, the consort of John, were all in existence at the same period. In these instances, and others where it has been necessary to avoid the evil of a twice-told tale, or confusion of dates, the sequel of the queen-dowager's memoirs has been related among the chronological events of the era to which it belonged.

The biographies of the queens of England commence, in their natural order, with the life of Matilda, the consort of William the Conqueror, the first of our Anglo-Norman queens, and the mother of the succeeding line of kings, whose dynasty, in the person of our present sovereign lady, queen Victoria, occupies the throne of England. Independently of her important position among the queens of England, the incidents of the life of Matilda are peculiarly interesting, and it affords me much pleasure to make her better known to the English reader, since the rich materials of which her memoir is composed are chiefly derived from untranslated Norman and Latin chronicles.

The history of the empress Matilda is incorporated with those of the contemporary queens of England, with whose annals the events of her life are inseparably connected.

As the uniting link of the Anglo-Saxon and Anglo-Norman dynasties, as the mother of the royal line of Plantagenet kings, the empress Matilda is a character of great importance in the annals of England; but she has never been included by any historian, either ancient or modern, in the catalogue of English sovereigns. Even on her great seal she claimed no other title than that of "Domina of England;" and as she was neither a crowned nor anointed sovereign, and, though queen *de jure*, she failed to establish her rights by force, and voluntarily ceded them to her son Henry II., a separate memoir of this princess could not with propriety appear among those of the queens of England.

The life of Berengaria, the crusading queen of Richard Cœur de Lion, is for the first time presented to the public, in the second volume of this work.

The memoir of Isabella of Valois, the virgin widow of Richard II., with whose eventful history some authors are little acquainted, is included in these biographies.

The memoir of Margaret of Anjou contains a portion of her life which is at present unknown to English historians—the details of her childhood and early youth. These are derived from the most authentic sources, and comprise many new particulars, both of her personal and public life as queen of England, and the mournful epoch of her widowhood.

The life of Katharine Parr will, I venture to hope, form an attractive portion of the fifth volume of the Lives of the Queens of England;— my ancestral connexion with that queen affording me peculiar facilities as her biographer.

The personal histories of the Anglo-Norman and several of the Plantagenet queens are involved in such great obscurity, that it has cost years of patient research, among English and foreign chronicles, ancient records, antiquarian literature, and collateral sources of information of various kinds, to trace out the events of their lives, from the cradle to the grave. The most difficult part of the undertaking is now achieved; for the concluding volumes of the lives and times of the queens of England belong to eras abounding in authentic materials for royal biography. State papers, autograph letters, and other important documents, which the antiquarian taste of the present age has drawn forth, from repositories, where they have slumbered among the dust of centuries, to afford their silent, but incontrovertible evidence, on matters connected both with the public and private history of royalty, enable those writers who, unbiassed by the leaven of party spirit, deal in facts, rather than opinions, to unravel the tangled web of falsehood, and to set forth the truth in all sincerity.

In conclusion, I have to acknowledge my obligations to his grace the duke of Norfolk, and to Mr. Howard of Corby, the descendants of queen Adelicia, for some important particulars connected with the life of that princess, for which I was indebted to the "Memorials of the Howard Family." To Mr. Howard, indeed, my thanks are peculiarly due, as well as to his accomplished son, Philip H. Howard, Esq. M.P. for Carlisle. I am likewise deeply indebted to my learned friends, Sir Thomas Phillips of Middlehill, Sir Harris Nicolas, and Sir Cuthbert Sharp, for their inestimable kindness in regard to MSS. and books of reference.

The courteous attention I have received from Sir William Woods, garter king-at-arms, and the valuable assistance afforded by G. F. Beltz, Esq. Lancaster Herald, and C. G. Young, Esq. York Herald, claim also my grateful remembrance.

My acknowledgments must likewise be offered to the Earl of Stradbroke, Lord Manners, D. E. Davey, Esq., and other learned and noble individuals in my native county, who have facilitated my arduous undertaking, by placing their extensive and valuable libraries at my disposal; nor can I omit to express my sincere appreciation of the courteous attention and assistance I have received during my researches, from Mr. Cates and Mr. Grabham, librarians at the British Museum, and other gentlemen connected with that national treasury of learning.

My warmest thanks are due to my accomplished friend, Mademoiselle Fontaine, of Neuilly, for her unwearied kindness in supplying me with foreign chronicles, and in transcribing French documents from the "Bibliothèque du Roi," not always accessible in England: also to the Rev. J. Hunter, of the augmentation Record Office; to J. Bruce, Esq., the treasurer of the Camden Society, and the learned editor of some of its publications; to J. O. Halliwell, Esq., to whose research and literary labours that Society is so much indebted; and last, not least, to that dear sister who is my fellow-labourer and faithful assistant in the Lives of the Queens of England, though she has forbidden her name to be united on the title-page with that of

AGNES STRICKLAND.

Reydon Hall, Suffolk,
Dec. 16th, 1839.

PREFACE

TO

THE SECOND EDITION.

~~~~~~~~~

THE demand for the three volumes of the " Lives of the Queens of England," already before the public, has been so unexpectedly rapid, that a very large edition has been exhausted, and a reprint of the commencing portion of the work is required, before the concluding volumes could be brought through the press.

This unusual, but most gratifying circumstance, has afforded an opportunity for corrections and additions, which, it is hoped, will render the publication more worthy of the flattering reception with which it has been honoured, both by the critical press and the public, to whom my grateful acknowledgments are due. I likewise avail myself of this circumstance to express my warmest thanks to that great historian, Dr. Lingard, for the valuable assistance he has rendered me in the present edition.

(xi)

PREFACE

TO

THE THIRD EDITION.

In introducing a third edition of these volumes of the " Lives of the Queens of England," it may be proper to state, that they have again undergone a complete and very careful revision, and that various additions have been made tending to increase the interest of the work. The publication of the seventh volume, containing the sequel of queen Elizabeth's memoirs, and the life of the first queen of Great Britain, Anne of Denmark, has been somewhat delayed, in consequence, but will be forthcoming very early in the new year.

The unequivocal tokens of national approbation, indicated by the repeated call for reprints of the series of the " Lives of the Queens of England," already before the public, while they convey a proud reward for the time and labour employed in the undertaking, will, at the same time, afford an additional stimulus for endeavouring to render the concluding volumes more worthy the attention of the lovers of historical literature.

Reydon Hall, Suffolk,
    Dec. 14th, 1843.

(xii)

INTRODUCTION.

"The Queen of England," says that learned commentator on the laws and constitution of this country, Blackstone, "is either queen-regnant, queen-consort, or queen-dowager." The first of these is a female sovereign reigning in her own right, and exercising all the functions of regal authority in her own person,—as in the case of her present majesty, queen Victoria, who ascended the throne, both by rightful inheritance, the consent of the people, and also in full accordance with the ancient British custom, noticed by Tacitus in these remarkable words:—"Solent fœminarum ducta bellare, et sexum in imperiis non discernere."[1]

No other princess has, however, been enthroned in this land, under such auspicious circumstances as our present sovereign lady.

Mary I. was not recognised without bloodshed. Elizabeth's title was disputed. Mary II. was only a sovereign in name, and as much dependent on the will of her royal husband as a queen-consort. The archbishop of Canterbury forfeited the primacy of England, for declining to assist at her coronation, or to take the oaths. The same scruples of conscience withheld the nonjuring bishops and clergy, and many of the nobility and gentry, of England, from performing their homage either to her or to queen Anne.

Not one of those four queens, therefore, was crowned with the unanimous consent of her people. But the rapturous acclamations that drowned the pealing of the bells and the thunders of the artillery, at the recognition of our beloved liege lady, queen Victoria, in Westminster Abbey, can never be forgotten, by those who then heard the voices of a united nation uplifted in assent. I was present, and felt the massy walls of the Abbey thrill, from base to tower, with the mighty sound, as the burst of loyal enthusiasm within that august sanctuary was echoed by the thronging multitude without, hailing her queen by universal suffrage.

The queen-regnant, in addition to the cares of government, has to preside over all the arrangements connected with female royalty, which, in the reign of a married king, devolve on the queen-consort; she has, therefore, more to occupy her time and attention than a king,

---

[1] Life of Agricola.

for whom the laws of England expressly provide, that he is not to be troubled with his wife's affairs, like an ordinary husband.

There have been but three unmarried kings of England, William Rufus, Edward V., and Edward VI. The two latter were removed at a very tender age; but the Red King was a determined bachelor, and his court, unrestrained by the presence and beneficial influence of a queen, was the focus of profaneness and all evil-doing.

The queens of England, commencing the series with Matilda, the wife of William the Conqueror, are forty in number, including her present majesty queen Victoria, the sovereign of these realms, and Adelaide, our revered queen-dowager.

Of these, five are queen-regnants, or sovereigns, and thirty-five queen-consorts. Our present series begins, not according to rank, but chronological order, with the queen-consorts, of whom there were twenty-six, before a female monarch, ascending the throne, combined in her own person the high office of queen and sovereign of England. The lives of the queen-regnants will appear in due course, our great object being to present, in a regular and connected chain, the history of female royalty, to trace the progress of civilization, learning, and refinement in this country, and to show how greatly these were affected by queenly influence in all ages.

The wives of the kings of England, though wisely excluded by the constitution of the realm from any share in the government, have frequently exercised considerable authority in affairs of state, and some have been regents of the kingdom; every one has been more or less a character of historical importance, as will be shown in their respective biographies.

The earliest British queen named in history is Cartismandua, who, though a married woman, appears to have been the sovereign of the Brigantes, reigning in her own right. This was about the year 50.

Boadicea, or Bodva, the warrior queen of the Iceni, succeeded her deceased lord, king Prasutagus, in the regal office. Speed gives us a curious print of one of her coins, in his chronicle. The description of her dress and appearance, on the morning of the battle, that ended so disastrously for the royal amazon and her country, quoted from a Roman historian, is remarkably picturesque:—

"After she had dismounted from her chariot, in which she had been driving from rank to rank to encourage her troops, attended by her daughters and her numerous army, she proceeded to a throne of marshy turfs, apparelled after the fashion of the Romans, in a loose gown of changeable colours, under which she wore a kirtle very thickly plaited, the tresses of her yellow hair hanging to the skirts of her dress. About her neck she wore a chain of gold, and bore a light spear in her hand, being of person tall, and of a comely, cheerful, and modest countenance; and so a while she stood, pausing to survey her army, and being regarded with reverential silence, she addressed to them an impassioned and eloquent speech on the wrongs of her country."

The overthrow and death of this heroic princess took place in the year 60.

There is every reason to suppose that the majestic code of laws, called the common law of England, usually attributed to Alfred, were by him derived from the laws first established by a British queen. "Martia," says Holinshed,[1] "surnamed Proba, or the Just, was the

---

[1] Holinshed's Description of England, vol. i., p. 298, 4to. ed.

widow of Gutiline, king of the Britons, and was left protectress of the realm during the minority of her son. Perceiving much in the conduct of her subjects which needed reformation, she devised sundry wholesome laws which the Britons, after her death, named the Martian statutes. Alfred caused the laws of this excellently learned princess, whom all commended for her knowledge of the Greek tongue, to be established in the realm." These laws, embracing trial by jury and the just descent of property, were afterwards collated and still farther improved by Edward the Confessor, and were as pertinaciously demanded from the successors of William the Conqueror, by the Anglo-Normans, as by their Anglo-Saxon subjects.

Rowena, the wily Saxon princess, who, in an evil hour for the unhappy people of the land, became the consort of Vortigern in the year 450, is the next queen whose name occurs in our early annals.

Guiniver, the golden-haired queen of Arthur, and her faithless successor and namesake, have been so mixed up with the tales of the romance poets and troubadours, that it would be difficult to trace a single fact connected with either.

Among the queens of the Saxon Heptarchy, we hail the nursing mothers of the Christian faith in this island, who firmly established the good work begun by the British lady Claudia and the empress Helena.

The first and most illustrious of these queens was Bertha, the daughter of Cherebert, king of Paris, who had the glory of converting her pagan husband, Ethelbert, the king of Kent, to that faith of which she was so bright an ornament, and of planting the first Christian church at Canterbury. Her daughter, Ethelburga, was in like manner the means of inducing her valiant lord, Edwin, king of Northumbria, to embrace the Christian faith. Eanfled, the daughter of this illustrious pair, afterwards the consort of Oswy, king of Mercia, was the first individual who received the sacrament of baptism in Northumbria.

In the eighth century, the consorts of the Saxon kings were excluded, by a solemn law, from sharing in the honours of royalty, on account of the crimes of the queen Edburga, who had poisoned her husband, Brihtric, king of Wessex; and even when Egbert consolidated the kingdoms of the Heptarchy into an empire, of which he became the Bretwalda, or sovereign, his queen Redburga was not permitted to participate in his coronation.

Osburga, the first wife of Ethelwulph, and the mother of the great Alfred, was also debarred from this distinction; but when, on her death, or, as some historians say, her divorce, Ethelwulph espoused the beautiful and accomplished Judith, the sister of the emperor of the Franks, he violated this law, by placing her beside him on the King's Bench, and allowing her a chair of state, and all the other distinctions to which her high birth entitled her.

This afforded a pretence to his ungallant subjects, for a general revolt, headed by his eldest son Ethelbald, by whom he was deprived of half his dominions. Yet Ethelbald, on his father's death, was so captivated by the charms of the fair cause of his parricidal rebellion, that he outraged all Christian decency, by marrying her.

The beautiful and unfortunate Elgiva, the consort of Edwy, has afforded a favourite theme for poetry and romance; but the partisans of her great enemy, Dunstan, have so mystified her history, that it would be no easy matter to give an authentic account of her life.

Elfrida, the fair and false queen of Edgar, has acquired an infamous celebrity, for her remorseless hardness of heart. She did not possess the talents necessary to the accomplishment of her design, of seizing the reins of government, after she had assassinated her unfortunate step-son at Corfe Castle: for in this she was entirely circumvented by the political genius of Dunstan, the master spirit of the age.

Emma of Normandy, the beautiful queen of Ethelred, and afterwards of Canute, plays a conspicuous part in the Saxon Annals. There is a Latin treatise, written in her praise by a contemporary historian, entitled, "*Encomium Emmæ*;" but, notwithstanding the florid commendations there bestowed upon her, the character of this queen must be considered a doubtful one. The manner in which she sacrificed the interests of her children by her first husband, Ethelred, to those by her second unnatural marriage with the Danish conqueror, is little to her credit, and was certainly never forgiven by her son, Edward the Confessor; though that monarch, after he had witnessed the triumphant manner in which she cleared herself of the charges brought against her by her foes, by passing through the ordeal of walking barefoot, unscathed, over the nine red-hot ploughshares in Winchester Cathedral, threw himself at her feet in a transport of filial penitence, implored her pardon with tears, and submitted to the discipline at the high altar, as a penance for having exposed her to such a test of her innocence.[1]

Editha, the consort of Edward the Confessor, was not only an amiable, but a learned lady. The Saxon historian, Ingulphus, himself a scholar at Westminster Monastery, close by Editha's palace, affirms that the queen used frequently to intercept him and his schoolfellows in her walks, and ask them questions on their progress in Latin, or, in the words of his translator, "moot points of grammar with them, in which she oftentimes posed them." Sometimes she gave them a piece of silver or two out of her own purse, and sent them to the palace buttery, to breakfast. She was skilful in the works of the needle, and with her own hands she embroidered the garments of her royal husband, Edward the Confessor. Editha is perhaps the most interesting of all our Saxon queens, and it was not without regret that we felt precluded, by the nature of the plan we have adopted, from including her life in the present series of the Lives of the Queens of England.

---

[1] Milner's Winchester.

MATILDA OF FLANDERS,

QUEEN OF WILLIAM THE CONQUEROR.

CHAPTER I.

Title of queen—Regina—Matilda first so called—Her descent from Alfred—Parents—Education—Learning—Beauty—Character—Skill in embroidery—Sought in marriage by William of Normandy—His passionate love—Unsuccessful courtship—Brihtric Meaw, the English envoy—Matilda's love for him—Perseverance of William of Normandy—Furious conduct of William to Matilda—Their marriage—Rich apparel—William's early life—William and Matilda excommunicated—Dispensation—Matilda's taste for architecture—Matilda's sister married to Tostig—Birth of Matilda's eldest son—Harold's visit—Betrothed to Matilda's daughter—William's invasion of England—Letter to Matilda's brother—Matilda appointed Regent of Normandy—Her son Robert—Happy arrival of Matilda in the Mora—Ship presented by her—William sails in it to England—Matilda's delineations—Battle of Hastings—News of victory brought to Matilda—Our Lady of Good Tidings.

MATILDA, the wife of William the Conqueror, was the first consort of a king of England who was called *regina*.[1] This was an innovation in the ancient customs of the land, for the Saxons simply styled the wife of the king " the lady his companion,"[2] and to them it was displeasing to hear the Normans speak of Matilda as *la reine*, as if she were a female sovereign, reigning in her own right:—so distinct in those days was the meaning attached in this country to the lofty title of *reine*, or *regina*, from that of queen, which, though at present the highest female title of honour used in England, then only signified companion.

---

[1] Thierry's Anglo-Normans. In the Doomsday-book, Matilda, the wife of the Conqueror, is called Matilda Regina.

[2] *Hlafdige se cwene* is the Saxon phrase. Hlafdige, or lady, means the giver of bread. Cwene, or Quen, was anciently used as a term of equality, indiscriminately applied to both sexes. In the old Norman chronicles and poems, instead of the Duke of Normandy and his peers, the phrase used is the Duke of Normandy and his Quens. "The word *quen*, signifying companion," says Rapin, vol. i. p. 148, "was common both to men and women." So late as the thirteenth century, a collection of poems written by Charles of Anjou and his courtiers, is quoted as the songs of the Quens of Anjou. Also in a chant of the twelfth century, enumerating the war-cries of the French provinces, we find

"And the *quens* of Thibaut
'Champagne and passavant' cry!"

The people of the land murmured among themselves at this unprecedented assumption of dignity, in the wife of their Norman sovereign; yet " the strange woman," as they called Matilda, could boast of royal Saxon blood.[1] She was, in fact, the direct descendant of the best and noblest of their monarchs, Alfred, through the marriage of his daughter, Elstrith, with Baldwin II. of Flanders, whose son, Arnold the Great, was the immediate ancestor of Matilda,—an interesting circumstance which history passes over in silence. Few of the queens of England, indeed, can claim a more illustrious descent than this princess. Her father, Baldwin V., surnamed the Gentle, Earl of Flanders, was the son of Baldwin IV. by Eleanora, daughter of duke Richard II. of Normandy; and her mother was Adelais, daughter of Robert, king of France, and sister to Henry, the reigning sovereign of that country. She was nearly related to the emperor of Germany, and to most of the royal families in Europe.

Matilda was born about the year 1031, and was very carefully educated. She was possessed of fine natural talents, and was no less celebrated for her learning than for her great beauty. William of Malmsbŭry, when speaking of this princess, says, " She was a singular mirror of prudence in our days, and the perfection of virtue."

Among her other acquirements, Matilda was particularly famed for her skill in ornamental needlework, which, in that age, was considered one of the most important and desirable accomplishments which princesses and ladies of high rank could possess. We are told by a worthy chronicler,[2] " That the proficiency of the four sisters of King Athelstane, in spinning, weaving, and embroidery, procured these royal spinsters the addresses of the greatest princes in Europe."

The fame of this excellent stitchery is, however, all the memorial that remains of the industry of Matilda's Saxon cousins; but her own great work, the Bayeux tapestry, is still in existence, and is, beyond all competition, the most wonderful achievement, in the gentle craft of needlework, that ever was executed by fair and royal hands. But of this we shall have to speak more fully in its proper place, as a pictorial chronicle of the conquest of England.

The earl of Flanders, Matilda's father, was a rich, powerful, and politic prince, equally skilled in the arts of war and of peace. It was to him that the town of Lille, which he rebuilt and greatly beautified, owed its subsequent greatness; and the home manufactures of his native country, through his judicious encouragement, became a source of wealth and prosperity to Flanders. His family connexion with the king of France, his *suzerain* and ally, and his intimate relationship to most of the royal houses in Europe, rendered his alliance very desirable to several of the reigning princes, his neighbours, who became suitors for the hand of his beautiful daughter.

The most accomplished of these was the young duke William of Normandy, who was not only desirous of this union in a political point

[1] See Matilda's pedigree in Ducarel's Norman Antiquities.
[2] Malmsbury, vol. i. book ii. p. 26.

of view, but passionately enamoured of his fair cousin. Yet William, though no less remarkable for the manly beauty of his person than for his knightly prowess in the field, and his great talents as a legislator, had, in the first instance, the mortification of receiving a very discouraging reply to his suit, not only from the parents and kindred of the young lady, but also from herself. The fact was, Matilda had bestowed her first affections on a young Saxon nobleman, named Brihtric Meaw, who had visited her father's court in the quality of ambassador from Edward the Confessor, king of England.[1]

Brihtric, surnamed Snaw, or Snow, from the fairness of his complexion, was the son of Algar, the lord of the honour of Gloucester, and possessed of very extensive domains in that county. He appears, however, to have been insensible to the regard with which he was distinguished by Matilda. This, together with the dark sequel of the tale, which will be subsequently related, is one of those authentic but obscure facts which occasionally tinge the page of history with the semblance of romance.

It is more than probable that the passion which Matilda cherished for the fair-haired English envoy, was the most formidable of all the obstacles with which her cousin, William of Normandy, had to contend during the tedious period of his courtship.

A less determined character would have given up the pursuit as hopeless; but William, having once fixed his mind upon this marriage, was not to be deterred by difficulties or discouragements. It was in vain that his foes and jealous kinsmen intrigued against him in the Flemish court; that the parents of the lady objected to his illegitimate birth, and his doubtful title to the duchy of Normandy; that the church of Rome interdicted a marriage between parties within the forbidden degrees of consanguinity; and, worse than all, the lady herself treated him with coldness and hauteur. After seven years' delay, William appears to have become desperate; and if we may trust the evidence of the chronicle of Inger, he, in the year 1047, waylaid Matilda in the streets of Bruges, as she was returning from mass, seized her, rolled her in the dirt, spoiled her rich array, and, not content with these outrages, struck her repeatedly, and then rode off at full speed. This Teutonic method of courtship, according to our author, brought the affair to a crisis; for Matilda, either convinced of the strength of William's passion by the violence of his behaviour, or afraid of encountering a second beating, consented to become his wife.[2] How he ever presumed to enter her presence again, after such a series of enormities, the chronicle saith not, and we are at a loss to imagine.

The marriage between the royal cousins took place in 1052, at William's own castle of Angi, in Normandy, whither Matilda was, with great pomp, conducted by her illustrious parents, and a noble company of knights and ladies.

---

[1] Chronicle of Tewkesbury, Cotton. MSS. Cleopatra, c. 111, 220. Leland's Collections, vol. i. p. 78. Monasticon, 111, 59. Palgrave's Rise and Progress, vol. i. p. 294. Thierry's Anglo-Normans, vol. i. p. 335.

[2] Chronicle of Inger, likewise called Ingerius. The anecdote has been translated by J. P. Andrews.

Wace,[1] in his poetical chronicle of the dukes of Normandy, says, "that the count, her father, gave Matilda joyfully, with very rich *appareilement*, that she was very fair and graceful, and that William married her by the advice of his baronage."[2]

The royal mantle, garnished with jewels, in which Matilda was arrayed on the day of her espousals, and also that worn by her mighty lord on the same occasion, together with his helmet, were long preserved in the treasury of the cathedral of Bayeux. Lancelot mentions an inventory of precious effects belonging to the church, dated 1476, in which these costly bridal garments are enumerated. Immediately after the marriage solemnity, William conducted his fair and royal bride to Rouen, "where," says Wace, "she was greatly served and honoured."

Nothing could be more perilous than the position of William's affairs at the period of his marriage with Matilda of Flanders. He was menaced on every side by powerful neighbours, who were eager to appropriate and parcel out the fertile fields of Normandy, to the enlargement of their respective borders; and at the same time a formidable party was arraying itself against him within his own dominions, in favour of Guy of Burgundy, the eldest son of his aunt Alice. This prince was the nearest legitimate male descendant of duke Richard the Second of Normandy; and as the direct line had failed with duke Robert, the late sovereign, he was, notwithstanding the operation of the Salic law, considered by many to possess a better right to the dukedom than the son of duke Richard by Arlotta, the skinner's daughter of Falaise. The particulars of William's birth are too well known to require recapitulation; but it is proper to notice that there are historians who maintain that Arlotta was the wife of duke Robert, though not of rank or breeding fit to be acknowledged as his duchess.[3] This we are disposed to regard as a mere paradox, since William, who would have been only too happy to avail himself of the plea of even a contract or promise of marriage between his parents, in order to strengthen his defective title by a pretence of legitimacy, never made any such assertion. On the contrary, not only before his victorious sword had purchased for him a more honourable surname, but even afterwards, he submitted to the use of the one derived from his mother's shame, and in the charter of the lands which he bestowed on his son-in-law, Alan, duke of Bretagne, in Yorkshire, he subscribed himself "William surnamed Bastardus."[4]

It is a general opinion that Arlotta was married to Herlewin of Conteville during the lifetime of duke Robert, and that this circumstance prevented any possibility of William attempting to assert that he was the legitimate offspring of his royal sire.[5]

---

[1] The author of the Roman de Rou.

[2] The nobles of Normandy, minding their duke of succession, persuaded him to marry Matilda, or Maud, daughter of Baldwin V., of Flanders.—Sandford.

[3] William of Malmsbury. Ingulphus.   [4] Leland.

[5] After the accession of Henry the Second to the throne, a Saxon pedigree was ingeniously invented for Arlotta, which is too great a curiosity to be omitted. "Edmund Ironside," says the Saxon genealogist, "had two sons, Edwin and Edward, and an only daughter, whose name does not appear in history because of

According to all historians, William was, from the very moment of his birth, regarded as a child of the most singular promise. The manful grasp with which his baby hand detained the rushes of which he had " *taken seizin* "[1] the moment after his entrance into life, when, in consequence of the danger of his mother, he was permitted to lie unheeded on the floor of his chamber, where he first saw the light,[2] gave occasion to the oracular gossips in attendance on Arlotta to predict " that the child would become a mighty man, ready to acquire everything within his reach, and that which he acquired he would with a strong hand steadfastly maintain against all challengers."

It does not appear that duke Robert bestowed much notice on the babe during the early stages of infancy; indeed, the contrary may be inferred from the testimony of the historian,[3] who says, " When William was a year old, he was introduced into the presence of his father; and when duke Robert saw what a goodly and fair child he was, and how closely he resembled the royal line of Normandy, he embraced him, and acknowledged him to be his son, and caused him to receive princely nurture in his own palace. When William was five years old, a battalion of boys, of his own age, was placed under his command, with whom he practised the military exercise, according to the custom of those days. Over these infant followers William assumed the authority of a sovereign in miniature; and if dissensions arose among them, they always referred to his decision, and his judgments are said to have been remarkable for their acuteness and equity."[4] Thus early in life did the mighty Norman learn to enact the character of a leader and legislator. Nature had, indeed, eminently fitted him for the lofty station which he was afterwards destined to fill; and his powerful talents were strengthened and improved by an education such as few princes in that rude, unlettered age were so fortunate as to receive. At the age of eight years he was able to read and explain Cæsar's Commentaries.[5]

The beauty and early promise of this boy caused him to be regarded with peculiar interest by the Normans; but as a child of illegitimate birth, William possessed no legal claim to the succession. His title was simply founded on the appointment of the duke, his father. This prince, having no other issue, had centered all the doting affection of a father's

her bad conduct, seeing that she formed a most imprudent alliance with the king's skinner. The king, in his anger, banished the skinner from England, together with his daughter. They both went to Normandy, where they lived on public charity, and had successively three daughters. Having one day come to Falaise to beg at duke Richard's door, the duke, struck with the beauty of the woman and her children, asked, ' who she was?' ' I am an Englishwoman,' she said, ' and of the royal blood.' The duke, on this answer, treated her with honour, took the skinner into his service, and had one of his daughters brought up in the palace. She was Arlotte or *Charlotte*, the mother of the Conqueror."— Thierry.

[1] The feudal term for taking possession.   [2] William of Malmsbury.
[3] Henderson's Life of the Conqueror.   [4] Ibid.
[5] According to William of Malmsbury, the importance which the Conqueror placed on mental culture was great. Throughout life he was used to say " that an illiterate king was a crowned ass."

heart on the young William; and feeling naturally desirous of securing
to him the ducal crown, before he set out on his mysterious pilgrimage
for the Holy Land, he called the peers of Normandy together, in the
Hotel de Ville, and required them to swear fealty to his son, whom he
then solemnly appointed for his successor. When the princely boy,
then a child of seven years old, was brought in to receive the homage
of the assembled nobles, duke Robert took him in his arms, and, after
kissing and passionately embracing him, he presented him to his valiant
"*Quens*" as their future sovereign, with this remark, "He is little, but
he will grow." [1]

The peers of Normandy gratified their departing lord by paying the [2]
homage required to the young William. The duke then appointed his
vassal, kinsman and friend, Alan, duke of Bretagne, seneschal of his dominions, with full power to govern the state of Normandy in his absence. Then he carried his son to Paris, and delivered him into the
hands of the king of France, his *suzerain*, or paramount lord : and having received his promise of protecting and cherishing the boy with a
loving care, he made William perform the same homage to that monarch
as if he were already the reigning duke of Normandy; by which he
secured his sovereign's recognition of the title of his little vassal-peer to
the ducal crown. After these arrangements, duke Robert departed on
that expedition from which he never again returned to his own dominions.[3]

At the court of his sovereign, Henry I. of France, the uncle of his
future spouse, Matilda of Flanders, William completed his education, and
learned the science of diplomacy, secure from all the factions and intrigues
with which Normandy was convulsed. The states, true to the fealty
they had sworn to the son of their deceased lord, sent ambassadors to

[1] Il est petit, mais il croitera.—Wace.

[2] Chronicle of Normandy. Malmsbury.

[3] It was whispered by some that duke Robert undertook this pilgrimage to Jerusalem as an expiatory penance for the death of his elder brother and sovereign, duke Richard III., which he was suspected of having hastened; while
others believed he was impelled from motives of piety alone to pay his vows at
the holy grave, according to a new but prevailing spirit of misdirected devotion,
which manifested itself among the princes and nobles of that age of superstition
and romance. Whether duke Robert ever reached the place of his destination,
is uncertain. The last authentic tidings respecting him that reached his capital
were brought by Pirou, a returned pilgrim from the Holy Land, who reported
that he met his lord, the duke of Normandy, on his way to the Holy City, borne
in a litter on the shoulders of four stout Saracens, being then too ill to proceed
on his journey on foot. When the royal pilgrim recognised his vassal, he exclaimed, with great animation, " Tell my valiant peers that you have seen your
sovereign carried towards heaven on the backs of fiends."—William of Malmsbury. Whether this uncourteous allusion to the spiritual darkness of his pagan
bearers was sufficiently intelligible to them to have the effect of provoking them
into shortening his journey thither, we know not. Some chronicles, indeed,
assert that he died at Nicea, in Bithynia, on his return; but there is a strange
uncertainty connected with his fate, and it appears that the Norman nobles long
expected his return—an expectation that was probably most favourable to the
cause of his youthful successor, whose title might otherwise have been more
effectually disputed by the heirs of the sisters and aunts of duke Robert.

Paris, to claim their young duke.[1] The king of France resigned him to
the deputies, but soon after invaded his dominions. William, however,
was possessed of energies equal to any difficulties in which he might be
placed, and he had some faithful and powerful friends among the counsellors of his late father. Raoul de Gace and Roger de Beaumont stoutly
maintained the cause of their young duke, both in the court and in the
camp. They were his tutors in the art of war, and through their assistance and advice he was enabled to defeat the king of France, and to
maintain the dignity of a sovereign and military chief, at a period of life
when princes are generally occupied in childish amusements, or the
pleasures of the chase.[2]

One by one, almost every Norman noble who could boast any portion
of the blood of Rollo, the founder of the ducal line of Normandy, was
incited by king Henry of France to stir up an insurrection, as a rival
claimant of the crown. On one occasion, William would in all probability have fallen a victim to the plot which his cousin Guy of Burgundy
had laid to surprise him, when he was on a hunting excursion, and was
to pass the night without any of his military retinue, at the castle of
Valognes; but from this peril he was preserved by the fidelity of his
fool, who, happening to overhear the conspirators arranging their plan,
travelled all night at full speed to give the duke notice of his danger;
and finding means to make an entrance into the castle at four o'clock in
the morning, he struck violently with the handle of his whip at the
chamber-door of his sleeping sovereign, and shouted, "Levez, levez,
Seigneur!" till he succeeded in rousing him. So close at hand, however, were Guy of Burgundy and his confederates, that it was only by
mounting his swiftest steed, half-dressed, and riding with fiery speed for
many hours, that William could effect his escape from his pursuers; and
even then he must have fallen into their hands, if he had not encountered
a gentleman on the road, with whom he changed horses, his own being
thoroughly spent. Guy of Burgundy was afterwards taken prisoner by
the young duke; but having been on affectionate terms with him in his
childhood, he generously forgave him all the trouble he had occasioned
him, and his many attempts against his life.[3]

The king of France was preparing to attack William with redoubled
fury, at the period when, by his fortunate marriage with Matilda, he
strengthened his defective title to the throne of Normandy, by uniting
himself with a legitimate descendant of the royal line, and at the same
time acquired a powerful ally, in the person of his father-in-law, the earl
of Flanders. The death of Henry averted the dark storm that lowered
over Normandy; and the young Philip of France, his son and successor,
having been left during his minority under the guardianship of his aunt's
husband, Baldwin of Flanders, Matilda's father, William found himself
entirely relieved from all present fears of hostility on the part of France.[4]
Scarcely, however, was he preparing himself to enjoy the happiness of

[1] Chronicle of Normandy.　[2] Ibid. Malmsbury. Wace.
[3] Chronicle of Normandy. Mezerai. Wace.
[4] St. Marthe. Wace.

wedded life, when a cause of annoyance arose, which had been little anticipated.[1]

Mauger, the archbishop of Rouen, an illegitimate uncle of the young duke, who had taken great pains to prevent his marriage with Matilda of Flanders, finding all the obstacles which he had raised against it were unavailing, proceeded to pronounce sentence of excommunication against the newly-wedded pair, under the plea of its being a marriage within the forbidden degrees of consanguinity,[2] and therefore unlawful in the sight of man, and abominable to God.

William indignantly appealed to the pope against this sentence, who, on the parties submitting to the usual fines, nullified the archbishop's ecclesiastical censures, and granted the dispensation for the marriage, on condition of the young duke and duchess each building and endowing an abbey at Caen, and an hospital for the blind. Lanfranc, afterwards the celebrated archbishop of Canterbury, but at that time an obscure individual, to whom William had extended his protection and patronage, was intrusted with this negotiation, which he conducted with such ability as to secure to himself the favour and confidence both of William and Matilda, by whom he was, in after years, advanced to the office of tutor to their royal offspring, and finally to the highest ecclesiastical rank and power.

William and Matilda cheerfully submitted to the conditions on which the dispensation for their marriage had been granted, by founding the sister abbeys of St. Stephen and the Holy Trinity. That of St. Stephen was built and endowed by William, for a fraternity of monks, of which he made Lanfranc abbot. Matilda founded and endowed that of the Holy Trinity, for nuns. It should appear that the ground on which these holy edifices were erected was not very honestly obtained, as we shall have occasion to show hereafter.[3]

All that Mauger gained by his impertinent interference with the matrimonial concerns of his royal nephew, was the exposure and punishment of his own evil deeds; for William, highly exasperated at the archbishop's attempt to separate him from his bride, retaliated upon him, by calling a convocation of all the bishops of Normandy, at Lisieu, before whom he caused Mauger to be accused of several crimes and misdemeanors, especially of selling consecrated chalices, and other articles of church-plate, to supply his luxury.[4] Mauger, being convicted of these malpractices, was deposed from his office, and Maurilliers was elected in his room.[5]

All things being now tranquilly settled, William proceeded to build a royal palace within the precincts of St. Stephen's abbey, for his own residence and that of his young duchess. The great hall, or council-chamber, of this palace, was one of the most magnificent apartments at that time in Europe.

[1] Chronicle of Normandy. Rapin.
[2] Chronicle of Normandy. Matilda was the granddaughter of Eleanor of Normandy, William's aunt. [3] Montfaucon. Malmsbury. [4] Rapin.
[5] This council was held at Lisieu, anno 1055. Vide Sir Harris Nicholas's Chronology of History.

Matilda, inheriting from her father, Baldwin of Lille, a taste for architecture, took great delight in the progress of these stately buildings; and her foundations are among the most splendid relics of Norman grandeur. She was a munificent patroness of the arts, and afforded great encouragement to men of learning, co-operating with her husband most actively in all his paternal plans for the advancement of trade, the extension of commerce, and the general happiness of the people committed to their charge. In this they were most successful. Normandy, so long torn with contending factions, and impoverished with foreign warfare, began to taste the blessings of repose; and, under the wise government of her energetic sovereign, soon experienced the good effects of his enlightened policy.

At his own expense William built the first pier that ever was constructed, at Cherbourg.[1] He superintended the building and organization of fleets, traced out commodious harbours for his ships, and in a comparatively short time rendered Normandy a very considerable maritime power, and finally the mistress of the Channel.

Meantime the domestic happiness which William enjoyed with his beautiful duchess appears to have been very great. All historians have agreed that they were a most attached pair, and that, whatever might have been the previous state of Matilda's affections, they were unalterably and faithfully fixed upon her cousin from the hour she became his wife; and with reason, for William was the most devoted of husbands, and always allowed her to take the ascendant in the matrimonial scale. The confidence he reposed in her was unbounded, and very shortly after their marriage he intrusted the reins of government to her care, when he crossed over to England, to pay a visit to his friend and kinsman, Edward the Confessor. By his marriage with Matilda, William had strengthened this connexion, and added a nearer tie of relationship to the English sovereign; and he was, perhaps, willing to remind the childless monarch of that circumstance; and to recall to his memory the hospitality he had received, both at the Flemish and the Norman courts, during the period of his adversity.[2]

Edward "received him very honourably, and presented him with hawks and hounds, and many other fair and goodly gifts," says Wace, "as tokens of his love." Duke William had chosen his time for this visit during the exile of Godwin and his sons; and it is probable that he availed himself of their absence, to obtain from Edward the promise of being adopted as his successor to the English throne, and also to commence a series of political intrigues, connected with that mighty project, which, fourteen years afterwards, he carried into effect.

In pursuing the broad stream of history, how few writers take the trouble of tracing the under-currents by which the tide of events is influenced! The marriage of Tostig, the son of Godwin, with Judith of Flanders, the sister of Matilda, wife of William of Normandy, was one great cause of the treacherous and unnatural conduct, on his part, which decided the fate of Harold, and transferred the crown of England to the

---

[1] Henderson's Life of William the Conqueror. [2] Higden Polychronicon.

Norman line.' During the period of their exile from England, Godwin
and his family sought refuge at the court of the earl of Flanders, Tostig's father-in-law, from whom they received friendly and hospitable entertainment, and were treated by the duke and duchess of Normandy
with all the marks of friendship that might reasonably be expected, in
consideration of the family connexion to which we have alluded.'

Nine months after her marriage, Matilda gave birth to a son, whom
William named Robert, after his father, thinking that the name of a
prince, whose memory was dear to Normandy, would ensure the popularity of his heir.' The happiness of the royal pair was greatly increased
by this event. In fact, nothing could exceed the terms of affection and
confidence in which they lived. They were at that period reckoned the
handsomest and most tenderly united couple in Europe. The fine natural talents of both had been improved, by a degree of mental cultiva-
tion very unusual in that age; and there was a similarity in their tastes
and pursuits, which rendered their companionship delightful to each
other in private hours, and gave to all their public acts that graceful una-
nimity, which could not fail of producing the happiest effects on the
minds of their subjects.

The birth of Robert was followed in quick succession by that of
Richard, William-Rufus, Cecilia, Agatha, Constance, Adela, Adelaide, and
Gundred. During several years of peace and national prosperity, Matilda and her husband employed themselves in superintending the education of their lovely and numerous family; several of whom, according
to the report of contemporary chronicles, were children of great promise.'

No very remarkable event occurs in the records of Matilda's court,
till the arrival of Harold in the year 1065. Harold, having undertaken
a voyage to Normandy in an open fishing-boat, was driven by stress of
weather into the river Maye, in the territories of the earl of Ponthieu,
by whom, with the intention of extorting a large ransom, he was seized,
and immured in the dungeons of Beaurain.

The duke of Normandy, however, demanded the illustrious captive,
and the earl of Ponthieu, understanding that Harold's brother was husband to the duchess of Normandy's sister, thought it most prudent to
resign his prey to the family connexion by whom it was claimed.

Harold was treated with apparent friendship by William and Matilda.
They even offered to bestow one of their daughters upon him in marriage,—a young lady whose age did not exceed seven years; and to her
Harold permitted himself to be affianced, though without any intention
of keeping his plight.

William then confided to his reluctant guest the tale of his own adoption, by Edward the Confessor, for his successor, and proceeded to extort
from him a solemn oath, to render him all the assistance in his power, in
furtherance of his designs on the crown of England.'

Harold, on his return to England, came to an open rupture with his

' Wace. Ingulphus. Eadmer.   ' Malmsbury. Wace.
' Malmsbury. Ordericus Vitalis.   ' Wace. Malmsbury. Thierry.

brother Tostig. Probably he had, during his late visit to Normandy, discovered how entirely the latter was in the interest of his Flemish wife's connexions. Tostig then fled, with his wife and children, to the court of his father-in-law, the earl of Flanders, and devoted himself entirely to the cause of William of Normandy.

At this perilous crisis, when so dark a storm was slowly but surely gathering over England, a woful deterioration had taken place in the national character of the people, especially among the higher classes, who had given way to every species of luxury and licentiousness. William of Malmsbury draws the following quaint picture of their manners and proceedings at this period. "Englishmen," says he, "had then transformed themselves into the strange manners of the French, not only in their speech and behaviour, but in their deeds and characters. Their fashion in dress was to go fantastically appointed, with garments shortened to the knee. Their heads shorn, and their beards shaven all but the upper lip, on which they wore long moustaches. Their arms they loaded with massive bracelets of gold, carrying withal pictured marks upon their skins, pounced in with divers colours;" by which it is evident that the Anglo-Saxons had adopted the barbarous practice of tattooing their persons, like the rude aborigines of the island eleven centuries previous. "They were," continues our author, "accustomed to eat to repletion, and to drink to excess; while the clergy wholly addicted themselves to light and trivial literature, and could scarcely read their own breviaries." In a word, they had, according to the witness of their own chronicles, arrived at that pass of sensuality and folly which is generally supposed to provoke a national visitation, in the shape of pestilence or the sword.

"The Normans of that period," says Malmsbury, " were proudly apparelled, delicate in their food, but not gluttonous; a race inured to war, which they could scarcely live without; fierce in rushing upon the foe, and, when unequal in force, ready to use stratagem or bribery to gain their ends. They live in large houses with economy. They wish to rival their superiors. They envy their equals, and plunder their inferiors, but not unfrequently intermarry with their vassals."

Such were the general characteristics of the men whom William had rendered veterans in the art of war, and, both by precept and example, stimulated to habits of frugality, temperance, and self-control. A mighty sovereign and a mighty people, possessing within themselves the elements of every requisite that might ensure the success of an undertaking which, by every other nation in Europe, must have been considered as little short of madness.

When the intelligence of king Edward's death, coupled with the news of Harold's assumption of the regal dignity, reached the court of Normandy, William was struck speechless with indignation and surprise, and is said to have unconsciously tied and untied the rich cordon that fastened his cloak, several times, in the first tumults of his agitation and anger.[2] He then gave vent to his wrath, in fierce animadversions on

---

[1] W. Malmsbury.   [2] Wace.

Harold's broken faith, in causing himself to be crowned king of England, in defiance of the solemn oath he had sworn to him, to support his claims.

William also complained of the affront that had been offered to his daughter by the faithless Saxon, who, regardless of his contract to the little Norman princess, just before king Edward's death, strengthened his interest with the English nobles, by marrying Algitha, sister to the powerful earls Morcar and Edwin, and widow to Griffith, prince of Wales. This circumstance is mentioned with great bitterness in all William's proclamations and reproachful messages to Harold, and appears to have been considered by him to the full as great a villany as the assumption of the crown of England. Some of the historians who wrote near that period say, that the lady Adeliza, the affianced bride of Harold, was dead at that time; but if so, William could have had no pretext for upbraiding him with the insult he had offered to his family, by entering into another matrimonial alliance.[1]

When William first made known to his Norman peers his positive intention of asserting, by force of arms, his claims to the crown of England, on the plea of Edward the Confessor's verbal adoption of himself as successor to that realm, there were stormy debates among them on the subject. They were then assembled in the hall of Lillebon, where they remained long in council, but chiefly employed in complaining to one another of the warlike temper of their lord. There were, however, great differences of opinion among them, and they separated themselves into several distinct groups, because many chose to speak at once, and no one could obtain the attention of the whole assembly, but harangued as many hearers as could be prevailed on to listen to him. The majority were opposed to the idea of the expedition to England, and said they had already been grievously taxed to support the duke's foreign wars, and observed, that " they were not only poor, but in debt;" while others were no less vehement in advocating their sovereign's project, and spake " of the propriety of contributing ships and men, and crossing the sea with him." Some said, " they would," others, " that they would not;" and at last the contention among them became so fierce, that Fitz-Osborn, of Breteul, surnamed the Proud Spirit, stood forth and harangued the malcontent portion of the assembly in these words :—

" Why should you go on wrangling with your natural lord, who seeks to gain honour? You owe him service for your fiefs, and you ought to render it with all readiness. Instead of waiting for him to entreat you, you ought to hasten to him, and offer your assistance, that he may not hereafter complain that his design has failed through your delays."

" Sir," replied they, " we fear the sea, and we are not bound to serve beyond it; but do you speak to the duke for us, for we do not seem to know our own minds, and we think you will decide better for us than we can do for ourselves."[2]

Fitz-Osborn, thus empowered to act as their deputy, went to the duke

---

[1] Wace's Chronicles of the Dukes of Normandy.   [2] Wace.

at their head, and in their names made him the most unconditional proffers of their assistance and co-operation.

"Behold," said Fitz-Osborn, "the loving loyalty of your lieges, my lord, and their zeal for your service. They will pass with you over sea, and double their accustomed service. He who is bound to furnish twenty knights, will bring forty; he who should serve you with thirty will now serve you with sixty; and he who owes one hundred, will cheerfully pay two hundred.[1] For myself, I will, in good love to my sovereign, in his need, contribute sixty well-appointed ships charged with fighting men." Here the dissentient barons interrupted him with a clamour of disapprobation, exclaiming, "That he might give as much as he pleased himself, but they had never empowered him to promise such unheard-of aids for them;" and they would submit to no such exactions from their sovereign, since if they once performed double service, it would henceforth be demanded of them as a right.

"In short," continues the lively chronicler,[2] "they raised such an uproar, that no one could hear another speak—no one could either listen to reason, or render it for himself. Then the duke, being greatly perplexed with the noise, withdrew, and sending for the barons one by one, exerted all his powers of persuasion, to induce them to accede to his wishes, promising ' to reward them richly with Saxon spoils for the assistance he now required at their hands; and if they felt disposed to make good Fitz-Osborn's offer of double service at that time, he should receive it as a proof of their loyal affection, and never think of demanding it as a right on any future occasion.' "

The nobles, on this conciliatory address, were pacified; and feeling that it was a much easier thing to maintain their opposition to their sovereign's wishes in the council than in the presence-chamber, began to assume a different tone, and even to express their willingness to oblige him as far as it lay in their power.[3]

William next invited his neighbours, the Bretons, the Angevins, and men of Boulogne, to join his banners, bribing them with promises of good pay, and a share in the spoils of *merrie* England. He even proposed to take the king of France into the alliance, offering, if he would assist him with the quota of money, men, and ships, which he required, to own him for the *suzerain*, or paramount lord of England, as well as Normandy, and to render him a liegeman's homage for that island, as well as for his continental dominions. Philip treated the idea of William's annexing England to Normandy, as an extravagant chimera,[4] and asked him, "Who would take care of his duchy while he was running after a kingdom?" To this sarcastic query, William replied, "That is a care that shall not need to trouble our neighbours; by the grace of God we are blessed with a prudent wife and loving subjects, who will keep our border securely during our absence."[5]

William entreated the young count Baldwin of Flanders, the brother of his duchess, to accompany him as a friendly ally; but the wily Fleming, with whom the family connexion seems to have had but little

[1] Wace's Chronicle of Normandy. [2] Ibid. [3] Ibid. [4] Ibid. [5] Ibid.
3*

weight, replied by asking William : " What share of England he intended to bestow on him by way of recompence ?" [1]

The duke, surprised at this demand, told his brother-in-law, " That he could not satisfy him on that point till he had consulted with his barons on the subject ;" but instead of naming the matter to them, he took a piece of fair parchment, and having folded it in the form of a letter, he superscribed it to count Baldwin of Flanders, and sealed it with the ducal seal, and wrote the following distich on the label that surrounded the scroll—

> " Beau frère, en Angleterre vous aurez
> Ce qui dedans escript vous trouverez ;" [2]

which is to say, " Brother-in-law, I give you such a share of England as you shall find within this letter."

He sent the letter to the young count by a shrewd-witted page, who was much in his confidence. When Baldwin had read this promising endorsement, he broke the seal, full of expectation, but finding the parchment blank, he showed it to the bearer; and asked what was the duke's meaning.

" Nought is written here," replied the messenger, " and nought shalt thou receive, therefore look for nothing. The honour that the duke seeks will be for the advantage of your sister and her children, and their greatness will be the advancement of yourself, and the benefit will be felt by your country ; but if you refuse your aid, then, with the blessing of God, my lord will conquer England without your help." [3]

But though William ventured, by means of this sarcastic device, to reprove the selfish feelings manifested by his brother-in-law, he was fain to subscribe to the only terms on which the aid of Matilda's father could be obtained, which was by securing to him and his successors a perpetual pension of 300 marks of silver annually, in the event of his succeeding in establishing himself as king of England. [4] According to the Flemish historians, this pension was actually paid during the life of Baldwin V. and his son Baldwin VI., but afterwards discontinued. It is certain that Matilda's family connexions rendered the most important assistance to William in the conquest of England, and her countrymen were among his bravest auxiliaries. [5] The earl of Flanders was, in fact, the first person to commence hostilities against Harold, by furnishing the traitor Tostig with ships, and a military force, to make a descent on England.

Tostig executed his mission more like a pirate-brigand than an accredited leader. The brave earls Morcar and Edwin drove him into Scotland, whence he passed into Norway, where he succeeded in persuading

---

[1] Wace.   [2] Henderson. Wace.   [3] Wace.

[4] Will. Gemiticen. p. 665, and Daniels' Histoire de France, vol. iii. p. 90. Baldwin Earl of Flanders furnished Tostig with sixty ships. Malmsbury Saxon Annals.

[5] Tradition makes the famous Robin Hood a descendant of Matilda's nephew, Gilbert de Gant, who attended the Conqueror to England. Hist. of Sleaford by Dr. Yerborough.

king Harfager to invade England at one point, simultaneously with William of Normandy's attack in another quarter of the island.[1]

The minds of the people of England in general were, at this momentous crisis, labouring under a painful depression, occasioned by the appearance of the splendid three-tailed comet, which became visible in their horizon at the commencement of the memorable year 1066, a few days before the death of king Edward. The unsettled state of the succession, and the superstitious spirit of the age, inclined all classes of persons to regard, with ominous feelings of dismay, any phenomenon which could be construed into a portent of evil: moreover the astrologers who had foretold the approach of this comet had thought proper to announce their prediction in an oracular Latin distich, of which the following rude couplet is a literal translation:—

> " In the year one thousand and sixty-six,
> Comets to England's sons an end shall fix."[2]

" About this time," says Malmsbury, " a comet or star, denoting as they say, a change in kingdoms, appeared trailing its extended and fiery train along the sky; wherefore a certain monk of our monastery named Elmer, bowing down with terror when the bright star first became visible to his eye, prophetically exclaimed, ' Thou art come! a matter of great lamentation to many a mother art thou come. I have seen thee long before; but now I behold thee in thy terrors, threatening destruction to this country.' "[3]

Wace, whom we may almost regard in the light of a contemporary chronicler, in still quainter language describes the appearance of this comet, and the impression it made on the unphilosophical star-gazers of the eleventh century. " This year a great star appeared in the heavens, shining for fourteen days, with three long rays streaming towards the south. Such a star as is wont to be seen when a kingdom is about to change its ruler. I have seen men who saw it—men who were of full age at the time of its appearance, and who lived many years afterwards."[4]

The descriptions which I have just quoted, from the pen of the Norman poet and the monastic chronicler, fall far short of the marvellousness of Matilda's delineation of this comet, in the Bayeux tapestry, where the royal needle has represented it of dimensions that might well have justified the alarm of the terror-stricken group of Saxon princes, priests, and ladies, who appear to be rushing out of their pigmy dwellings, and pointing to it with unequivocal signs of horror; for, independently of the fact that it looks near enough to singe all their noses, it would inevitably have whisked the world and all its sister planets out of their orbits, if it had been of a hundredth part proportionable to the magnitude there portrayed.[5] Some allowance, however, ought to be made, for the exaggeration of feminine reminiscences, of an object which we can scarcely suppose to have been transferred to the embroidered

[1] Brompton. Saxon Annals.   [2] Henderson.   [3] Malmsbury.
[4] Wace.   [5] Bayeux tapestry.

chronicle of the conquest of England, till after the triumphant termination of William of Normandy's enterprise afforded his queen-duchess so magnificent a subject, for the employment of the skill and ingenuity of herself and the ladies of her court, in recording his achievements on canvass, by dint of needlework. But, on the eve of this adventurous expedition, we may naturally conclude, that Matilda's time and thoughts were more importantly occupied than in the labours of the loom, or the fabrication of worsted pictures; when, in addition to all her fears and anxieties in parting with her lord, we doubt not but she had, at least, as much trouble in reconciling the Norman ladies to the absence of their husbands and lovers,[1] as the duke had to prevail on these his valiant *quens* to accompany him on an expedition so full of peril to all parties concerned in it.

Previously to his departure to join his ships and forces assembled at the port of St. Valleri, William solemnly invested Matilda with the regency of Normandy, and entreated, "that he and his companions in arms might have the benefit of her prayers, and the prayers of her ladies, for the success of their expedition." He appointed for her council some of the wisest and most experienced men among the prelates and elder nobles of Normandy.[2] The most celebrated of these, for courage, ability, and wisdom, was Roger de Beaumont, and by him William recommended the duchess to be advised in all matters of domestic policy. He also associated with the duchess, in the regency, their eldest son, Robert, and this youth, who had just completed his thirteenth year, was nominally the military chief of Normandy during the absence of his sire.

The invasion of England was by no means a popular measure with any class of William's subjects; and during the time that his armament remained wind-bound at St. Valleri, the common soldiers began to murmur in their tents. "The man must be mad," they said, "to persist in going to subjugate a foreign country, since God, who withheld the wind, opposed him; that his father, who was surnamed *Robert le Diable*, purposed something of the kind, and was in like manner frustrated; and that it was the fate of that family to aspire to things beyond them, and to find God their adversary."[3]

When the duke heard of these disheartening reports, he called a council of his chiefs, at which it was agreed that the body of St. Valleri should be brought forth, to receive the offerings and vows of those who should feel disposed to implore his intercession for a favourable wind.[4] Thus artfully did he, instead of interposing the authority of a sovereign, and a military leader, to punish the language of sedition and mutiny among his troops, oppose superstition to superstition, to amuse the short-sighted instruments of his ambition. The bones of the patron saint of the port were accordingly brought forth, with great solemnity, and exposed in their shrine, on the green turf, beneath the canopy of heaven, for the double purpose of receiving the prayers of the pious and

---

[1] Wace.
[3] Malmsbury. Wace.   William of Poitou. Wace. Malmsbury.
[4] Ibid.

the contributions of the charitable.[1] The Norman chroniclers affirm that the shrine was half-buried in the heaps of gold, silver, and precious things which were showered upon it by the crowds of votaries who came to pay their respects to the saint. Thus were the malcontent Normans amused till the wind changed.

In the meantime William was agreeably surprised by the arrival of his duchess at the port, in a splendid vessel of war, called the Mora,[2] which she had caused to be built unknown to him, and adorned in the most royal style of magnificence, for his acceptance. The effigy of their youngest son (William), formed of gilded bronze, some writers say of gold, was placed at the prow of this vessel, with his face turned towards England, holding a trumpet to his lips with one hand, and bearing in the other a bow, with the arrow aimed at England.[3] It seemed as if the wind had only delayed in order to enable Matilda to offer this gratifying and auspicious gift to her departing lord; for scarcely had the acclamations with which it was greeted by the admiring host died away, when the long-desired breeze sprang up, " and a joyful clamour," says Malmsbury, " then arising, summoned every one to the ships." The duke himself, first launching from the continent into the deep, led the way in the Mora, which, by day, was distinguished by a blood-red flag,[4] and, as soon as it was dark, carried a light at the mast-head, as a beacon to guide the other ships. The first night the royal leader so far outsailed his followers, that when morning dawned, the Mora was in the mid-seas alone, without a single sail of her convoy in sight, though these were a thousand in number. Somewhat disturbed at this circumstance, William ordered the master of the Mora to go to the topmast and look out, and bring him word what he had seen.

The reply was, " Nothing but sea and sky." " Go up again," said the duke, " and look out." The man cried out, " That he saw four specks in the distance, like the sails of ships."

" Look once again," cried William; then the master exclaimed, " I see a forest of tall masts and a press of sails bearing gallantly towards us."[5]

Rough weather occurred during the voyage, but it is remarkable that, out of so numerous a fleet, only two vessels were lost. In one of these was a noted astrologer, who had taken upon himself to predict that the expedition would be entirely successful, for that Harold would resign England to the duke without a battle. William neither believed in omens nor encouraged fortune-telling, and when he heard the catastrophe of the unfortunate soothsayer, who had thought proper to join himself to the armament, shrewdly observed, " Little could he have known of the fate of others who could not foresee his own."[6]

On the 28th of September, 1066, the Norman fleet made the port of Pevensey, on the coast of Sussex.

Wace's Chronicle of the Norman Conquest affords a graphic picture

---

[1] Malmsbury. Wace.   [2] Wace.   [3] Ibid.
[4] Thierry's Anglo-Normans.   [5] Ibid.   [6] Wace. Henderson.

of the disembarkation of the duke and his armament. The knights and archers landed first.[1]

After the soldiers, came the carpenters, armorers, and masons, with their tools in their hands, and planes, saws, axes, and other implements slung to their sides. Last of all came the duke, who, stumbling as he leaped to shore, measured his majestic height upon the beach.

Forthwith all raised a cry of distress. "An evil sign is here!" exclaimed the superstitious Normans; but the duke, who, in recovering himself, had filled his hands with sand, cried out in a loud and cheerful voice, " See, *seigneurs!* by the splendour of God I have seized England with my two hands.[2] Without challenge no prize can be made, and that which I have grasped I will, by your good help, maintain."

On this, one of his followers ran forward, and snatching a handful of thatch from the roof of a hut, brought it to the duke,[3] exclaiming merrily, " Sire, come forward and receive *seizin.* I give you *seizin,* in token that this realm is yours."

" I accept it," replied the duke, " and may God be with us!"[4]

They then sat down, and dined together on the beach; after which they sought for a spot on which to rear a wooden fort, which they had brought in disjointed pieces, in their ships, from Normandy.

Matilda has, in a curious section of the Bayeux tapestry, shown us the manner in which the trusty followers of her lord carried the disjointed frame-work of this timber fortress to the shore. The soldiers assisted the carpenters and other craftsmen in this arduous undertaking, and the duke encouraged and stimulated them, in this union of labour, to such good purpose, that before even-fall they had finished their building, fortified it, and supped merrily therein. Here the duke tarried four days. William had, through the agency of Matilda's brother-in-law, Tostig, arranged measures with Harfager, king of Norway, that their attacks upon England should be simultaneous; but the contrary winds which had detained his fleets so long at St. Valleri, had speeded the sails of his northern ally, so that Harfager and Tostig entered the Tyne with three hundred ships, and commenced their work of rapine and devasta-

---

[1] There is a tradition in the north of England, that the foremost man of this company to touch the land of promise, was the ancestor of the Stricklands of Sizergh Castle, in Westmoreland, who derive their name and arms from this circumstance. They show the sword in the ancient banqueting-room in the D'Eincourt tower of Sizergh Castle, with which it is asserted by that venerable gossip, tradition, that the redoubted chief first struck the land at Pevensey. The weapon, which appears formed for a giant's grasp, is not, however, we imagine, of earlier date than the days of Edward III., and greatly resembles the sword of state belonging to that monarch, which is shown in Westminster Abbey. It is more probable that it pertained to Sir Thomas Strickland, who attended the victorious Edward in his French campaigns, than to the Norman founder of his lineage.

[2] Wace. Ordericus Vitalis.

[3] Wace. Simon Dunelm. Matthew of Westminster. This ceremony is still observed in the transfer of some copyhold estates. Formerly a turf from a field, and a piece of thatch from the roof of a tenement, were all the conveyance required to give the purchaser a legal title of possession.

[4] Wace.

tion a full fortnight before the arrival of the Norman armament. Harold was thus at liberty to direct his whole strength against his fraternal foe and Harfager; and the intelligence of his decisive victory at Stanford Bridge, where both Tostig and Harfager were defeated and slain, reached William four days after his landing at Pevensey,[1] while he lay entrenched in his wooden citadel, waiting for a communication from his confederates, before he ventured to advance farther up the country. On receiving this unfavourable news, William manifested no consternation or surprise, but, turning to his nobles, said, " You see the astrologer's prediction was false. We cannot win the land without a battle; and here I vow that if it shall please God to give me the victory, that on whatever spot it shall befall I will there build a church to be consecrated to the blessed Trinity, and to St. Martin, where perpetual prayers shall be offered for the sins of Edward the Confessor, for my own sins, the sins of Matilda my spouse, and the sins of such as have attended me in this expedition, but more particularly for the sins of such as may fall in the battle."[2]

This vow greatly reassured his followers, and appears to have been considered by the valiant Normans as a very comfortable arrangement. Hard work, however, it must have prepared for the priests, who had to sing and pray away the sins of all the parties specified, if we take into consideration who and what manner of people they were.

Harold, meantime, was far beyond the Humber, and in high spirits at the signal victory he had obtained at Stanford Bridge, supposing at the same time that the duke of Normandy had delayed his threatened invasion till the spring,[3] as the father of Matilda had deceitfully informed him. But the intelligence of the arrival of these unwelcome guests was too soon conveyed to him, by a knight from the neighbourhood of Pevensey, who had heard the outcry of the peasants on the coast of Sussex, when they saw the great fleet arrive, and being aware of the project of the Norman duke, had posted himself behind a hill, where, unseen himself, he had watched the disembarkation of this mighty host, and their proceedings on the shore, till they had built up and entrenched their wooden fortress; which, being done with such inconceivable rapidity, appeared to him like the work of enchantment. Sorely troubled at what he had seen, the knight girded on his sword, and taking lance in hand, mounted his fleetest steed, and tarried not by the way, either for rest or refreshment, till he had found Harold, to whom he communicated his alarming tidings, in these words: " The Normans have come — they have landed at Hastings, and built up a fort which they have enclosed with a foss and palisades; and they will rend the land from thee and thine, unless thou defend it well."[4]

In the forlorn hope of ridding himself of his formidable invader, Harold offered to purchase the departure of the Norman duke, telling him " that if silver or gold were his object, he, who had enriched himself with the spoils of the defeated king of Norway, would give him enough to satisfy both himself and his followers."

[1] Saxon Annals. Malmsbury. Simon Dunelm. Henry Huntingdon. Wace.
[2] Wace.　　　[3] Speed.　　　[4] Wace.

"Thanks for Harold's fair words," replied William, "but I did not bring so many *écus* into this country to change them for his *esterlins*.[1] My purpose in coming is to claim this realm, which is mine, according to the gift of king Edward, which was confirmed by Harold's oath."

"Nay, but you ask too much of us, sire," returned the messenger, by whom the pacific offer had been made; "my lord is not so pressed that he should resign his kingdom at your desire. Harold will give you nothing but what you can take from him, unless in a friendly way, as a condition for your departure, which he is willing to purchase with large store of silver and gold and fine garments; but if you accept not his offer, know that he is ready to give you battle on Saturday next, if you be in the field on that day."[2]

The duke accepted this challenge, and on the Friday evening preceding that fatal day for the Saxon cause, Harold planted his ganfanon on the very spot where Battle Abbey now stands.

The Normans and English being equally apprehensive of attack during the season of darkness, kept watch and ward that night, but employed their vigils in a very different manner.

The English, according to the report of contemporary chroniclers, kept up their spirits with a riotous carouse, crying *Wassail* and *Drink heal*,[3] dancing, laughing, and gambling all night. The Normans, on the contrary, being in a devout frame of mind, made confessions of their sins, and employed the precious moments in recommending themselves to the care of God. The day on which the battle was to take place being Saturday withal, they, by the advice of their spiritual directors, vowed that if the victory were awarded to them, they would never more eat flesh on that day of the week: an obligation which, till very recently, was observed by the Catholics in England.

"Odo, the warrior bishop of Bayeux, William's half-brother by the mother's side, and Goisfred, bishop of Coutances, received confessions, bestowed benedictions, and imposed penances not a few."[4]

The battle joined on the 14th of October, Harold's birth-day, on a spot about seven miles from Hastings, called Heathfield, where the town of Battle now stands.

When William was arming for the encounter, in his haste and agitation he unwittingly put on his hauberk the hind part before.[5] He quickly changed it: but, perceiving, from the looks of consternation among the bystanders, that his mistake had been observed, and construed into an omen of ill, he smilingly observed, "I have seen many a man who, if such a thing had happened to him, would not have entered the battle-field; but I never believed in omens, nor have I ever put my faith in fortune-tellers nor divinations of any kind, for my trust is in God. Let not this mischance discourage you, for if this change import aught, it is

[1] Wace. A play on words meaning *crowns* and *shillings*; *écu*, meaning a shield as well as the coin called a crown.
[2] Malmsbury. Matthew of Westminster. Wace.
[3] Meaning "Wish health" and "Drink health."   [4] Wace.
[5] Malmsbury. Wace. William of Poitou.

that the power of my dukedom shall be turned into a kingdom — yea, a king shall I be, who have hitherto been but a duke." [1]

Then the duke called for the good steed which had been presented to him as a token of friendship by the king of Spain.

Matilda has done justice to this noble charger, in her Bayeux tapestry. It is represented as caparisoned for the battle, and led by Gualtier Giffart, the duke's squire. There is in the same group the figure of a knight armed cap-à-pié, in the close-fitting ring armour, and nasal conical helmet, worn by the Norman chivalry of that era, with a gonfanon attached to his lance, something after the fashion of the streamer which forms part of the paraphernalia of the modern lancer, with this difference only, that the gonfanon of the ancient knight was adorned with his device or armorial bearing, and served the purpose of a banner or general rallying point for his followers.

The knightly figure in the Bayeux tapestry, which I have just described, is generally believed to have been designed for the veritable effigies of the redoubtable conqueror of this realm, or at any rate as correct a resemblance of him as his loving spouse Matilda could produce in cross-stitch. He is delineated in the act of extending his hand to greet his favourite steed.

"The duke," says Wace, "took the reins, put foot in stirrup, and mounted; and the good horse pawed, pranced, reared himself up, and curveted." The viscount of Toazay, who stood by, thus expressed to those around him his admiration of the duke's fine appearance and noble horsemanship: [2]

"Never," said he, "have I seen a man so fairly armed, nor one who rode so gallantly, and became his hauberk so well, or bore his lance so gracefully. There is no other such knight under heaven! A fair count he is, and a fair king he will be. Let him fight, and he will overcome; and shame be to him who shall fail him." [3]

The Normans were drawn up in three bodies. Montgomery and Fitz-Osborn led the first, Geoffrey Martel led the second, and the duke himself headed the third, which was composed of the flower of Normandy, and kept in reserve till the proper moment for its most effective advance should be ascertained by its skilful and puissant leader.

Taillefer, the warrior minstrel of Normandy, rode gallantly at the head of the chivalry of his native land, singing the war-song of Rollo. [4] William had that day three horses killed under him, without losing a drop of his own blood; finding, however, that Harold had succeeded in rallying a strong body of men around him on one of the heights, with the evident intention of keeping possession of that vantage ground, till the approaching night should favour the Saxon's retreat, he made his last desperate charge upon the people of the land. In this attack it was supposed that Harold was slain by a random arrow, which was shot through the left eye into his brain.

---

[1] Wace.   [2] Ibid.   [3] Ibid. Chronicle of the Dukes of Normandy.
[4] Malmsbury. Matthew of Westminster. Henry Huntingdon. Speed. Rapin. Chronicle de Bello Will. Gemeticensis.

The victorious duke pitched his tent that night in the field of the dead, which, in memory of the dreadful slaughter that had dyed the earth to crimson, was ever after called by him the vale of *Sanguelac*.[1] This fiercely contested battle cost William the lives of six thousand of his bravest followers; but Malmsbury, and other accredited historians of that time, rate the loss of the Saxons at threescore thousand men.[2]

When the duchess-regent of Normandy, Matilda, received the joyful tidings of the victory which her lord had obtained at Hastings, she was engaged in her devotions, in the chapel of the Benedictine priory of Notre Dame, in the fields near the suburbs of St. Sevre; and after returning her thanksgivings to the God of battles, for the success of her consort's arms, she ordered that the priory should henceforth be called, in memory of that circumstance, *Notre Dame de Bonnes Nouvelles* And by that name it is distinguished to this day.[3]

The coronation of the mighty forefather of our present line of sovereigns took place at Westminster, on Monday the 25th of December, being Christmas-day, or, as it was called by our Saxon ancestors, Midwinter-day. Splendid preparations were made in the sister cities of London and Westminster, for the celebration of the twofold festival, of the nativity of our Lord and the inauguration of the new sovereign. On the afternoon of Christmas eve, William of Normandy entered the city on horseback, and was greeted by the acclamations of the Londoners. He took up his lodgings that night at the palace in Blackfriars, where Bridewell now stands. Early in the morning he went by water to London-bridge, where he landed and proceeded to a house near London-stone, where, after reposing a while, he set forth with a stately cavalcade gallantly mounted, and rode to Westminster, amidst the shouts of a prodigious multitude, who were reconciled, by the excitement of the pageant, to the idea of receiving for their sovereign a man whom nature had so admirably qualified to set off the trappings of royalty.[4]

---

[1] Saxon Annals. Speed. Ordericus says it was called so long before this battle.

[2] The following day was devoted by the Norman conquerors to the interment of their dead; and William gave leave and licence to the Saxon peasants to perform the like charitable office to the remains of their unfortunate countrymen. Search was made for the body of Harold, but at first in vain. The spoilers had stripped and gashed the victims of the fight, so that it was difficult to distinguish between the mortal remains of the leader and the serf. Githa, the mother of Harold, had been herself unable to identify the body of her beloved son; but there was one whose fond eye no change in the object of her affection could deceive; this was a Saxon lady of great beauty, Edith, surnamed Swans-Hals, or the Swan-necked; she had formerly been on those terms with Harold which had rendered her only too familiar with his personal characteristics, and by her the corpse of her false lover was recognised. Githa, it is said, offered to purchase it of William, at the price of its weight in gold; but he yielded it without a ransom to the afflicted mother, either through a generous impulse of compassion, or with a view of conciliating the kindred of the deceased. He also cashiered a Norman soldier, who boasted of having gashed the leg of the royal Saxon after he had fallen. The mother of Harold buried her son at his royal foundation of Waltham Abbey, placing over his tomb the simple but expressive sentence, "Harold Infelix."—Thierry. Chron. of Waltham. Malmsbury.

[3] Ducarel's Norman Antiquities.   [4] Ingulphus. Ordericus Vitalis.

Next to his person rode the nobility of England, and those of Normandy followed. Up to that period, so brilliant a coronation had never been witnessed, and perhaps there have been few since that have surpassed it in splendour: it is certain that there has never been one at which so many foreign princes and peers have assisted.

In consequence of the dispute between Stigand, archbishop of Canterbury, and the Pope, William chose to be crowned and consecrated by the hand of Aldred, archbishop of York,[1] to avoid the possibility of the ceremony being questioned at any future time. He took not the crown, however, as a right of conquest, but by consent of the people, for the archbishop, before he placed the royal circlet on his head, paused, and turning to the English nobles, asked them "if they were willing to have the duke of Normandy for their king;" to which they replied with such continuous acclamations of assent, that the vehemence of their loyalty, more noisy than sincere, had nearly been productive of the most fatal consequences. William had surrounded the abbey, and guarded its approaches with a large body of Norman soldiers, as a prudential measure, in case any attempt upon his life should be made by his new vassals; and those trusty guards without the abbey, mistaking the clamorous applause within for a seditious rising amongst the Saxons, with intent to massacre their lord and his Norman followers, in the first emotions of surprise and rage, set fire to the adjoining houses by way of reprisals. The flames rapidly communicating to the wooden buildings round about, produced great consternation, and occasioned the loss of many lives. William, and the pale and trembling assistant prelates and priests within the church, were dismayed, and faltered in the midst of the ceremonial, and with good cause; for if great exertions had not been used by the more sober-minded portion of the Norman guards, to extinguish the conflagration, which presently extended to the abbey, that magnificent edifice, with all the illustrious company within its walls, must have been consumed together. Some persons have considered this fire as the work of the Saxon populace, with intent to destroy at one blow the Norman conqueror and his followers, with such of their own countrymen as had forgotten their honour so far as to become, not only witnesses, but assistants, at the coronation of their foe. And this indeed is not improbable, if the Anglo-Saxons of that period had evinced a spirit capable of conceiving and carrying into execution a design of such terrific grandeur, for the deliverance of their country. We are, therefore, inclined to agree with all contemporary chroniclers, in attributing the conflagration to the Norman soldiery, who could by no means be appeased, till their beloved chief came out of the abbey, and shewed himself to them, in his coronation robes and diadem.[2]

---

[1] "Then on Midwinter-day, archbishop Aldred hallowed him to king at Westminster, and gave him possession with the books of Christ; and also swore him, ere that he would set the crown upon his head, that he would so well govern this nation, as any king before him best did, if they would be faithful to him."—Saxon Chronicle.   [2] William of Poitou. Lingard.

MATILDA OF FLANDERS,

QUEEN OF WILLIAM THE CONQUEROR.

CHAPTER II.

Matilda assumes the title of queen of England in Normandy—Her regency there
—Patronage of learning—Charities—Her vengeance on Brihtric Meaw—
Obtains his lands—His imprisonment—Death in prison—William's court at
Berkhamstead—Triumphant return to Normandy—Matilda awaits his landing
—Triumphal Norman progresses—Revolts in England—William re-appoints
Matilda regent—Embarks for England in a storm—William sends for Ma-
tilda—She arrives in England with her children—Her coronation at Winchester—Champion at her Coronation—Birth of her son Henry—Bayeux tapestry
—Her dwarf artist Turold—Her daughter betrothed to Earl Edwin—Contract
broken—Queen Matilda's return to Normandy—Regent there the third time—
Her passionate love for her eldest son—Death of her father—Dissensions of
her brothers—Ill effects of her absence—English miseries—Separate govern-
ments of William and Matilda—King of France attacks Matilda—Her able
government—Discontent of Norman ladies—Scandalous reports—William's
supposed conjugal infidelity—Matilda's cruelty to her rival—Duke of Bretagne
invades Normandy — Marriage with Matilda's second daughter — Princess
Cicely professed—Dissensions in the royal family—Matilda's partiality to her
son Robert—Her second son, Prince Richard—His death—New Forest.

" OUR mistress Matilda," says William of Poitou,[1] the chaplain of the
Conqueror, " had already assumed the name of queen, though she was
not yet crowned. She had governed Normandy during the absence of
her lord with great prudence and skill." So firmly, indeed, had that
authority been sustained, that, though the whole flower and strength of
Normandy had followed the fortunes of their warlike duke to the shores
of England, not one of the neighbouring princes had ventured to molest
the duchess-regent.

It is true that her kinsman, the emperor Henry, had engaged, in event
of any aggression on the part of France or Bretagne, to defend Normandy with the whole strength of Germany; and she also had a powerful neighbour and protector in the earl of Flanders, her father; but
great credit was certainly due to her own political conduct, in keeping
the duchy free, both from external embroilments and internal strife, at
such a momentous period. Her government was very popular, as well
as prosperous in Normandy,[2] where, surrounded by the most learned
men of the age, she advanced, in no slight degree, the progress of civilization and refinement. The encouragement afforded by her to arts and

---

[1] This elegant author, who is also called Pictaviensis, was archdeacon of Lisieu.
His Chronicle of the Conquest of England is written in very flowing language,
greatly resembling in style an heroic poem. It abounds with eulogiums on his
royal patron, but is extremely valuable on account of the personal history which
it contains. It is sometimes called the Domestic Chronicle of William of Normandy.   [2] Ordericus Vitalis. William of Poitou.

letters, has won for this princess golden reports in the chronicle lore of that age.

Well aware was Matilda of the importance which it is to princes, to enlist in their service the pens of those who possess the power of defending or undermining thrones, and whose influence continues to bias the minds of men after the lapse of ages.

" This princess," says Ordericus Vitalis, " who derived her descent from the kings of France and emperors of Germany, was even more distinguished for the purity of her mind and manners than for her illustrious lineage. As a queen she was munificent, and liberal of her gifts. She united beauty with gentle breeding and all the graces of Christian holiness. While the victorious arms of her illustrious spouse subdued all things before him, she was indefatigable in alleviating distress in every shape, and redoubled her alms. In a word, she exceeded all commendations, and won the love of all hearts."

Such is the character which one of the most eloquent and circumstantial historians of the eleventh century has given of Matilda. Yet Ordericus Vitalis, as a contemporary witness, could scarcely have been ignorant of the dark stain which the first exercise of her newly acquired power in England has left upon her memory.

The Chronicle of Tewkesbury,[1] which states that Brihtric Meaw, the lord of the honour of Gloucester, when he resided at her father's court as ambassador from Edward the Confessor,[2] had refused to marry Matilda, adds, that in the first year of the reign of William the Conqueror, Matilda obtained from her lord the grant of all Brihtric's lands and honours, and that she then caused the unfortunate Saxon to be seized at his manor of Hanelye, and conveyed to Winchester, where he died in prison and was privately buried.[3]

Thus, then, does it appear that Matilda, after having filled for fourteen years a most exalted station, and enjoying the greatest happiness as a wife and mother, had secretly brooded over the bitter memory of the slight that had been offered to her in early youth, for the purpose of inflicting the deadliest vengeance in return, on the man who had rejected the love she had once condescended to offer.

This circumstance is briefly related, not in a general, but a topographical history, without comment, and it is in no slight degree confirmed by the records of the Domesday-book, where it appears that Avening,

---

[1] Chron. Tewkesbury Bib. Cottonian MSS. Cleopatra, c. 111. Monasticon, vol. iii., p. 59. Leland's Coll., vol. i., p. 78.

[2] The Author of the continuation of Brut, born in the same age, and written in the reign of Henry I., son of this queen, thus alludes to this circumstance :—

"La quele jadis quant fu pucelle,	Who when she was maiden
Ama un conte d'Angleterre,	Loved a count of England,
Brihtric Mau, le oi nomer,	Brihtric Mau he was named,
Apres le roi ki fu riche ber,	Except the king was no richer man,
A lui la pucell envoeia messager,	To him the virgin sent a messenger,
Pur sa amour a lui procurer :	His love for her to obtain :
Mais Brihtric Maude refusa."	But Brihtric Maude refused.

[3] Chronicle of Tewkesbury. Thierry's Anglo-Normans.

4 *

Tewkesbury, Fairford, Thornbury, Whitenhurst, and various other possessions in Gloucestershire, belonging to Brihtric, the son of Algar, were granted to Matilda by the Conqueror, and, after her death, reverting to the crown, were by William again bestowed on their second son, William Rufus.[1]

Matilda, moreover, deprived Gloucester of its charter and civic liberties, merely because it was the city of the unfortunate Brihtric—perhaps, for showing some sign of resentment for his fate.

We fear that the first of our Norman queens must, on this evidence, stand convicted of the crime of wrong and robbery, if not of absolute murder; and if it had been possible to make a *post-mortem* examination on the body of the unfortunate son of Algar, sufficient reason might have been seen, perhaps, for the private nature of his interment. All this wrong was done by agency; for, if dates be correct, Matilda had not yet entered England.

A few days after his coronation, William, feeling some reason to distrust the Londoners, withdrew to his old quarters at Berkhamstead, where he kept his court, and succeeded in drawing round him many of the most influential of the Saxon princes and thanes, to whom, in return for their oaths of allegiance, he restored their estates and honours.

His next step, for the mutual satisfaction of his Norman followers and Saxon subjects, was to lay the foundation of the church and abbey of St. Martin, now called Battle Abbey, where perpetual prayers were directed to be offered up, for the repose of the souls of all who had fallen in that sanguinary conflict.

The high altar of this magnificent monument of the Norman victory was set up on the very spot where Harold's body was found, or, according to others,[2] where he first pitched his gonfanon.

Tranquillity was now restored in England, or things were fast progressing to that most desired consummation. William having been now six months separated from his wife and family, his desire to embrace them once more, and to display to his Norman subjects his newly acquired grandeur, induced him to revisit his native country, at a time when it would have been far more conducive to his interests to have remained in England. Previous to his departure, he placed strong Norman garrisons in all his castles; he appointed his half-brother, Odo, bishop of Bayeux,[3] with his faithful kinsman and friend, William Fitz-Osborn, regents of England; and carried with him to Normandy all the leading men among the Anglo-Saxons. Among these were Edgar Atheling, Morcar, Edwin, and Waltheof.[4] These lords, who certainly had no wish to become the companions of his voyage, were not over-pleased at the idea of swelling the pride of the Normans, by forming a part of William's triumphant pageant.

[1] "Infra scriptas terras tenuit Brihtric et post Regina Matilda."—Domesday-book, tom. ii., p. 100. History of Gloucester.
[2] Malmsbury. William of Poitou.
[3] The son of his mother Arlotta, by Herlewin of Conteville.
[4] William of Poitou. Malmsbury. S. Dunelm. Walsingham. Y-Podigma.

William was determined to spend the Easter festival in Normandy, with his queen; and reckless of the seeds of disaffection and disgust which he was sowing in the bosoms of his new subjects, he re-embarked in the Mora, in the month of March, 1067, and with the most splendid company that ever sailed from England, he crossed the seas, and landed on his native shore, a little below the abbey of Fescamp.

Matilda was already there, with her children,[1] in readiness to receive and welcome her illustrious lord, who was greeted with the most enthusiastic rapture by all classes of his subjects. For joy of William's return the solemn fast of Lent was this year kept as a festival; all labour was suspended, and nothing but mirth and pleasure prevailed in his native Normandy.[2]

William appears to have had infinite pleasure in displaying, not only to his wife and family, but to the foreign ambassadors, the costly spoils which he had brought over from England.[3] The quantity and exquisite workmanship of the gold and silver plate, and withal, the richness of the embroidered garments, wrought by the skilful hands of the Anglo-Saxon ladies, (then esteemed so inestimably precious in all parts of Europe, that they were called, by distinction, *Anglicum opus*,[4]) excited the admiration and astonishment of all beholders; but more particularly did the splendid dress of his guards, and the magnificence and beauty of the long-haired and moustached Anglo-Saxon nobles, by whom he was attended, attract the wonder of the foreign princes and peers.

The whole summer was spent by William in a series of triumphant progresses, through the towns and cities of Normandy, with his queen-duchess.[5] Meanwhile, England, in addition to all the recent horrors of war and rapine, was suffering at one and the same time the evils attendant on a system of absenteeism, and the oppressive weight of a foreign yoke. The spirit of freedom was crushed, but not extinguished, among the people of the land; and the absence of the Conqueror was regarded as a favourable opportunity for expelling the unwelcome locusts who had fastened upon the land, and were devouring its fatness; and a secret plot was in agitation, for a simultaneous rising throughout England, for the purpose of a general massacre of the Normans.[6] But though the terror of William's actual presence was withdrawn for a season, he kept up a strict espionage on the proceedings of the English. The first rumour of what was going on among them, roused him from the career of pleasure which he had been pursuing. Relinquishing the idea of keeping a splendid Christmas with his beloved family, he re-appointed Matilda and his son Robert regents of Normandy, and embarking on a stormy sea, he sailed from Dieppe on the 6th of December.[7] On the 7th he arrived at Winchelsea, and proceeded immediately to London, to the consternation of the malcontents, who thought they were sure of him for the winter season.

He kept Christmas in London, and though he used very prompt and

[1] William of Poitou. Henderson.   [2] William of Poitou.   [3] Ibid.
[4] English work.   [6] Ordericus Vitalis. Saxon Chronicle.
[5] William of Poitou.   [7] Ordericus Vitalis.

energetic measures for crushing the insurrection, he gave a conciliatory reception to such of the English prelates and nobles as ventured to attend his summons.

After the suppression of the revolt caused by the imposition of Dane-gelt, William, perceiving the disadvantages attendant on a queenless court, and feeling withal the greatest desire to enjoy the society of his beautiful consort, despatched a noble company into Normandy, to conduct Matilda and her children to England.[1] She joyfully obeyed the welcome mandate of her lord, and crossed the sea, with a stately cortège of nobles, knights, and ladies.[2] Among the learned clerks by whom she was attended was the celebrated Gui, bishop of Amiens, who had distinguished himself by an heroic poem on the defeat and fall of Harold.

Matilda arrived in England soon after Easter, in the month of April, 1068, and proceeding immediately to Winchester, was received with great joy by her lord; and preparations were instantly commenced for her coronation, which was appointed to take place in that city on Whit-Sunday.[3] The great festivals of the church appear in the middle ages to have been considered by the English as peculiarly auspicious days for the solemnization of coronations and marriages, if we may judge by the frequency of their occurrence at those seasons. Sunday was generally chosen for a coronation-day.

William, who had been exceedingly anxious to share his newly acquired honours with Matilda, chose to be re-crowned at the same time, to render the pageant of her consecration more imposing; and farther to conciliate the affections of his English subjects, he repeated for the second time the oath by which he engaged to govern with justice and moderation, and to preserve inviolate that great palladium of English liberty, the right of trial by jury.[4]

This coronation was far more splendid than that which had preceded it in Westminster Abbey, at William's first inauguration, where the absence of the queen and her ladies deprived the ceremony of much of its brilliancy, and the alarming conflagration by which it was interrupted must have greatly abridged the pomp and festivities that had been anticipated on that occasion. Here everything went off auspiciously. It was in the smiling season of the year, when the days were long and bright, without having attained to the oppressiveness of summer heat. The company, according to the report of contemporary historians, was exceedingly numerous and noble; and the Conqueror, who appears to have been in a wonderfully gracious mood on that day, was very sprightly and facetious on the occasion, and conferred favours on all who solicited. The graceful and majestic person of queen Matilda, and the number and beauty of her fine children, charmed the populace, and every one present was delighted with the order and regularity with which this attractive pageant was conducted.[5]

The nobles of Normandy attended their duchess to the church; but

[1] Ordericus Vitalis.   [2] Ibid.
[3] Florence of Worcester. S. Dunelm. M. Westminster.
[4] S. Dunelm. Saxon Chronicle.   [5] Henderson.

after the crown was placed on her head by Aldred, archbishop of York, she was served by her new subjects, the English.

The first occasion on which the office of champion was instituted, is said to have been at this splendid coronation at Winchester, where William caused his consort to be associated with himself, in all the honours of royalty.[1]

The splendid ceremonial of Matilda's inauguration banquet afforded precedents for most of the grand feudal offices at subsequent coronations.[2] Among these, the office of grand pannetier has been for some time extinct. His service was to bear the salt and the carving-knives from the pantry to the king's dining-table, and his fees were the salt-cellars, spoons, and knives laid on the royal table; "forks were not among the royal luxuries at the board of the mighty William and his fair Matilda, who both, in feeding themselves, verified the proverb which says 'that fingers were made before forks.'" "The grand pannetier likewise served the bread to the sovereigns, and received, in addition to the rest of his fees, the bread-cover, called the cover-pane. For this service the Beauchamps held the manor of Beauchamp Kibworth. The manor of Addington was likewise granted by the Conqueror to Tezelin, his cook, for composing a dish of white soup called dillegrout, which especially pleased the royal palate."

"When the noble company had retired from the church, and were seated at dinner in the banqueting hall," says Henderson, in his life of the Conqueror, "a bold cavalier called Marmion,[3] completely armed, rode into the hall, and did at three several times repeat this challenge :—

"If any person denies that our most gracious sovereign, Lord William, and his spouse Matilda, are not king and queen of England, he is a false-hearted traitor and a liar; and here I, as champion, do challenge him to single combat."

No person accepted the challenge, and Matilda was called *la reine* ever after.

The same year, Matilda brought into the world her fourth son, Henry, surnamed Beauclerk. This event took place at Selby, in Yorkshire, and was productive of some degree of satisfaction to the people, who considered the English-born prince with far more complacency than his three Norman brethren, Robert, Richard, and William Rufus. Matilda settled upon her new-born son all the lands she possessed in England and Normandy; they were to revert to him after her death.

Tranquillity now appeared to be completely restored; and Matilda,

---

[1] Henderson.   [2] Glories of Regality.

[3] Henderson inaccurately says Dymock; it was Marmion. This ceremony, unknown among the Saxon monarchs, was of Norman origin. The lands of Fontenaye, in Normandy, were held by Marmion, one of the followers of William the Conqueror, on the tenure of championship. The office was hereditary in the family of Marmion, and from them, by heirship, descended to the Dymocks of Scrivelshye.—See Dugdale. The armorial bearings of the Marmions, from the performance of this great feudal service, were, sable, an arming sword, the point in chief argent.—Glories of Regality.

enjoying every happiness as a wife, a mother, and a queen, seemed to be placed at the very summit of earthly prosperity.

Whether it be by accident, or owing to a close attention to the reality he saw before him, it is certain that the antique limner who drew Matilda's portrait, has represented the organ of constructiveness in her head, as very decidedly developed. It is singular, too, that of this propensity, her tastes and pursuits afforded remarkable instances, in the noble ecclesiastical buildings of which she was the foundress; and in her ingenious and curious example of industry, in the Bayeux tapestry, wherein she has wrought the epic of her husband's exploits, from Harold's first landing in Normandy to his fall at Hastings.

It is, in fact, a most important historical document, in which the events and costume of that momentous period have been faithfully preserved to us, by the indefatigable fingers of the first of our Norman queens, and certainly deserves a particular description.

This curious monument of antiquity is still preserved in the cathedral of Bayeux, where it is distinguished by the name of "the duke of Normandy's *toilette*;" which simply means the duke's great cloth.

It is a piece of canvas, about nineteen inches in breadth, but upwards of sixty-seven yards in length, on which, as we have said, is embroidered the history of the Conquest of England by William of Normandy, commencing with the visit of Harold to the Norman court, and ending with his death at the battle of Hastings, 1066.

The leading transactions of these eventful years, the death of Edward the Confessor, and the coronation of Harold, in the chamber of the royal dead, are represented in the clearest and most regular order, in this piece of needlework, which contains many hundred figures of men, horses, birds, beasts, trees, houses, castles, and churches, all executed in their proper colours, with names and inscriptions over them, to elucidate the story.[1]

This pictorial chronicle of her mighty consort's achievements appears

---

[1] The Bayeux tapestry has lately been much the subject of controversy among some learned individuals, who are determined to deprive Matilda of her traditionary fame, as the person from whom this specimen of female skill and industry emanated. Montfaucon, Thierry, Planché, Ducarel, Taylor, and many other equally important authorities, may be quoted in support of the historical tradition, that it was the work of Matilda and her ladies. The brief limits to which we are confined in these Biographies, will not admit of our entering into the arguments of those who dispute the fact, though we have carefully examined them; and, with due deference to the judgment of the lords of the creation, on all subjects connected with policy and science, we venture to think our learned friends, the archæologists and antiquaries, would do well to direct their intellectual powers to more masculine objects of inquiry, and leave the question of the Bayeux tapestry, (with all other matters allied to needle-craft,) to the decision of the ladies, to whose province it peculiarly belongs. It is matter of doubt to us whether one out of the many gentlemen who have disputed Matilda's claims to that work, if called upon to execute a copy of either of the figures on canvas, would know how to put in the first stitch. The whole of the Bayeux tapestry has been engraved, and coloured like the original, by the Society of Antiquaries, who, if they had done nothing else to merit the approbation of the historical world, would have deserved it for this alone.

to have been, in part at least, designed for Matilda by Turold, a dwarf artist, who, moved by a natural desire of claiming his share in the celebrity which he foresaw would attach to the work, has cunningly introduced his own effigies and name, thus authenticating the Norman tradition, that he was the person who illuminated the canvas with the proper outlines and colours.[1]

It is probable that the wife of the Conqueror, and her Norman ladies, were materially assisted in this stupendous work of feminine skill and patience, by some of the hapless daughters of the land, who, like the Grecian captives described by Homer, were employed in recording the story of their own reverses, and the triumphs of their haughty foes.

About this period William laid the foundation of that mighty fortress and royal residence, the Tower of London, which was erected by a priestly architect and engineer, Gundulph, bishop of Rochester. He also built the castle of Hurstmonceaux, on the spot which had, in the first instance, been occupied by the wooden fort which he had brought over from Normandy, and, for the better security of his government, built and strongly garrisoned many other strong fortresses, forming a regular chain of military stations, from one end of England to the other.[2] These proceedings were regarded with jealous displeasure, by such of the Anglo-Saxon nobles as had hitherto maintained a sort of passive amity with their Norman sovereign, and they began gradually to desert his court. Among the first to withdraw from the royal circle were the mighty Saxon brethren, Edwin and Morcar. They were the darlings of the people, and secretly favoured by the clergy. A third part of England was under their authority, and the reigning prince of Wales was their nephew. William had in the first instance endeavoured, by the most insidious caresses, to conciliate Edwin, who was the youngest of the two, and remarkable for the beauty of his person, and his noble and engaging qualities. The Conqueror had actually promised to give him one of his daughters in marriage.[3] When, however, the young nobleman demanded his bride, he met with a denial, at which he was so much exasperated, that he retired with his brother into the north, where they organized a plan with the kings of Scotland and Denmark, and the princes of Wales, for separate but simultaneous attacks upon William, in which the disaffected Saxons were to join. The prompt and energetic measures of the Conqueror defeated their projects before they could be brought to maturity; the brother earls were compelled to sue for pardon, and obtained a deceitful amnesty.

---

[1] Thierry's History of the Anglo-Normans. The figures were, in fact, always prepared for tapestry work by some skilful artist, who designed and traced them out in the same colours that were to be used in silk or woollen by the embroideress; and we are told in the life of St. Dunstan, "that a certain religious lady, being moved with a desire of embroidering a sacerdotal vestment, earnestly entreated the future chancellor of England, who was then a young man in an obscure station of life, but creeping into notice through his excellent taste in such delineations, to draw the flowers and figures which she afterwards formed with threads of gold."

[2] At Norwich, Warwick, Lincoln, York, Nottingham, &c. &c.

[3] Ordericus Vitalis.

The repeated and formidable revolts of the English, in 1069, compelled William to provide for the safety of Matilda and her children in Normandy.[1] The presence of the queen-duchess was, indeed, no less required there, than that of her warlike lord in England. She was greatly beloved in the duchy, where her government was considered exceedingly able, and the people were beginning to murmur at the absence of the court and the nobility, which, after the states of Normandy had been so severely taxed to support the expense of the English wars, was regarded as a national calamity. It was therefore a measure of great political expediency on the part of William, to re-appoint Matilda, for the third time, to the regency of Normandy. The name of his eldest son, Robert, was, as before, associated with that of Matilda in the regency; and at parting, the Conqueror entreated his spouse " to pray for the speedy termination of the English troubles, to encourage the arts of peace in Normandy, and to take care of the interests of their youthful heir." [2]

The latter injunction was somewhat superfluous; for Matilda's fondness for her first-born betrayed her into the most injudicious acts of partiality in his favour, and in all probability was the primary cause of the dissensions between him and his brothers, and the subsequent rupture between that wrong-headed prince and his royal father.

The death of the earl of Flanders, Matilda's father, and the unsettled state of her native country, owing to the strife between her brothers and nephews, who appeared bent on effecting the ruin of each other, and the fall of the ancient royal house of Flanders, greatly troubled her, and added in no slight degree to the feelings of anxiety and sorrow with which her return to Normandy was clouded, after the brief splendour of her residence in England as queen.[3]

The year 1069 was a season of peculiar misery in England.[4] The breaking up of the court at Winchester, and the departure of queen Matilda and her children for Normandy, cast a deep gloom on the aspect of William's affairs, while it was felt as a serious evil by the industrious classes, whose prosperity depended on the encouragement extended to their handiworks, by the demands of the rich and powerful, for those articles of adornment and luxury, in the fabrication of which many hands are profitably employed, employment being equivalent to wealth with those whose time, ingenuity, or strength, can be brought into the market in any tangible form. But where there is no custom, it is useless to tax the powers of the craftsman or artisan to produce articles which are no longer required. This was the case in England from the year 1069, when, the queen and ladies of the court having quitted the country, trade languished, employment ceased, and the horrors of civil war were aggravated by the distress of a starving population. The most peaceably disposed were goaded by their sufferings to desperation.

It was, according to most accounts, in this year that William, to prevent the people of the land from confederating together in nocturnal assemblies, for the purpose of discussing their grievances, and stimulat-

[1] Ordericus Vitalis. Henry Huntingdon.   [2] Ordericus Vitalis. Malmsbury.
[3] Ordericus Vitalis.   [4] W. Poitou. Ordericus Vitalis. Saxon Chronicle.

ing each other to revolt, compelled them to *couvre feu*, or to extinguish the lights and fires in their dwellings, at eight o'clock every evening, at the tolling of a bell, called, from that circumstance, the curfew, or *couvre feu*.[1] Such, at any rate, has been the popular tradition of ages, and traces of the custom in many places still remain. The curfew has become so thoroughly identified with the institutions of William the Conqueror, that we doubt not, it originated with him, especially as there is great reason to believe that he had previously resorted to the same measure, in his early career as duke of Normandy, to secure the better observance of his famous edict for the suppression of brawls and murders in his dominions, called emphatically "God's peace."[2]

When William took the field after Matilda's departure, and commenced one of his rapid marches towards York, where Waltheof had encouraged the Danish army to winter, he swore " by the splendour of God," his usual oath, that he would not leave one living soul in Northumberland. As soon as he entered Yorkshire, he began to execute his terrible threats of vengeance, laying the whole country waste with fire and sword. After he had bribed the Danish chief to withdraw, and the long defended city of York was surrendered at discretion by Waltheof, he won that powerful Saxon leader to his cause, by bestowing upon him in marriage his beautiful niece Judith.

These fatal nuptials were solemnized among the ruins of the vanquished city of York, where the Conqueror kept his Christmas, amidst the desolation he had wrought.[3]

Not to enter into the melancholy details of William's work of devastation in the north of England, which are so pathetically recorded by the Saxon Chronicle, we will close the brief annals of the direful years 1070 and 1071, with the death of earl Edwin, the affianced husband of one of the daughters of the Conqueror and Matilda. He was proceeding from Ely to Scotland, charged, as was supposed, with a secret mission from his disinherited countrymen to the king of Scots, when his route was betrayed by three brothers in whom he had rashly confided, and, after a valiant defence against a band of Normans, he was slain, with twenty of his followers. His death was passionately bewailed by the English, and even the stern nature of the Conqueror was melted into compassion, and he is said to have shed tears when the bleeding head of the young Saxon, with its long flowing hair, was presented to him by the traitors, who had beguiled him into the Norman ambush; and, instead of conferring the expected reward on the murderers, he condemned them to perpetual exile.[4]

A singular curiosity was turned up by the plough, 1694, in a field near Sutton, in the Isle of Ely, where Edwin and Morcar are said to have met. It is a small shield of silver, about six inches long. On it was a Saxon inscription, which has been found to express that it had the

[1] Speed. It was first established at Winchester. Cassan's Lives of the Bishops of Winchester. Polydore Vergil is the first chronicler who mentions the curfew.
[2] Ordericus Vitalis. The curfew is still tolled in some districts of Normandy, where it is called "*La Retraite*."—Ducarel.
[3] Matthew Paris.   [4] Ordericus Vitalis, p. 521.—J. Brompton.

double property, of protecting the person who wore it, and the lover for whose sake it was worn. If it belonged to the young earl Edwin, it was perhaps a returned love-pledge from the betrothed princess.[1]

The Saxon bishops had stood forth as champions for the rights and ancient laws of the people; and William, finding it impossible to awe or silence these true patriots, proceeded to deprive them of their benefices, and to plunder the churches and monasteries without scruple; and, according to the report of Roger Wendover, and other ancient chroniclers, he appropriated to his own use all the chalices and rich shrines on which he could lay his hands.[2]

It was in vain for the English clergy to appeal to the Roman pontiff for protection; for William was supported by the authority of the new system of church government adopted by the Norman bishops, which was to deprive the people of the use of the Scriptures in the Saxon tongue; thereby rendering one of the best and noblest legacies bequeathed to them by that royal reformer, king Alfred,—the translation commenced by him of the Word of God,—a dead letter. It also became an understood thing, that no scholar, of English birth, was to be admitted to any degree of ecclesiastical preferment.[3]

The Norman language was at that time introduced, by royal authority, into all schools, colleges, and public foundations for the instruction of youth. The laws and statutes of the country were written in that language, and no other was permitted to be used in courts of justice, to the great perplexity and vexation of the people of the land, who were thus under the necessity of employing Norman advocates to plead for redress against the wrongs of Normans.[4]

The luckless Saxons were, of course, sure to obtain more law than justice in such cases, being for the most part wholly unconscious of the purport of the proceedings; so that unless they had the good fortune to

---

[1] Ingram, the learned translator of the Saxon Chronicle, has given this elegant translation of the inscription:—

"Edwinus me pignori dat;
 Illa, O Domine, Domine,
 Cum semper defendat,
 Quæ me ad pectus suum gestet,
 Nisi illa me alienaverit
 Sua sponte."

"Edwin his pledge has left in me,
 Now to the battle prest;
His guardian angel may *she* be,
 Who wears me on her breast.

To him the true-hearted may she prove,
 O God, to thee I pray:

Edwin shall well requite her love,
 Returning from the fray.

But if, forgetful of her vows,
 (May Heaven avert the thought!)
She sell this love-charm of her spouse,
 Which never could be bought;—

If of her own free will she cast
 This talisman away;
May Edwin's life no longer last,
 To rue that fatal day."

As this talisman was found where earl Edwin fell, or, at least, where he was last heard of, circumstances seem to say, that *he* was in possession of it, and not the lady he loved, who had, in all probability, been forced to return it to him.

[2] Ingulphus. Malmsbury. Brompton.
[3] Ingulphus. Halket. Eadmer. Saxon Annals.
[4] Ingulphus. Halket. Polydore Vergil. Mills. Brady.

fall into the hands of *very conscientious* Norman pleaders, they were sacrificed to the superior interest of their opponents, and, for aught they could tell to the contrary, the advocates whom they had paid might have employed their eloquence on the contrary side, or, at the least, in betraying all the weaker points of their clients' causes.

It was the earnest desire of our Norman sovereigns to silence the Saxon tongue for ever, by substituting in its place the Norman dialect, which was a mixture of French and Danish.[1] It was, however, found to be a more easy thing to subjugate the land, than to suppress the natural language of the people. A change was all that could be effected, and that change was an amalgamation between the two languages, the Normans gradually acquiring as many of the Saxon words and idioms as the Anglo-Saxons were compelled to use of theirs. Latin was used by the learned as a general medium of communication, and thus became, in a slight degree, mingled with the parlance of the more refined portion of society. From these mingled elements our own copious and expressive language was in process of time formed.

One of the Conqueror's most difficult undertakings was the reduction of the Isle of Ely, which had been fortified with the most consummate military skill, by the Saxon patriot, Hereward, who was accounted one of the bravest champions and most accomplished leaders.

The unsettled state of England had the effect of dividing William from his beloved queen, and forced them for a considerable time to reign separately—he in England, and she in Normandy.

Matilda, meantime, who appears to have possessed no inconsiderable talents in the art of government, had conducted the regency of Normandy, during all the troubles in which her lord was involved, with great prudence and address. She had been placed in a position of peculiar difficulty, in consequence of the revolt of the province of Maine, and the combined hostilities of the king of France and the duke of Bretagne, who had taken advantage of the manner in which William was occupied with the Scotch invasion and the Saxon revolt, to attack his continental dominions; and Matilda was compelled to apply to her absent lord for succour. William immediately despatched the son of Fitz-Osborn to assist his fair regent in her military arrangements for the

---

[1] While the Provençal language was yet in its infancy in the South of France, the Romance Walloon, or Latin, corrupted by German, was the dialect spoken in the North of France, and, with a further mixture of Norse, became the polite and poetical language of the ducal court of Normandy. It was called the *langue d'oil*, or tongue of *oui*, from its affirmative. The appellation of Walloon was derived from the word Waalchland, the name by which the Germans to this day designate Italy. William the Conqueror was so much attached to the Romance Walloon, that he encouraged its literature among his subjects, and forced it on the English by means of rigorous enactments, in place of the ancient Saxon, which closely resembled the Norse of his own ancestors. It was from Normandy that the first poets in the French language sprang. A digest of the laws which William imposed on his English subjects, is the most ancient work existing in the Romance Walloon. Then the Book of Brut, a fabulous history of the Britons; next Wace's Romance de Rou, or History of Rollo; the word *romance* meaning narrative, and not a fiction.

defence of Normandy, and expedited a peace with the king of Scotland, that he might the sooner come to her aid in person, with his veteran troops.

The Norman ladies were at that period extremely malcontent at the long-protracted absence of their lords.[1] The wife of Hugh Grantmesnil, the governor of Winchester, had caused them great uneasiness, by the reports which she had circulated of the infidelities of their husbands. These representations had induced the indignant dames to send peremptory messages, for the immediate return of their lords. In some instances the warlike Normans had yielded obedience to these conjugal mandates, and returned home, greatly to the prejudice of William's affairs in England. This was the aim of the lady of Grantmesnil, who had for some reason conceived a particular ill-will against her sovereign; and, not contented with doing everything in her power to incite his Norman subjects to revolt, she had thought proper to cast the most injurious aspersions on his character as a husband, and insinuated that he had made an attempt on her virtue.[2]

Githa, the mother of Harold, eagerly caught at these reports, which she is said to have taken great pleasure in circulating. She communicated them to Sweno, king of Denmark, and added, that the reason why Merleswen, a Kentish noble of some importance, had joined the late revolt in England, was, because the Norman tyrant had dishonoured his fair niece, the daughter of one of the canons of Canterbury.[3] This tale, whether false or true, came in due course to Matilda's ears, and caused the first conjugal difference that had ever arisen between her and her lord. She was by no means of a temper to take any affront of the kind patiently, and it is said that she caused the unfortunate damsel to be put to death, with circumstances of great cruelty.[4] Hearne, in his notes to Robert of Gloucester, furnishes us with a curious sequel to this tale, extracted from a very ancient chronicle among the Cottonian MSS., which, after relating " that the priest's daughter was privily slain by a confidential servant of Matilda, the queen," adds, " that the Conqueror was so enraged at the barbarous revenge taken by his queen, that, on his return to Normandy, he beat her with his bridle so severely, that she soon after died." Now, it is certain Matilda lived full ten years after the period at which this matrimonial discipline is said to have been inflicted upon her by the strong arm of the Conqueror; and the worthy chronicler himself seems to regard that part of the tale as apocryphal, and merely relates it as one of the current reports of the day. We are willing to hope that the story altogether has originated from the scandalous reports of that malign busy-body of the eleventh century, the lady Grantmesnil; though at the same time it is to be feared, that the woman who was capable of inflicting such deadly vengeance on the

---

[1] Ordericus Vitalis. Malmsbury.   [2] Henderson. Ordericus Vitalis.
[3] Henderson's Life of the Conqueror. It must be remembered that the marriages of the English clergy were allowed by the Anglo-Saxon Catholic Church till near a quarter of a century afterwards.
[4] She caused her to be hamstrung.—Rapin. Henderson says Matilda ordered her jaws to be slit.

unfortunate Saxon nobleman who had been the object of her earliest affections, would not have been very scrupulous in her dealings with a female whom she suspected of having rivalled her in her husband's regard. At this distance of time it is impossible, after most careful investigation, to speak with any certainty, as to the degree of credit which may be attached to this dark tale; but as it is recorded by several of the oldest chroniclers, it becomes a matter of duty in the biographers of Matilda of Flanders to relate it, and leave the readers to form their own conclusions.

William was attended, on his voyage to Normandy, by a great military retinue; many English as well as Norman troops accompanied him,[1] and performed good service for him, in the reduction of the rebel province of Maine. The king of France made a hasty retreat before the terror of his warlike neighbour's arms, and peace was quickly restored within the circle of William's continental dominions.

If any cause of anger or mistrust had occurred, during their long separation, to interrupt the conjugal happiness of Matilda and her husband, it was but a passing cloud, for historians all agree that they were living together in a state of the most affectionate union, during the year 1074, great part of which was spent by the Conqueror with his family in Normandy.[2] It was at this period that Edgar Atheling came to the court at Caen, to make a voluntary submission to the Norman sovereign, and to entreat his forgiveness for the several insurrections in which he had been engaged. The Conqueror freely accorded an amnesty, treated him with great kindness, and pensioned him with a daily allowance of a pound of silver,[3] in the hope that this amicable arrangement would secure his government in England from all future disturbances. He was mistaken: fresh troubles had already broken out in that quarter, but this time they proceeded from his own turbulent Norman chiefs; one of them, withal, was the son of his great favourite and trusty kinsman, Fitz-Osborn; who was defeated and taken prisoner[4] by the nobles and prelates of Worcester. The Danish fleet, which had vainly hovered on the coast, waiting for a signal to land troops to assist the conspirators, was fain to retreat without effecting its object. As for the great Saxon earl, Waltheof, who had been drawn into the plot, and betrayed by his Norman wife, Judith, to her uncle, the Conqueror, he was, after a long suspense, beheaded on a rising-ground, just without the gates of Winchester; being the first English nobleman who had died by the hand of a public executioner.[5]

---

[1] Ordericus Vitalis.   [2] Ibid. Malmsbury. Saxon Annals.
[3] Saxon Annals. Malmsbury. Brompton.
[4] Fitz-Osborn was a relation of his sovereign, and, before this act of contumacy, stood high in his favour. He was only punished with imprisonment, for his share in the conspiracy. After a time his royal master, as a token that he was disposed to pardon him, sent him a costly suit of clothes; but Fitz-Osborn, instead of tendering his grateful acknowledgments for this present, ordered a large fire to be made, and, in the presence of the messenger, burned the rich garments, one by one, with the most insolent expressions of contempt. William was very angry at the manner in which his unwonted graciousness was received by his vassal kinsman, but inflicted no severer punishment than a lengthened term of imprisonment.—Henderson.   [5] Ordericus Vitalis.

William next pursued his Norman traitor, Ralph de Guader, to the continent, and besieged him in the city of Dol, where he had taken refuge. The young duke of Bretagne, Allan Fergeant, assisted also by the king of France, came with a powerful army to the succour of the besieged earl; and William was not only compelled to raise the siege, but to abandon his tents and baggage, to the value of fifteen thousand pounds. His diplomatic talents, however, enabled him to extricate himself from the embarrassing strait in which he had placed himself; and a pacific treaty was entered into, between him and the valiant young duke of Bretagne, the conclusion of which was a marriage between Alan and his daughter Constance. This alliance was no less advantageous to the princely bridegroom, than agreeable to William and Matilda. The nuptials were celebrated with great pomp, and the bride was dowered with all the lands of Chester, once the possessions of the unfortunate earl Edwin, who had formerly been contracted to one of her sisters.[1]

At the close of this year died Editha, the widow of Edward the Confessor. She had retired to a convent, but was treated with the respect and honour of a queen-dowager, and was buried by the side of her royal husband, in Westminster Abbey. She was long survived by her unfortunate sister-in-law, Algith, the widow of Harold, the other Saxon queen-dowager, who, having had woful experience of the calamities of greatness, and the vanity of earthly distinctions, voluntarily resigned her royal title, and passed the residue of her days in obscurity.

In the year 1075, William and Matilda, with their family, kept the festival of Easter with great pomp, at Fescamp, and attended in person the profession of their eldest daughter Cicely, who was there veiled a nun, by the archbishop John.[2] "This royal maid," says Ordericus Vitalis, "had been educated with great care, in the convent of Caen, where she was instructed in all the learning of the age, and several sciences. She was consecrated to the holy and indivisible Trinity, and took the veil under the venerable abbess Matilda, and faithfully conformed to all the rules of conventual discipline. Cicely succeeded this abbess in her office, having, for fourteen years, maintained the highest reputation for sanctity and wisdom. From the moment that she was dedicated to God by her father, she became a true servant of the Most High, and continued a pure and holy virgin, attending to the pious rules of her order, for a period of fifty-two years."

Soon after the profession of the lady Cicely, those fatal divisions began to appear in the royal family, of which Matilda is accused of having sown the seeds, by the injurious partiality which she had shown for Robert, her first-born.

This prince, having been associated with his royal mother, in the regency of Normandy, from the age of fourteen, had been brought more into public than was perhaps desirable, at a period of life when presumptuous ideas of self-importance are only too apt to inflate the mind. Robert, during his father's long absence, was not only emancipated from all control, but had accustomed himself to exercise the functions of a sove-

---

[1] Saxon Annals. S. Dunelm. Malmsbury.   [2] Ordericus Vitalis. Malmsbury.

reign, in Normandy, by anticipation, and to receive the homage and flattery of all ranks of people, in the dominions to which he was the heir. The Conqueror, it seems, had promised that he would one day bestow the duchy of Normandy on him; and Robert, having represented the ducal majesty for nearly eight years, considered himself an injured person when his royal father took the power into his own hands once more, and exacted from him the obedience of a subject, and the duty of a son.[1] There was also a jealous rivalry between Robert and his two younger brothers, William Rufus and Henry. William Rufus, notwithstanding his rude, boisterous manners, and the apparent recklessness of his disposition, had an abundant share of world-craft, and well knew how to adapt himself to his father's humour, so that he was no less a favourite with the Conqueror than Robert was with Matilda. Robert was a prince of a generous disposition, but of an irritable temperament, proud, and quick to take offence. From his low stature his father had bestowed on him the cognomen of Court-hose,[2] and this appellation, like all names derived from some personal peculiarity, was, no doubt, very displeasing to a haughty young man, and tended in no slight degree to increase the mortification attendant on the loss of power, and to create feelings of ill-will against his royal sire. He had, withal, many injurious flatterers and pretended friends, among the dissipated young nobles of Normandy, who took every occasion to persuade him that he was an injured person, especially with regard to the province of Maine. Robert had in his infancy been espoused to Margaret, the heiress of Herbert, the last earl of that province. The little countess died while they were yet children, and William of Normandy, who had, during her minority, taken her lands under his wardship, annexed them to his own dominions after her death. When the juvenile widower became of age, he considered himself entitled to the earldom and lands of Maine, in right of his deceased wife, and claimed them of his father, who put him off with fair words, but withheld the territory, though the people of Maine demanded Robert for their lord; and at the surrender of the revolted city of Mans, it was among the articles of capitulation, that he should receive the investiture of the earldom. This condition was violated by the Conqueror, who had no mind to part with any portion of his acquisitions during his life; verifying, in this as in every other action, the predictions of the gossips at his birth, " that he would grasp everything within his reach, and that which he had once grasped he would keep."[3]

In the year 1076, while Matilda and William were with their family, at the castle of L'Aigle, their two younger sons, William and Henry, in wanton play, threw some dirty water from the balcony of an upper apartment, on Robert and some of his partisans, who were walking in the court below. The fiery heir of Normandy construed this act of boyish folly into an act of studied contempt; and being just then in an irritable and excited frame of mind, he drew his sword, and rushed up stairs, with a threat of taking deadly vengeance on the youthful transgressors who had offered this insult to him before the whole court.

---

[1] Ordericus Vitalis.   [2] Robert of Gloucester.   [3] Ordericus Vitalis.

This occasioned a prodigious tumult and uproar in the castle, and nothing but the presence and stern authority of the king, who, hearing the alarm, burst into the room with his drawn sword in his hand, could have prevented fatal consequences.[1]

Robert, not obtaining the satisfaction he expected, for the affront he had received, privately retired from the court that very evening, followed by a party of the young nobility whom he had attached to his cause.[2]

Richard, the second son of William and Matilda, does not appear to have taken any part in these quarrels. He was the pupil of the learned Lanfranc, and was probably occupied with studious pursuits, as he is said to have been a prince of great promise, and of an amiable disposition.[3] He died in England, in the flower of his youth. According to popular tradition, he was gored by a stag, while hunting in the New Forest, which caused his death; but some historians record that he died of a fever, occasioned by the malaria in the depopulated district of Hampshire, at the time when so many thousands of the unfortunate Saxons perished by famine, in consequence of having been driven from their homes, when the Conqueror converted that once fertile part of England into a chase, for the enjoyment of his favourite amusement of hunting.

Prince Richard was buried in Winchester Cathedral: a slab of stone marked with his name is still seen there.

Drayton gives a political reason for the depopulation of the shore of Hampshire, occasioned by the enclosure of the New Forest, which is well worth the consideration of the historical reader.

> "Clear Avon, coming in, her sister Stour doth call,
>   And at New Forest's foot into the sea doth fall;
>   That Forest now, whose sight e'en boundless seems to lie,
>   Its being erst received from William's tyranny,
>   Who framed laws to keep those beasts he planted then,
>   His lawless will from hence before had driven men:
>   That where the earth was warmed with Winter's festal fires,
>   The melancholic hare now forms in tangled brakes and briers;
>   And on sites of churches, grown with nettles, fern, and weeds,
>   Stands now the aged ranpick trunk, where ploughmen cast their seeds.
>   The people were, by William here, cut off from every trade:
>   That on this spot the Norman still might enter to invade,
>   And, on this desolated place and unfrequented shore,
>   New forces evermore might land to aid those here before."

The Saxon Chronicle comments on the oppressive statutes enacted by the Norman Conqueror, for the preservation of game, in an eloquent strain of indignant irony, and says, "he loved the tall deer as if he had been their father."

That game-laws were in existence at a much earlier period, is most certain; but it was during this reign that they were rendered a grievance to the people, and assumed the character of a moral wrong in the legislature of the country. The more enlightened policy of modern jurisprudence, has in some degree ameliorated the rigorous penalties enacted by our Norman line of sovereigns, against poaching in its various de-

---

[1] Ordericus Vitalis.   [2] Malmsbury.   [3] Camden. Saxon Chronicle.

partments; but the bitterness engendered by the spirit of those laws remains in full force, in the hearts of those classes against whom the statutes are supposed to point, and is constantly acted upon by persons assuming the office of political agitators, for the purpose of creating divisions between the people and their rulers.

MATILDA OF FLANDERS,

QUEEN OF WILLIAM THE CONQUEROR.

CHAPTER III.

Matilda mediates between her husband and son—Robert's insolence and rebellion—Matilda supplies him with money—Conqueror seizes Matilda's agent—Conqueror's remonstrance—Queen's answer—Robert's military prowess—Field of Archembraye—Robert wounds the Conqueror—His penitence—Matilda intercedes—Conqueror writes to his son—Robert pardoned—Conqueror's legislation in England—Domesday Book—Royal revenue—Queen of England's perquisites and privileges—Her dues at Queenhithe—Officers of royal household—Matilda's court the model of succeeding ones—She continues to govern Normandy—Her visit to the monastery of Ouche—Illness and death of her second daughter—Fresh cause of sorrow to the queen—Robert's dissensions with his father—Matilda's distress—Applies to a hermit—His vision, and message to the queen—Her grief and lingering illness—Dying of a broken heart—The Conqueror hastens from England—She dies—Her obsequies—her alms—Tomb—Epitaph—Will—Articles of dress named therein—Portrait and costume—Her children—The Conqueror's deep affliction—Disquiets after the death of the Queen—Fatal accident to the Conqueror—Death—His body plundered—Accidents and interruptions at his funeral—Monument—Portrait—Destruction of his tomb—Of Matilda's tomb—Her sapphire ring—Their bodies re-interred—Matilda's tomb restored—Final destruction at French Revolution.

THE feud between her royal husband and her first-born was very painful to Matilda, whose anxious attempts to effect a reconciliation were unavailing. When Robert's passion was somewhat cooled, he consented to see his father, but the interview was anything but friendly. Ordericus Vitalis gives the following particulars of the conference.

Robert assumed a very high tone, and repeated his demand, of being invested with the duchies of Normandy and Maine. This was of course refused by the Conqueror, who sternly bade his ambitious heir "remember the fate of Absalom, and the misfortunes of Rehoboam, and not to listen to the evil counsellors who wished to seduce him from the paths of duty." On which Robert insolently replied, "That he did not come there to listen to sermons, with which he had been nauseated by his tutors when he was learning grammar, but to claim the investiture which had been promised to him. Answer me positively," continued he, " are not these things my right ?   Have you not promised to bestow them on me ?" [1]

" It is not my custom to strip till I go to bed," replied the Conqueror; " and as long as I live, I will not deprive myself of my native realm, Normandy, neither will I divide with another; for it is written in the holy evangelists, 'Every kingdom that is divided against itself shall become desolate.' [2] I won England by mine own good sword; the vicars of Christ placed the diadem of its ancient kings on my brow, and the sceptre in mine hand; and I swear that all the world combined shall not compel me to delegate my power to another. It is not to be borne, that he who owes his existence to me should aspire to be my rival in mine own dominions."

But Robert scornfully rejoined, with equal pride and disrespect, " If it be inconvenient for you to keep your word, I will withdraw from Normandy, and seek justice from strangers; for here I will not remain as a subject." [3]

With these words he quitted the royal presence, and, with a party of disaffected nobles, took refuge with Matilda's brother, Robert earl of Flanders, surnamed Le Frison, from his having married the countess of Friesland.

From this uncle, Robert received very bad advice, and the king of France endeavoured, by all the means in his power, to widen the breach between the undutiful heir of Normandy and his father. Encouraged by these evil counsellors, Robert busied himself in fomenting discontents, and organizing a formidable faction, in his father's dominions, whence he drew large sums, in the shape of presents and loans, from many of the vassals of the ducal crown, who were willing to ingratiate themselves with the heir apparent, and to conciliate the favour of the queen-duchess, whose partial fondness for her eldest son was well known.

The supplies thus obtained Robert improvidently lavished among his dissolute companions, both male and female. In consequence of this extravagance, he was occasionally reduced to the greatest inconvenience. When under the pressure of those pecuniary embarrassments, which could not fail to expose him to the contempt of the foreign princes who espoused his quarrel against his father, he was wont to apply to his too indulgent mother, Matilda, by whom he was so passionately beloved, that she could refuse him nothing; from her private coffers she secretly supplied him with large sums of silver and gold; and when these resources were exhausted by the increasing demands of her prodigal son, Matilda had the weakness to strip herself of her jewels and precious garments, for the same purpose. [4]

This system continued even when Robert had taken up arms against his father and sovereign. Roger de Beaumont, that faithful minister — whom William had, previous to his first embarkation on the memorable expedition from St. Vallerie, appointed as the premier of Normandy, —

[1] Ordericus Vitalis. Hemingford. Walsingham.
[2] Ordericus Vitalis. S. Dunelm.   P. Daniel.
[3] Ordericus Vitalis.   [4] Malmsbury. Ordericus Vitalis.

and who had ever since assisted his royal mistress, not only with his counsels in the administration of affairs of state, but even in the education of her children, felt it his duty to inform his sovereign of the under-hand proceedings of Matilda in favour of her rebel son.[1]

William was in England when the startling intelligence reached him, of the unnatural rebellion of his first-born, and the treachery of his beloved consort, in whom he had ever reposed the most unbounded confidence. He appears scarcely to have given credence to the representations of Roger de Beaumont, relating to the conduct of his queen, till, on his return to Normandy, he intercepted one of Matilda's private agents, named Sampson, who was charged with communications from the queen to Robert, which left no doubt on William's mind, of the identity of the secret friend by whom his undutiful son had been supplied with the means of carrying on his plots and hostile measures against his government.[2]

There was a stern grandeur, not unmixed with tenderness, in the reproof which he addressed to his offending consort on this occasion.

"The observation of a certain philosopher is true," said he, "and I have only too much cause to admit the force of his words—

'Naufragium rerum est mulier malefida marito:'

'The woman who deceives her husband is the destruction of her own house.'

"Where in all the world could you have found a companion so faithful and devoted in his affection?" continued he, passionately. "Behold my wife, she whom I have loved as my own soul, to whom I have confided the government of my realms, my treasure, and all that I possessed in the world, of power and greatness — she hath supported mine adversary against me — she hath strengthened and enriched him from the wealth which I confided to her keeping — she hath secretly employed her zeal and subtlety in his cause, and done everything she could to encourage him against me!"[3]

Matilda's reply to this indignant but touching appeal, which her royal husband, more, it should appear, in sorrow than in anger, addressed to her, is no less remarkable for its impassioned eloquence, than the subtlety with which she evades the principal point on which she is pressed, and entrenches herself on the strong ground of maternal love.

"My lord," said she, "I pray you not to be surprised if I feel a mother's tenderness for my first-born son. By the virtue of the Most High, I protest that if my son Robert were dead, and hidden far from the sight of the living, seven feet deep in the earth, and that the price of my blood could restore him to life, I would cheerfully bid it flow. For his sake I would endure any suffering, yea, things from which, on any other occasion, the feebleness of my sex would shrink with terror. How then can you suppose that I could enjoy the pomp and luxuries with which I was surrounded, when I knew that he was pining in want and misery? Far from my heart be such hardness, nor ought your authority to impose such insensibility on a mother."[4]

---

[1] Malmsbury.   [2] Orderious Vitalis.   [3] Ibid.   [4] Ibid.

William is reported to have turned pale with anger at this rejoinder. It was not, however, on Matilda, the object of his adoring and constant affection, that he prepared to inflict the measure of vengeance which her transgression against him had provoked. Sampson, the comparatively innocent agent whom she had employed in this transaction, was doomed to pay the dreadful penalty of the offence, with the loss of sight, by the order of his enraged sovereign.[1] In such cases it is usual for the instrument to be the sacrifice, and persons of the kind are generally yielded up, as a sort of scapegoat, or expiatory victim. But Matilda did not abandon her terrified agent in his distress; she contrived to convey a hasty intimation of his peril, and her desire of preserving him, to some of the persons who were devoted to her service; and Sampson, more fortunate than his illustrious namesake of yore, was enabled to escape the cruel sentence of his lord, by taking sanctuary in the monastery of Ouche, of which Matilda was a munificent patroness. Nevertheless, as it was a serious thing to oppose the wrath of such a prince as William, the abbot Manier found no other way of securing the trembling fugitive from his vengeance, than that of causing him to be shorn, shaven, and professed a monk of Ouche, the same day he entered the convent, " in happy hour both for his body and soul," observes the contemporary chronicler who relates this circumstance.[2]

It does not appear that William's affection for Matilda suffered any material diminution in consequence of these transactions, neither would he permit any one to censure her conduct in his presence.[3] She was the love of his youth, the solace of his meridian hours of life, and she preserved her empire over his mighty heart to the last hour of her life. But though the attachment of the Conqueror to his consort remained unaltered, the happiness of the royal pair was materially impaired. Robert, their first-born, was in arms against his father and sovereign, and at the head of a numerous army, supported by the hostile power of France on the one hand, and the disaffected portion of William's subjects on the other. He had made a formidable attack on Rouen, and in several instances obtained successes which at first astonished his indignant parent, who had certainly greatly underrated the military talents of his heir.

When, however, the Conqueror perceived that the filial foe who had thus audaciously displayed his rebel banner against him, had inherited all the martial prowess of his race, and was by no means unlikely to prove a match for himself in the art of war, he arrayed a mighty army, and advanced with all his wonted energy, to give him battle, not doubting but that success would, as usual, attend his arms. The royal chiefs of Normandy met in hostile encounter, on the plain of Archembraye, near the castle of Gerberg. William Rufus, the Conqueror's favourite son, was in close attendance on his father's person that day. This prince had already received the honour of knighthood from Lanfranc, archbishop of Canterbury, his tutor, and he was eager to assist in humbling

---

[1] Ordericus Vitalis.   [2] Ibid.   [3] Ibid.

the pride of his elder brother, over whom the Conqueror anticipated a
signal triumph.[1]

The battle was fought with no common fury on both sides; but Robert, who headed a choice body of cavalry, decided the fortune of the
day, by his impetuous charge upon the rearward of his foes, where his
royal father commanded, whose utmost endeavours to preserve order in
his ranks were ineffectual. It was in this charge that the memorable
personal encounter between the Conqueror and his rebel son occurred,
where Robert, unconscious who the doughty champion was against
whom he tilted, ran his father through the arm with his lance, and un-
horsed him.[2] This was the first time that William had ever been overcome in single combat, for he was one of the strongest men, and most
approved knights, of the age in which he lived; and it is a singular fact,
that in all the battles in which he had been engaged, he had never lost
a drop of blood, till it was in this field drawn by the lance of his first-
born. He was on this occasion in great danger of being slain in the
mêlée; but transported with rage at the smart of his wound, and the
disgrace of the overthrow, he called so loudly and angrily for rescue, that
Robert recognised him, either by his voice or some of his favourite exple-
tives, and hastily alighting, raised him from the ground in his arms, with
much tenderness and respect, expressed the deepest concern at the unin-
tentional crime of which he had been guilty, for which he most humbly
entreated his forgiveness, and then placing him on his own horse, he
brought him safely out of the press.[3] According to some of the historians of that period, William, instead of meeting this generous burst of
feeling, on the part of his penitent son, with answering emotions of paternal tenderness, was so infuriated at the humiliation he had received,
that he uttered a malediction against him, which all the after submissions
of Robert could not induce him to retract; while others, equally deserving of credit, assert that he was so moved with the proof of Robert's
dutiful reverence for his person, and the anxiety he had manifested for
his safety, that he presently forgave him, and ever after held him in
better respect. Both accounts may be true in part; for it is very possible, that when the Conqueror of England found himself defeated by his
rebel subjects, on his native soil, and his hitherto invincible arm overcome by the prowess of his son, (whose person he had hitherto been
accustomed to mention with a contemptuous allusion to his inferiority
in stature,) he might, while the smart of his wound lasted, have indulged in a strong ebullition of wrathful reproach, not unmixed with
execrations, of which it appears that he, in common with all Normans
of that era, had an evil habit. But after his passion was abated, it is
certain that he did, in compliance with the entreaties of his queen, consent to receive the submission of his victorious but penitent son.[4]

In this battle, William Rufus was severely wounded, as well as his
father, and there was a considerable slaughter of the English troops, of
which the Conqueror's army was chiefly composed; for Robert had

[1] Hoveden. S. Dunelm. M. Paris. Polydore Vergil.
[2] S. Dunelm. Malmsbury. Hoveden. M. Paris.
[3] S. Dunelm. M. Paris. [4] Ordericus Vitalis.

stolen the hearts of the Normans, while associated in the regency with
his mother Matilda, and his father considered it unsafe to oppose him
with his native troops. As it was, Robert remained the master of the
field, having that day given indubitable proofs of able generalship, and
great personal valour; but the perilous chance that had nearly rendered
him the murderer of his father, made so deep an impression on his mind,
that he remained for a time conscience-stricken, which caused him to
endeavour, by employing the intercession of his doting mother, to obtain
a reconciliation with his offended sire.[1]

Matilda had suffered greatly in mind, during the unnatural warfare between her husband and her first-born, especially after the frightful circumstance of their personal encounter in the field of Archembraye,
which was fought in the year 1077. Some feelings of self-reproach
might possibly mingle with her uneasiness on this occasion.

Her health began to decline, and William was at length moved by her
incessant pleading, and the sight of her tears, to write a letter with his
own hand to Robert, inviting him " to repair to Rouen, and receive a full
pardon for his late rebellion, promising at the same time to grant him
everything that he could expect from the affection of a father, consist-
ently with the duty of a king." On the receipt of this welcome letter,
Robert delayed not a moment to obey the summons. He came to Rouen,
attended only by three servants; he was received by his parents in the
most affectionate manner; and a temporary reconciliation was effected
between him and his brethren.[2]

Matilda did not long enjoy the society of this beloved son; for the
Conqueror's affairs in England requiring his presence, he thought proper
to carry Robert with him, under the pretence that he required his services in a military capacity, to defend the northern counties against the
aggression of Malcolm, king of Scotland, who had once more violated
the treaty of peace.

William's real motive for making Robert the companion of his voyage,
was because he considered Matilda was too much devoted to the interest
of her first-born, to render it expedient for him to remain with her in
Normandy.

The following spring, Robert was commissioned to chastise the Scottish monarch; but having been given an ineffectual force, he performed
nothing remarkable in that campaign. While in the north, he founded
the town of Newcastle-upon-Tyne, in the same place where Monkches-
ter, or the city of the monks, was situated.[3]

The year 1078[4] was remarkable, in this country, for the great national
survey, which was instituted by the Conqueror, for the purpose of ascertaining the precise nature of the lands and tangible property throughout
England; so that, says Ingulphus, " there was not a hide of land, water,
or waste, but he knew the valuation, the owners and possessors, together

[1] Ordericus Vitalis.   [2] Ordericus Vitalis. Henderson.
[3] Henry Huntingdon. M. Westminster.
[4] According to some historians, the survey was not generally begun till 1080.
It was not fully completed till 1086.—Tindal's Notes on Rapin.

with the rents and profits thereof; as also of all cities, towns, villages, hamlets, monasteries, and religious houses; causing, also, all the people in England to be numbered, their names to be taken, with notice what any one might *dispend* by the year; their substance, money, and bond-men recorded, with their cattle, and what service they owed to him, who held of him in fee; all which was certified upon the oaths of commissioners." [1]

Such is the account given by the learned abbot of Croydon, of the particulars of William's "Great Terrar," or "Domesday-book," as it was called by the Saxons. The proceedings of the commissioners were inquisitorial enough, no doubt, since they extended to ascertaining how much money every man had in his house, and what was owing to him. That in some instances, too, they were partial in their returns, is evident, by the acknowledgment of Ingulphus, when, speaking of his own monastery of Croyland, he says, " the commissioners were so kind and civil, that they did not give in the true value of it:" we may therefore conclude that, whenever the proprietors made it worth their while, they were equally obliging elsewhere. Yet it was at the risk of severe punishment that any fraud, favour, connivance, or concealment, was practised, by either the owners of the property, or the commissioners. [2] Robert of Gloucester, in his rhyming chronicle, gives the following quaint description of the Domesday-book.

> " Then King William, to learn the worth of his land,
> Let enquiry stretch throughout all England;
> How many plough land, and hiden also,
> Were in every shire, and what they were worth thereto;
> And the rents of each town, and the waters each one,
> The worth, and woods eke, and wastes where lived none;
> By that he wist what he were worth of all England,
> And set it clearly forth that all might understand,
> And had it clearly written, and that *script* he put, I wis,
> In the treasurie of Westminster, where it still is."

The king's great object in instituting this survey, was to form an exact calculation of his own revenues, and especially how much money he might be enabled to realize in the way of a land-tax. Accordingly, he laid an impost of six shillings on every hide of land [3] throughout England as soon as he had ascertained this point; which tax affected the Normans, who had become, generally speaking, the lords of the soil, far more than it did the English, who were for the most part reduced to abject poverty.

The description or survey of England was written in two books, the Great and Little Domesday-book, [4] and when finished, they were carefully laid up in the king's treasury or exchequer, to be consulted on occasion,

---

[1] Ingulphus.

[2] This survey was made by presentment of juries, that is, certain persons who were appointed from every hundred, wapentake, or county, and sworn in before commissioners, consisting of the greatest earls, bishops, or leading persons in the district.—Brady.

[3] This was called Hydage.

[4] The little book contains only Norfolk, Suffolk, and Essex.

or as Polydore Vergil shrewdly observes, " when it was required to know of how much more wool the English flocks might be fleeced."

By the aid of this survey, William was enabled to raise the royal revenue to the sum of four hundred thousand pounds per year, which is computed by Brady to be upwards of five millions of our present money. In addition to this settled income, he was entitled to many perquisites, as mulcts, fines, forfeitures, licences for buying and selling, for granting leave to marry, and many other profitable contingencies, which were in those days constantly bringing supplies into the royal purse. Then there were certain occasions on which subsidies were granted, as a matter of course, as on the marriage of an eldest daughter, or when knighthood was conferred on a son.

Matilda, though residing chiefly in Normandy, had her distinct revenues, perquisites, and privileges, as queen of England. She was allowed to claim her *aurum reginæ*, or queen-gold; that is, the tenth part of every fine voluntary that was paid to the crown.[1] She received, from the city of London, sums to furnish oil for her lamp, wood for her hearth, and tolls or imposts on goods landed at Queenhithe; with many other immunities, which the queen-consorts in latter days have not ventured to claim.

The table at which the queen herself sat was furnished with viands, at the daily expenditure of forty shillings. Twelve pence each was allowed for the sustenance of her hundred attendants.[2]

The royal revenues were never richer than in this reign, and they were not charged with any of the expenses attending on the maintenance of the military force of the country, for the king had taken care to impose that burden on such persons, among his followers, who had been enriched with the forfeited lands of the Anglo-Saxons. Almost every landed proprietor then held his estates on the tenure of performing crown service, and furnishing a quota of men-at-arms, at the king's need or pleasure. In this reign the Court of Exchequer was instituted, so called from the chequered cloth, figured like a chess-board, that was laid on the table when the court was sitting.[3]

The principal or supreme court of judicature in ordinary was called *curia regis*,[4] or King's Court, which was always at the royal residence. There councils were held, and all affairs of state transacted. There the throne was placed, which was an ordinary court of judicature,[5] where justice was administered to the subjects by the king, as chief magistrate. The chief officers of this court were:—1st. The grand justiciary: he was next to the king in power and authority, and in his absence governed the realm as viceroy: if the king were not present in person in *curia regis*, he acted as chief judge, both in criminal and civil causes. 2d. The constable: he was a high officer, both in peace and war; this office was anciently hereditary. 3d. The mareschal: this office is still here-

[1] Prynne's " Aurum Reginæ."
[2] The household book of Edward IV. called the " Black Book," which cites precedents from extreme antiquity.
[3] Madox's History of the Exchequer.　　[4] Ibid.　　[5] Ibid.

ditary, and is at present exercised by his grace the duke of Norfolk.
The office of the mareschal, or earl marshal, was to provide for the security of the royal person, in the palace, to distribute lodgings there, (not
always the most enviable task in those bellicose days,) and to preserve
peace and order in the king's household. How the latter duty was performed when the mareschal chanced to be himself one of the most quar-
relsome persons in the court, as in the case of Bigod earl of Norfolk,
our authority saith not. It was also the business of the earl marshal to
assist in determining all controversies : there is a notable one on record,
that took place between king Edward the First and his mareschal, the
said Bigod, which we shall relate, among the events of that reign.

The 4th great officer of the King's Court was the seneschal or steward
of the palace, called the dapifer. The 5th was the chamberlain, who
presided over all matters of courtly ceremonial. The 6th was the king's
chancellor, generally some famous ecclesiastic. The chancellor was the
king's prime counsellor, and was accustomed to supervise the charters
to be sealed with the king's seal; and likewise to supervise and seal the
acts and precepts that issued in proceedings from *curia regis*, or the
king's court.

The 7th officer was the king's treasurer, and he was also most frequently a prelate or noted churchman. Besides these, there were *le
boteler*, or the king's butler, who presided over the royal cellars, and
served the wine-cup to the sovereign; the sewer, whose business it was
to place the dishes on the royal table; and many other officers, of inferior reckoning in the household, but who were nevertheless nobles or
knights.

We have been thus minute in our particulars of the first Anglo-Norman court, because, although it was little graced by the presence of the
queen, its arrangements formed the model and precedent for those in the
succeeding reigns, and cast no little light on the habits and customs of
royalty in the middle ages of English history.

We must now return to the personal history of Matilda. The latter
years of this queen were spent in Normandy, where she continued to
exercise the functions of government, for her royal husband.[1]

Ordericus Vitalis relates the particulars of a visit which she paid to
the monastery of Ouche, to entreat the prayers of the abbot Manier, and
his monks, in behalf of her second daughter, the lady Constance, the
wife of Alan Fergeant, duke of Bretagne. This princess, who was passionately desirous of bringing an heir to Bretagne, was childless, and to
the grief of her mother, had fallen into a declining state of health. Matilda, in the hope of averting the apprehended death of the youthful
duchess, sought the shrine of St. Eurole, the patron of the monks of
Ouche, with prayers and offerings. She was most honourably received
by the learned abbot Manier, and his monks, who conducted her into
the church. She offered a mark of gold on the altar there, and presented
to the shrine of St. Eurole a costly ornament, adorned with precious
stones, and she vowed many benefits in reversion, if the saint were pro-

---

[1] Ordericus Vitalis.

pitious. After this the queen-duchess dined in the common refectory, behaving at the same time with the most edifying humility, so as to leave an agreeable remembrance of her visit, on the minds of the brethren, of whom the worthy chronicler (who relates this circumstance, to the honour and glory of his convent) was one.[1]

Matilda found that her visit and offerings to the shrine of St. Eurole were unavailing, to prolong the life of her daughter, for the duchess Constance died in the flower of her age, after an unfruitful marriage of seven years. Her remains were conveyed to England, and interred in the abbey of St. Edmund's Bury. Like all the children of William and Matilda, she had been carefully educated, and is said to have been a princess possessed of great mental acquirements. After her death, Alan duke of Bretagne married again, and had a family by his second wife; but the rich grant of English lands, with which the Conqueror had dowered his daughter Constance, he was permitted to retain, together with the title of earl of Richmond, which was long borne by the dukes of Bretagne, his successors.

The grief which the early death of her daughter caused Matilda, was soon succeeded by feelings of a still more painful nature, the result of a fresh difference between her royal husband and her beloved son Robert. Some historians[2] assert that this was occasioned by the refusal of the prince to marry the young and lovely heiress of Earl Waltheof, which greatly displeased his father, who was desirous of conciliating his English subjects by such an alliance, and, at the same time, of making some atonement for the murder of the unfortunate Saxon chief, which always appears to have been a painful subject of reflection to him.

About this time, Matilda, hearing that a German hermit, of great sanctity, was possessed of the gift of prophecy, sent to entreat his prayers for her jarring son and husband, and requested his opinion on the subject of their dissension.[3]

The hermit gave a very affectionate reception to the envoys of the queen, but demanded three days before he delivered his reply to her questions. On the third day he sent for the messengers, and gave his answer, in the following strain of oracular allegory. "Return to your mistress," said he, "and tell her I have prayed to God in her behalf, and

---

[1] Ordericus Vitalis, the most eloquent of all the historians of that period, and the most minute and faithful in his personal records of the Conqueror, his queen, and family, was, nevertheless, born in England, and of Anglo-Saxon parentage. He was ten years old at the epoch of the Norman invasion, when for better security he was, to use his own language, "conveyed with weeping eyes from his native country, to be educated in Normandy, at the convent of Ouche," which finally became so dear to him, that all the affections of his heart appear to have been centred within its bounds. In his chronicle of the Norman sovereigns, he sometimes makes digressions of a hundred pages, to descant on St. Eurole, and the merits of the brethren of Ouche.

[2] Henderson, in his Life of the Conqueror, states that Robert was much taken with the beauty of the young Saxon lady; but that his regard was by no means of an honourable nature, and his conduct to her displeased the Conqueror so much, that, to punish his son for insults offered to his beautiful ward, he forbade him the court. [3] Ordericus Vitalis.

the Most High has made known to me in a dream the things she desires to learn. I saw in my vision a beautiful pasture, covered with grass and flowers, and a noble charger feeding therein. A numerous herd gathered round about, eager to enter and share the feast, but the fiery charger would not permit them to approach near enough to crop the flowers and herbage.

"But, alas! the majestic steed, in the midst of his pride and courage, died, his terror departed with him, and a poor silly steer appeared in his place, as the guardian of the pasture. Then the throng of meaner animals, who had hitherto feared to approach, rushed in, and trampled the flowers and grass beneath their feet, and that which they could not devour they defiled and destroyed.[1]

"I will explain the mystery couched in this parable. The steed is William of Normandy, the Conqueror of England, who, by his wisdom, courage, and power, keeps the surrounding foes of Normandy in awe. Robert is the dull, inactive beast who will succeed him; and then those baser sort of animals, the envious princes, who have long watched for the opportunity of attacking this fair, fruitful pasture, Normandy, will overrun the land, and destroy all the prosperity which its present sovereign has established. Illustrious lady, if, after hearing the words of the vision, in which the Lord has vouchsafed to reply to my prayers, you do not labour to restore the peace of Normandy, you will henceforth behold nothing but misery, the death of your royal spouse, the ruin of all your race, and the desolation of your beloved country."[2]

This clever apologue, in which some sagacious advice was implied, Matilda took for a prediction; and this idea, together with the increasing dissensions in her family, pressed heavily on her mind, and are supposed to have occasioned the lingering illness which slowly but surely conducted her to the tomb.

This illness was attended with great depression of spirits. She endeavoured to obtain comfort, by redoubling her devotional exercises and alms. She confessed her sins frequently, and with bitter tears.[3] It is to be hoped that a feeling of true penitence was mingled with the affliction of the queen, who, at the highest pinnacle of earthly grandeur, afforded a melancholy exemplification of the vanity and insufficiency of the envied distinctions with which she was surrounded, and was dying of a broken heart.

As soon as William, who was in England, was informed of the danger of his beloved consort, he hastily embarked for Normandy, and arrived at Caen in time to receive her last farewell.[4]

After Matilda had received the consolations of religion, she expired on the 2d of November, or, according to some historians, the 3d of that month, anno 1083, in the fifty-second year of her age, having borne the title of queen of England seventeen years, and duchess of Normandy upwards of thirty-one.

Her body was carried to the convent of the Holy Trinity at Caen,

---

[1] Ordericus Vitalis.   [2] Ibid.
[3] Malmsbury. Hoveden. Ingulphus. Ordericus Vitalis.   [4] Ordericus Vitalis.

which she had built and munificently endowed. The corpse of the queen-duchess was reverentially received, at the portal of the church, by a numerous procession of bishops and abbots, conducted within the choir, and deposited before the high altar. Her obsequies were celebrated with great pomp and solemnity, by the monks and clerks, and attended by a vast concourse of the poor, to whom she had been throughout life a generous benefactress; " and frequently," says Ordericus Vitalis, " relieved with bounteous alms in the name of her Redeemer."

A magnificent tomb was raised to her memory, by her sorrowing lord, adorned with precious stones and elaborate sculpture; and her epitaph, in Latin verse, was emblazoned thereon in letters of gold, setting forth in pompous language the lofty birth and noble qualities of the illustrious dead. The following is a translation of the quaint monkish rhymes, which defy the imitative powers of modern poetry:—

> " Here rests within this fair and stately tomb,
> Matilda, scion of a regal line;
> The Flemish duke her sire;[1] and Adelais
> Her mother, to great Robert, king of France,
> Daughter, and sister to his royal heir.
> In wedlock to our mighty William joined.
> She built this holy temple, and endowed
> With lands and goodly gifts. She, the true friend
> Of piety, and soother of distress,
> Enriching others, indigent herself;
> Reserving all her treasures for the poor;
> And, by such deeds as these, she merited
> To be partaker of eternal life:
> To which she pass'd November 2d, 1083."

Matilda's will, which is in the Imperial Library of Paris, in the register of the Abbey of the Holy Trinity of Caen,[2] fully bears out the assertion of her epitaph, touching her poverty; since, from the items in this curious and interesting record, it is plain that the first of our Anglo-Norman queens had little to leave, in the way of personal property; and, as to the bulk of her landed possessions, they were already settled on her son Henry.[3]

" I give," says the royal testatrix, " to the Abbey of the Holy Trinity my tunic worked at Winchester, by Alderet's wife; and the mantle embroidered with gold, which is in my chamber, to make a cope. Of my two golden girdles, I give that which is ornamented with emblems, for the purpose of suspending the lamp before the great altar.

" I give my large candelabra, made at St. Lo, my crown, my sceptre, my cups in their cases, another cup made in England, with all my horse-trappings, and all my vessels; and, lastly, I give the lands of Quetchou and Cotentin, except those which I may already have disposed of in my

---

[1] Baldwin, Matilda's father, was the descendant of the six foresters, as the first sovereigns of Flanders were called.   [2] Ducarel's Norman Antiquities.
[3] I am indebted to the private communication of that great historian Dr. Lingard, for this information.

lifetime, with two dwellings in England; and I have made all these bequests with the consent of my husband."

It is amusing to trace the feminine feeling with regard to dress and *bijouterie*, which has led the dying queen to enumerate, in her last will and testament, her embroidered tunic, girdle, and mantle, with sundry other personal decorations, before she mentions the lands of Quetchou and Cotentin, and her two dwellings in England; which are evidently objects of far less importance, in her opinion, than her rich array.

Ducarel tells us, that among the records preserved in the archives of the Holy Trinity at Caen, there is a curious MS. containing an account of Matilda, the royal foundress's wardrobe, jewels, and toilette; but he was unable to obtain a sight of this precious document, because of the jealous care with which it was guarded by those holy ladies, the abbess and nuns of that convent.[1]

Till the middle of the seventeenth century, the portraits of Matilda and William were carefully preserved on the walls of St. Stephen's Chapel at Caen. The queen had caused these portraits to be painted when this magnificent endowment was founded.[2] We have seen, by the Bayeux tapestry, that Matilda took great delight in pictorial memorials; and if we may judge by the engraving from this portrait, preserved in Montfaucon, it were a pity that so much grace and beauty should fade from the earth without remembrance. Her costume is singularly dignified and becoming. The robe simply gathered round the throat, a flowing veil falling from the back of the head on the shoulders, is confined by an elegant circlet of gems. The face is beautiful and delicate, the hair falls in waving tresses round her throat; with one hand she confines her drapery, and holds a book; she extends her sceptre with the other, in an attitude full of grace and dignity. Montfaucon declares that this painting was actually copied from the wall, before the room in which it was preserved was pulled down. The elegance of the design and costume ought not to raise doubts of its authenticity, for it is well known that all remains of art were much better executed before the destruction of Constantinople than after that period. Female costume, with the exception of some tasteless attire which crept into the uproarious court of William Rufus, was elegant and dignified; the noble circlet, the flowing transparent veil, the natural curls parted on each side of the brow, the vestal stole drawn just round the neck, in regular folds, the falling sleeves, the gently belted waist with its gemmed zone, confining the plaits of a garment that swept the ground in rich fulness, altogether formed a costume which would not have disgraced a Grecian statue. We shall see this elegant dress superseded in time, by the monstrous Syrian caps, of sugar-loaf or horned form, and by the heraldic tabards, and surcoats, seemingly made of patchwork, which deformed female costumes in succeeding ages: but we must not look for these barbarisms at the date of Matilda's portrait.

Matilda bore ten children to her royal spouse, namely, four sons and

---

[1] Ducarel's Norman Antiquities.
[2] Montfaucon's Monumens de la Monarchie Française.

six daughters. Robert, surnamed Courthose, her eldest son, succeeded his father as duke of Normandy.

This darling son of Matilda's heart is thus described in the old chronicler's lines :—

> "He was y-wox (grown) ere his fader to England came,
> Thick man he was enow, but not well long;
> Square was he, and well made for to be strong.
> Before his fader, once on a time, he did sturdy deed,
> When he was young, who beheld him, and these words said:
> 'By the uprising of God, Robelyn me sall see
> The Courthose, my young son, a stalwart knight sall be;'—
> For he was somewhat short, so he named him Courthose,
> And he might never after this name lose.
> He was quiet of counsel and speech and of body strong,
> Never yet man of might in Christendom ne in Paynim,
> In battail from his steed could bring him down."

After the death of Matilda, Robert broke out into open revolt against his royal father once more; and the Conqueror, in his famous death-bed speech and confession, alluded to this conduct with great bitterness, when he spake of the disposition of his dominions: these were the words of the dying monarch. "The dukedom of Normandy, before I fought in the vale Sanguelac, with Harold, I granted unto my son Robert, for that he is my first begotten, and having received the homage of his baronage, that honour given cannot be revoked. Yet I know that it will be a miserable reign which is subject to the rule of his government; for he is a foolish, proud knave, and is to be punished with cruel fortune." [1]

After the death of his father, Robert acquired the additional cognomen of the Unready, from the circumstance of being always out of the way when the golden opportunity of improving his fortunes occurred.

Robert, though an indifferent politician, was a gallant knight and a skilful general. He joined the crusade under Godfrey of Boulogne, and, to obtain the funds for this purpose, mortgaged the dukedom of Normandy to his selfish brother William, for the sum of six thousand six hundred and sixty-six pounds of silver.[2] He so greatly distinguished himself at the taking of the holy city, that of all the Christian princes, his fellow-crusaders, he was judged most deserving of the crown of Jerusalem.[3] This election was made on the Easter-eve, as they all stood at the high altar in the temple, each holding an unlighted wax taper in his hand, and beseeching God to direct their choice; when the taper which duke Robert held, becoming ignited without any visible agency, it was regarded by the rest of the Croises as a miraculous intimation in his favour, and he was entreated to accept the kingdom.[4]

Robert, however, at that critical juncture, hearing of the death of William Rufus, refused the proffered diadem, and returned to Europe under the idea that he should obtain the crown of England; but not only did

[1] See death-bed speech of the Conqueror, in Speed's Chronicle.
[2] S. Dunelm. Hoveden. Brompton.
[3] Matthew Paris. Polychronicon. Speed.   [4] Matthew Paris.

he fail of dispossessing his brother Henry of England, but he was finally defeated by him at the battle of Tinchebray, stripped of his dukedom, and made prisoner. After a weary captivity of eight-and-twenty years, Robert died at Cardiff Castle. While in the Holy Land, he had married the beautiful and amiable Sybilla, daughter of the Count Conversana, by whom he had one son, named William.

Richard, the second son of William the Conqueror and Matilda, died in England in the lifetime of his parents, as we have already stated. William, their third son, surnamed Rufus or Rous,[1] from the colour of his hair, and called by the Saxon historians the "Red King," succeeded to the crown of England after his father's death. He was slain in the New Forest, by the erring shaft of his favourite hunting companion, Sir Walter Tyrrel, whom he familiarly called Wat de Poix, from the name of Tyrrel's estate in Picardy.

Henry, the fourth and youngest son of William and Matilda, won the surname of Beauclerc, by his scholastic attainments, and succeeded to the throne of England after the death of William Rufus. The personal history of this prince will be found in the memoirs of his two queens, Matilda of Scotland and Adelicia of Louvaine.

There is a great confusion among historians and genealogists, respecting the names of the daughters of Matilda and the Conqueror, and the order of their birth, no two writers appearing to agree on that point, except with regard to the eldest princess, Cecilia, who was veiled a nun in the Abbey of Fescamp, and became the abbess of the nunnery of the Holy Trinity, founded by her mother Matilda.[2] William of Malmsbury, who wrote in the reign of Henry I., when enumerating the daughters of the Conqueror, says, "Cecilia the abbess of Caen still survives."

The generality of historians mention Constance, the wife of Alan duke of Bretagne, as the second daughter of this illustrious pair. Ordericus Vitalis, a contemporary, calls her the third,[3] and Agatha the second daughter. Of Agatha he relates the following interesting particulars. "This princess, who had been formerly affianced to Harold, was demanded of her father in marriage, by Alphonso king of Galicia; but manifested the greatest repugnance to this alliance." She told her father "that her heart was devoted to her first spouse," as she called Harold,[4] "and that she should consider it an abomination if she gave her hand to another. She had seen and loved her Saxon betrothed, and she revolted from a union with the foreign monarch whom she had never seen;" and bursting into tears, she added, with passionate emotion, "that she prayed that the Most High would rather take her to himself than allow her ever to be transported into Spain." Her prayer was granted, and the reluctant bride died on her journey to her unknown lord. Her remains were conveyed to her native land, and interred at Bayeux, in the church of St. Mary the perpetual virgin.[5] Sandford calls this princess the sixth daughter. If so, she could not have been the betrothed of Harold, but of earl Edwin; and indeed, if we reflect on the great disparity in age

---

[1] "Après William Bastardus regna Will le Rous."—Fitz-Stephen's Chronicle.
[2] Ordericus Vitalis. William of Malmsbury.
[3] Ordericus Vitalis. Malmsbury.   [4] Ibid.   [5] Ibid.

between Harold and the younger daughters of William of Normandy and take into consideration the circumstances of his breach of contract with the little Norman lady, and that he died the husband of another woman, it is scarcely probable that his memory could have been cherished with such a degree of passionate fondness as Ordericus Vitalis attributes to the lady Agatha; whereas Edwin was young, and remarkable for his beauty; he had, in all probability, been privileged with some intimacy with the princess, whom the Conqueror had promised to bestow on him in marriage. The breach of this promise on the part of William, too, was the cause of Edwin's revolt, which implies that the youthful thane was deeply wounded at the refusal of the Norman monarch to fulfil his engagement; and it is at least probable, that to the princess who had innocently been made a snare to him by her guileful sire, he might have become an object of the tenderest and most lasting affection

Malmsbury, speaking of this princess, says, " Agatha, to whom God granted a virgin death, was so devoted to the exercises of religion, that after her decease it was discovered that her knees had become hard like horn with constant kneeling." [1]

W. Gemiticensis and some other ancient chroniclers assert, that it was to Adeliza, the fifth daughter of William and Matilda, that Harold was contracted, and that she died young. Perhaps this is the same princess whom Ordericus Vitalis mentions as their fourth daughter, of whom he says, " Adelaide, very fair and very noble, recommended herself entirely to a life of devotion, and made a holy end, under the direction of Roger de Beaumont."

Adela, or Adelicia, generally classed as the fourth daughter of William and Matilda, Ordericus Vitalis places as the fifth, and says, " She was sought in marriage by Stephen earl of Blois, who was desirous of allying himself with the aspiring family of the Conqueror, and by the advice of William's councillors she was united to him. The marriage took place at Breteuil, and the marriage fêtes were celebrated at Chartres. This princess was a learned woman, and possessed of considerable diplomatic talents. She had four sons: William, an idiot; Thibaut, surnamed the great earl of Champaigne; Stephen de Blois, who succeeded to the English throne after the death of Henry I.; and Henry, bishop of Winchester. After the death of the count de Blois, her husband, the countess Adela took the veil at Mareigney.[2]

Gundred, the sixth and youngest daughter of the Conqueror and Matilda, was married to William de Warren, a powerful Norman noble, and the first earl of Surrey in England. By him the lady Gundred had two sons, William, the successor of his father and the progenitor of a mighty line of earls of that family, and Rainold, who died without issue. The countess Gundred died in child-bed at Castleacre in Norfolk, and is buried in the chapter-house of St. Pancras church, within the priory, at Lewes in Sussex.[3]

The death of his beloved queen Matilda afflicted the Conqueror very deeply. He wept excessively, for many days after her decease; and to

[1] Ordericus Vitalis. Malmsbury.   [2] Ordericus Vitalis.   [3] Sandford.

testify how keenly he felt her loss, he renounced his favourite amusement of hunting, and all the boisterous sports in which he formerly delighted.[1] After this event his temper became melancholy and irritable, to which, indeed, a train of public calamities and domestic vexations might in a great measure contribute. To the honour of Matilda, it has been asserted by some of the historians of the period, that she used her influence over the mind of her mighty lord, for the mitigation of the sufferings of the people whom he had subjugated to his yoke. Thomas Rudbourne, the author of the Annals of Winton, says, "King William, by the advice of Matilda, treated the English kindly as long as she lived, but after the death of Matilda he became a thorough tyrant."[2] It is certainly true, that after Matilda left England in 1070, the condition of the people became infinitely worse, and it is possible that it might be aggravated by her death.

Not only the happiness, but the worldly prosperity, of William, appeared sensibly diminished during his widowed state. In the course of the four years that he survived his consort, he experienced nothing but trouble and disquiet.[3]

William met with the accident which caused his death, at the storming of the city of Mantes. He had roused himself from a sick bed, to execute a terrible vengeance on the French border, for the ribald joke which his old antagonist, the king of France, had passed on his malady; and in pursuance of his declaration "that he would set all France in a blaze at his uprising," he had ordered the city to be fired. While he was with savage fury encouraging his soldiers to pursue the work of destruction to which he had incited them, his horse, chancing to set his foot on a piece of burning timber, started, and occasioned his lord so severe an injury from the pummel of the saddle, as to bring on a violent access of fever.[4] Being unable to remount his horse, after an accident which must have appeared to him like a retributive chastisement for the barbarous deed in which he was engaged, he was conveyed in a litter to Rouen, where, perceiving he drew near his end, he began to experience some compunctious visitings of conscience, for the crimes and oppressions of which he had been guilty.

In the first place, he ordered large sums to be distributed to the poor, and likewise for the building of churches, especially those which he had recently burnt at Mantes; next he set all the Saxon prisoners at liberty whom he had detained in his Norman prisons; among them were Morcar, and Ulnoth, the brother of Harold, who had remained in captivity from his childhood, when he was given in hostage by earl Godwin to Edward the Confessor. The heart of the dying monarch being deeply touched with remorse, he confessed that he had done Morcar much wrong, and bitterly bewailed the blood he had shed in England, and the desolation and woe he had caused in Hampshire, for the sake of planting

[1] Ordericus Vitalis.
[2] "Istius Matildis consilio Wilhelmus Rex pacifice cum Anglis tractabat, quamdiu ipsa vixisset: post mortem verò ipsius Matildis omnem induit tyrannidem." Winton, Anglia Sacra, i. 257. Thomæ Rudborne Hist. Major.
[3] Malmsbury. Ordericus Vitalis. [4] Malmsbury. Higden.

the New Forest, protesting " that having so misused that fair and beautiful land, he dared not appoint a successor to it, but left the disposal of that matter in the hands of God." [1] He had, however, taken some pains, by writing a letter to Lanfranc, expressive of his earnest wish that William Rufus should succeed him in his regal dignity, and to secure the crown of England to this his favourite son—for whom he called, as soon as he had concluded his edifying acknowledgment of the errors of his past life;—and sealing the letter with his own seal, he put it into the hands of the prince, bidding him hasten to England with all speed, and deliver it to the archbishop. He then blessed him with a farewell kiss, and dismissed him.

. When the Conqueror had settled his temporal affairs, he caused himself to be removed to Hermentrude, a pleasant village near Rouen,[2] that he might be more at liberty to prepare himself for death. On the 9th of September the awful change which he awaited took place. Hearing the sound of the great bell in the metropolitan church of St. Gervis, near Rouen, William, raising his exhausted frame from the supporting pillows, asked " What it meant ?" [3]

One of his attendants replying, ".That it then rang prime to Our Lady," the dying monarch, lifting his eyes to heaven, and spreading abroad his hands, exclaimed, " I commend myself to that blessed Lady, Mary the mother of God, that she by her holy intercession may reconcile me to her most dear Son, our Lord Jesus Christ;" and with these words he expired, in the sixty-fourth year of his age, 1087, after a reign of fifty-two years in Normandy, and twenty-one in England.

His eldest son, Robert, was absent in Germany at the time of his death; [4] William was on his voyage to England; Henry, who had taken charge of his obsequies, suddenly departed on some self-interested business, and all the great officers of the court having dispersed themselves, some to offer their homage to Robert, and others to William, the inferior servants of the household, with some of their rapacious confederates, took the opportunity of plundering the house where their sovereign had just breathed his last, of all the money, plate, wearing apparel, hangings, and precious furniture; they even stripped the person of the royal dead, and left his body naked upon the floor.[5]

Every one appeared struck with consternation and dismay, and neither the proper officers of state, nor the sons of the deceased king, issuing the necessary orders respecting the funeral, the remains of the Conqueror were left wholly neglected, till Herlewin, a poor country knight, — but in all probability the same Herlewin who married his mother Arlotta, — undertook to convey the royal corpse to Caen at his own cost, for interment in the abbey of St. Stephen, where it was met by prince Henry and a procession of monks.[6] Scarcely, however, had the burial rites commenced, when there was a terrible alarm of fire in that quarter of the town; and as there was great danger of the devouring element communicating to the cloisters of St. Stephen, the monks, who were far

[1] See William's death-bed confession in Speed.   [3] Eadmer.
[2] Ordericus Vitalis. Malmsbury.   [4] Ordericus Vitalis. Brompton.
[5] Ordericus Vitalis. Brompton. Malmsbury. Speed.   [6] Ibid.

more concerned for the preservation of their stately abbey than for the lifeless remains of the munificent founder, scampered out of the church, without the slightest regard to decency, or the remonstrances of prince Henry and the faithful Herlewin. The example of the ecclesiastics was followed by the secular attendants, so that the hearse of the mighty William was in a manner wholly deserted, till the conflagration was suppressed.[1] The monks then re-entered the holy fane, and proceeded with the solemnity, if so it might be called; but the interruptions and accidents with which it had been marked were not yet ended; for when the funeral sermon was finished, the stone coffin set in the grave which had been dug in the chancel between the choir and the altar, and the body ready to be laid therein,[2] Anselm Fitz-Arthur, a Norman gentleman, stood forth and forbade the interment: "This spot," said he, "was the site of my father's house, which this dead duke took violently from him, and here, upon part of mine inheritance, founded this church. This ground I therefore challenge, and I charge ye all, as ye shall answer it at the great and dreadful day of judgment, that ye lay not the bones of the despoiler on the hearth of my fathers."[3]

The effect of this bold appeal of a solitary individual, was an instant pause in the burial rite of the deceased sovereign. The claims of Anselm Fitz-Arthur were examined, and his rights recognised by prince Henry, who prevailed upon him, as the lawful owner of the soil, to accept sixty shillings as the price of the grave, and to suffer the interment of his royal father to proceed, on the condition of his pledging himself to pay the full value of the rest of the land.[4] The compensation was stipulated between Anselm Fitz-Arthur and prince Henry, standing on either side the grave, on the verge of which the unburied remains of the Conqueror rested, while the agreement was ratified, in the presence of the mourners and assistant priests and monks, whereby Henry promised to pay, and Fitz-Arthur to receive, one hundred pounds of silver, as the purchase of the ground on which William had, thirty-five years previously, wrongfully founded the abbey of St. Stephen's, to purchase a dispensation from the pope for his marriage with his cousin Matilda of Flanders.

The bargain having been struck, and the payment of the sixty shillings earnest money (for the occupation of the seven feet of earth, required, as the last abode of the Conqueror of England) being tendered by the prince and received by Fitz-Arthur,—strange interlude as it was in a royal funeral,—the obsequies were suffered to proceed. According to some historians, an accident occurred in placing the lid on the stone coffin, attended with such unpleasant results that mourners, monks, and assistant priests, after vainly censing the chancel with additional clouds of incense, fled the church a second time before the interment was completed.[5] This tale, inasmuch as it was refuted by the appearance of the royal remains when the grave was opened upwards of four hundred and fifty years afterwards, we are disposed to regard as a piece of mingled

[1] Ordericus Vitalis. Speed. Brompton. Malmsbury.   [2] Speed.
[3] Eadmer. Malmsbury. Ordericus Vitalis.   [4] Ordericus Vitalis. M. Paris.
[5] See Speed's Chronicle.

marvellousness and malice on the part of the Saxon chroniclers, who have taken evident pleasure in enlarging on all the mischances and humiliations which befel the unconscious clay of their great national adversary, in its passage to the tomb. Yet surely so singular a chapter of accidents was never yet recorded, as occurring to the corpse of a mighty sovereign, who died in the plenitude of his power.

William of Normandy was remarkable for his personal strength, and for the majestic beauty of his countenance. It has been said of him, that no one but himself could bend his bow, and that he could, when riding at full speed, discharge either arblast or long-bow with unerring aim.[1]

His forehead was high and bald, his aspect stern and commanding; yet he could, when it pleased him to do so, assume such winning sweetness, in his looks and manner, as could scarcely be resisted; but when in anger, no man could meet the terror of his eye.[2] Like Saul, he was, from the shoulders upwards, taller than the rest of his subjects; but before he became too corpulent, his figure was finely proportioned. His eloquence was both powerful and persuasive. His habits were temperate, and his household was well regulated, with a view to the strictest economy; yet upon proper occasions he indulged his taste for magnificence, and took pleasure in appearing in all his royal state. He wore his crown three times in the year:[3] at Christmas or Midwinter-day, in the city of Gloucester; Easter at Winchester; and when he celebrated Whitsuntide, at Westminster. He wisely carried his court, it seems, at these festivals, to different parts of England.

William Rufus caused a stately monument, adorned with gold, silver, and precious stones, and very rich sculpture, to be erected to the memory of his father, before the high altar of St. Stephen's Abbey.[4]

The loftiness of stature which contemporary chroniclers have ascribed to William the Conqueror, was fully confirmed by the *post-mortem* examination of his body, which was made by the Bishop of Bayeux, in the year 1642, when, prompted by a strong desire to behold the remains of this great sovereign, he obtained leave to open his tomb.[5]

On removing the stone cover, the body, which was corpulent, and exceeding in stature the tallest man then known, appeared as entire as when it was first buried.

Within the tomb lay a plate of copper gilt, on which was engraved an inscription in Latin verse.[6]

---

[1] Robert of Gloucester. W. Malmsbury.   [2] W. Malmsbury.
[3] Saxon Annals. Ordericus Vitalis. Madox, Hist. Exchequer.
[4] Ordericus Vitalis.   [5] Ducarel's Norman Antiquities.
[6] Thomas, archbishop of York, was the author of the Latin verse, of which the following lines present a close translation not unpoetical in its antique simplicity:—

He who the sturdy Normans ruled, and over England reigned,
And stoutly won and strongly kept what he had so obtained;
And did the swords of those of Maine by force bring under awe,
And made them under his command live subject to his law;
This great King William lieth here entombed in little grave;
So great a lord, so small a house sufficeth him to have.
When Phœbus in the Virgin's lap his circled course applied,
And twenty-three degrees had past, e'en at that time he died.

The bishop, who was greatly surprised at finding the body in such perfect preservation, caused a painting to be executed of the royal remains, in the state in which they then appeared, by the best artist in Caen, and caused it to be hung up on the abbey wall, opposite to the monument. The tomb was then carefully closed, but in 1562, when the Calvinists under Chastillon took Caen, a party of the rapacious soldiers forced it open, in hope of meeting with a treasure, but finding nothing more than the bones of the Conqueror wrapped in red taffeta, they threw them about the church in great derision. Viscount Falaise, having obtained from the rioters one of the thigh-bones, it was by him deposited in the royal grave. Monsieur Le Bras, who saw this bone, testified that it was longer by the breadth of his four fingers than that of the tallest man he had ever seen.[1]

The picture of the remains, which had been painted by the order of the bishop of Bayeux, fell into the hands of Peter Ildo, the goaler of Caen, who was one of the spoilers, and he converted one part into a table, and the other into a cupboard door; which proves that this portrait was not painted on canvas, but as usual, on wood. Some years after, these curious relics were discovered, and reclaimed by M. Bras, in whose possession they remained till his death.[2]

No sooner had the Calvinist spoilers plundered the abbey of St. Stephen, and exhumed the bones of the Conqueror, than they entered the church of the Holy Trinity, threatening the same violence to the remains of Matilda. The entreaties and tears of the abbess and her nuns at first had no effect on the rapacious bigots, who considered the destruction of church ornaments and monumental sculpture an acceptable service to God, quite sufficient to atone for the sacrilegious violence of defacing a temple consecrated to his worship, and rifling the sepulchres of the dead.[3] In this instance they contented themselves with throwing down the monument, breaking to pieces the effigies of the queen, which lay thereon, and opening the grave in which the royal corpse was deposited. At that juncture, one of the party observing that there was a gold ring set with a fine sapphire on one of the queen's fingers, took it off, and, with more gallantry than might have been expected from such a person, presented it to the abbess, Madame Anna de Montmorenci, who afterwards gave it to her father, the baron de Conti, constable of France, when he attended Charles the Ninth to Caen, in the year 1563.[4]

In 1642 the monks of St. Stephen collected the bones of their royal patron, William of Normandy, and built a plain altar-shaped tomb over them, on the spot where the original monument stood in the chancel. The nuns of the Holy Trinity, with equal zeal, caused the broken fragments of Matilda's statue and monument to be restored, and placed over her grave, near the middle of the choir, on a tomb of black and white marble, three feet high and six long, in the shape of a coffin, surrounded with iron spikes, and hung with ancient tapestry.[5]

The restored monument of Matilda remained undisturbed till nearly the close of the last century, when the French republicans paid one of

[1] Ducarel's Norman Antiquities. [2] Ibid. [3] Ibid. [4] Ibid. [5] Ibid.

7*

their destructive visits to the church of the Holy Trinity at Caen, and, among other outrages against taste and feeling, swept away this memorial of its royal foundress;[1] but while a single arch of that majestic and time-honoured fane, the church of the Holy Trinity, survives, the first of our Anglo-Norman queens, Matilda of Flanders,[2] will require no other monument.

[1] Ducarel.

[2] In addition to our numerous authorities regarding Brihtric Meaw, we subjoin this important extract from a work containing great research among ancient monuments:—"Brietric, the son of Algar, a Saxon Thane, is stated, in Domesday, to have held this manor in the reign of Edward the Confessor; but having given offence to Maud, the daughter of Baldwin count of Flanders, previous to her marriage with William duke of Normandy, by refusing to marry her himself, his property was seized by that monarch on the conquest, and bestowed, seemingly in revenge, upon the queen."—ELLIS's *History of Thornbury Castle.*   Bristol, 1839.

MATILDA OF SCOTLAND,

QUEEN OF HENRY I.

CHAPTER I.

Ancestry of Matilda—Direct descent from Alfred—Margaret Atheling, her mother—Marries the king of Scotland—Matilda's birth—Her godfather—Education—First suitor—Her father invades England—His death—Her mother's
grief—Pious death—Revolution in Scotland—Edgar Atheling carries the royal
family to England—Princesses Matilda and Mary—Placed in Rumsey abbey—
Their aunt abbess Christina—Matilda's brother Edgar—Restored to the throne
of Scotland—The Atheling a crusader—Matilda at Wilton Abbey—Her literary education—Attachment between Matilda and Henry Beauclerc—Her
other suitors—Early life of Henry—Education at Cambridge—Surname—Literary work by him—Legacy at the Conqueror's death—Poverty of Henry—
Affronted by Matilda's suitor, earl Warren—Courtship of Matilda—Harsh rule
of lady Christina—Henry seizes English throne—Asks Matilda's hand—Opposition of her aunt—Council of the church—Matilda's evidence—Her scruples
—Importuned by Anglo-Saxons—Consents—Address to her by Anselm—Consent of the people—Her marriage and coronation—Saxon laws restored.

WHEN we consider the perils to which the representatives of our
ancient line of sovereigns, Edgar Atheling and his sisters, were exposed
during the usurpation of Harold, and the Norman reigns of terror, it
almost appears as if an overruling Providence had guarded these descendants of the great Alfred, for the purpose of continuing the lineage of that
patriot king on the throne of these realms, through the marriage of
Henry I. with the daughter of Margaret Atheling, Matilda of Scotland.
This princess, the subject of our present biography, is distinguished
among the many illustrious females that have worn the crown matrimonial of England, by the title of "the Good Queen;" a title which, eloquent in its simplicity, briefly implies that she possessed not only the
great and shining qualities calculated to add lustre to a throne, but that
she employed them in promoting the happiness of all classes of her
subjects, affording at the same time a bright example of the lovely and
endearing attributes which should adorn the female character.

Some historians call this princess Matilda Atheling, and by these she
is almost invested with the dignity of a queen-regnant, and styled the
heiress of the Anglo-Saxon monarchs. In the same spirit, her grandson
and representative, Henry II., is designated "the restorer of the English
royal line." This is, however, as Blackstone justly observes, "a great
error, for the rights of Margaret Atheling to the English succession were
vested in her sons, and not in her daughter."[1] James I., on his acces-

---

[1] Blackstone's Commentaries, vol. i.

sion to the throne of England, failed not to set forth that important leaf in his pedigree, and laid due stress on the circumstance of his descent from the ancient line of English sovereigns by the elder blood.

Alexander, the archdeacon of Salisbury (who wrote the tracts of the Exchequer, quoted by Gervase of Tilbury in his celebrated Dialogues of the Exchequer), has gravely set forth, in his red-book, a pedigree of Matilda of Scotland, tracing her descent in an unbroken line up to Adam. There is a strange medley of Christian kings and pagan sinners, such as Woden and Balder, with the Jewish patriarchs of holy writ, in this royal genealogy.[1]

Matilda is the only princess of Scotland who ever shared the throne of a king of England. It is, however, from her maternal ancestry that she derives her great interest, as connected with the annals of this country. Her mother, Margaret Atheling, was the grand-daughter of Edmund Ironside, and the daughter of Edward Atheling, surnamed the Outlaw, by Agatha, daughter of the emperor Henry II. of Germany. Her brother, Edgar Atheling, so often mentioned in the preceding biography, feeling some reason to mistrust the apparent friendship of William the Conqueror, privately withdrew from his court, and in the year 1068, (the same year in which Henry I. was born,) took shipping with Margaret, and their younger sister Christina, and their mother Agatha, intending to seek a refuge in Hungary, with their royal kindred; but, by stress of weather, the vessel in which they, with many other English exiles, were embarked, was driven into the Frith of Forth. Malcolm Canmore, the young unmarried king of Scotland, who had just regained his dominions from the usurper Macbeth, happened to be present when the royal fugitives landed, and was so struck with the beauty of the lady Margaret Atheling, that in a few days he asked her in marriage of her brother. Edgar joyfully gave the hand of the dowerless princess to the young and handsome sovereign, who had received the exiled English in the most generous and honourable manner, and whose disinterested affection was sufficient testimony of the nobleness of his disposition. The spot where Margaret first set her foot on the Scottish land was, in memory of that circumstance, called Queen's Ferry, the name it bears to this day.

The Saxon chronicler, of whom this lady is an especial favourite, indulges in a most edifying homily, on the providence which led the holy Margaret to become the spouse of the king of Scotland, who is evidently regarded by the cowled historian as little better than a pagan. Certain it is, that the mighty son of "the gracious Duncan" could neither read nor write. After her marriage, the Saxon princess became the happy instrument of diffusing the blessings of Christianity throughout her husband's dominions, commencing the work of conversion in the proper place, her own household and the court. The influence which her personal charms had in the first instance won over the heart of her royal husband, her virtues and mental powers increased and retained to the last hour of Malcolm's existence. He reposed the most unbounded confidence, not only in the principles, but the judgment, of his English

---

[1] Lib. Rub. fol. notata, 4.

consort, who became the domestic legislator of the realm. She dismissed from the palace all persons who were convicted of leading immoral lives, or who were guilty of fraud or injustice, and allowed no persons to hold offices in the royal household, unless they conducted themselves in a sober and discreet manner; observing, moreover, that the Scotch nobles had an irreverent habit of rising from table before grace could be pronounced by her pious chaplain Turgot, she rewarded those of the more civilized chiefs, who could be induced to attend the performance of that edifying ceremony, with a cup of the choicest wine. The temptation of such a bribe was too powerful to be resisted by the hitherto perverse and *graceless* peers, and by degrees the custom became so popular, that every guest was eager to claim his "grace-cup;" the fashion spread from the palace to the castles of the nobility, and thence descending to the dwellings of their humbler neighbours, became an established usage in the land.

Many deeply interesting, as well as amusing particulars, connected with the parents of Matilda of Scotland, the subject of our present memoir, have been preserved by the learned Turgot, the historian of this royal family, who, in his capacity of confessor to queen Margaret, and preceptor to her children,[1] enjoyed opportunities of becoming acquainted not only with all personal particulars respecting these illustrious individuals, but of learning their most private thoughts and feelings.

Turgot gives great commendation to his royal mistress, for the conscientious care she bestowed on the education of her children, whose preceptors she enjoined to punish them as often as their faults required correction.

Matilda, the subject of this memoir, was her eldest daughter, and was probably born in the year 1077. This we infer from the remarkable circumstance, of the elder brother of her future husband, Robert Courthose, being her godfather.[2] Malcolm Canmore, her father, invaded England in that year, and Robert of Normandy was, on his reconciliation with his father, William the Conqueror, sent with a military force to

---

[1] Turgot was a Saxon of good family, born in Lincolnshire. He was delivered as a hostage to William the Conqueror, and shut up by him in Lincoln Castle. From thence he escaped to Norway. Returning from that country, he was shipwrecked on the English coast, and having lost everything he possessed in the world, he became a priest, and distinguished himself so much by his learning and piety that he was promoted to be prior of Durham. When Margaret Atheling became queen of Scotland she preferred him to the office of her confessor. He followed the fortunes of his royal pupil Matilda, the daughter of his illustrious patroness, after her marriage with Henry I.; and we find that the English monarch, who possibly wished to remove him from the queen, in 1107 warmly recommended him to his royal brother-in-law, Edgar of Scotland, as a fit person to be appointed to the bishopric of St. Andrew's. Turgot, however, died prior of Durham. He is said to have been the author of the "Chronicle of Durham," which goes by the name of "Simeon of Durham," and has been appropriated by a contemporary monk of that name. Turgot's Chronicle of the Lives of his royal mistress, Margaret Atheling, and her consort, Malcolm Canmore, king of Scotland, has been preserved by Fordun, and is frequently cited by Sir David Dalrymple.—Nicholson. Henry.   [2] Sir J. Hayward.

F

repel this northern attack.[1] Robert, finding his forces inadequate to maintain successfully a war of aggression, entered into a negotiation with the Scottish monarch, which ended in a friendly treaty. Malcolm renewed his homage for Cumberland; and Robert, who, whatever his faults might be as a private character, was one of the most courteous knights and polished gentlemen of the age in which he lived, finally cemented the auspicious amity which he had established between his royal sire and the warlike husband of the heiress presumptive of the Saxon line of kings, by becoming the sponsor of the infant princess Matilda. Some historians assert that the name of the little princess was originally Editha, and that it was, out of compliment to the Norman prince her godfather, changed to Matilda, the name of his beloved mother; the contemporary chronicler, Ordericus Vitalis, says, "*Matildem quæ prius dicta est Editha,*"—Matilda, whose first name was Edith.[2]

Matilda the Good received her earliest lessons of virtue and piety from her illustrious mother, and of learning from the worthy Turgot, the preceptor of the royal children of king Malcolm and queen Margaret of Scotland. While Matilda was very young, there appears to have been an attempt on the part, either of the queen her mother, or her aunt Christina Atheling, the celebrated abbess of Rumsey, to consecrate her to the church, or at least to give her tender mind a conventual bias, greatly to the displeasure of the king her father; who once, as Matilda herself testified, when she was brought into his presence, dressed in a nun's veil, snatched it from her head in a great passion, and indignantly tore it in pieces, observing at the same time, to Alan duke of Bretagne, who stood by, " that he intended to bestow her in marriage, and not to devote her to a cloister."[3]

This circumstance, young as she was, appears to have made a very deep impression on the mind of the little princess, and probably assisted in strengthening her determination, in after years, never to complete the profession of which she was, at one period of her life, compelled to assume the semblance.

Alan duke of Bretagne, to whom king Malcolm addressed this observation, was the widower of William the Conqueror's daughter Constance; and though there was a great disparity of years between him and Matilda, it appears certain, from his after-proposals, that the object of his visit to the Scottish court was to form a matrimonial alliance with the young Matilda;[4] and this was indubitably one of the unsuitable matches to which we shall find that Matilda afterwards alluded.

Matilda's uncle, Edgar Atheling, became resident at the court of her father and mother for some time, in the year 1091, Robert Courthose having sacrificed his friendship to the temporary jealousy of William Rufus. This displeasure did not last long, for both the eldest sons of William the Conqueror seem to have cherished an affection for the Atheling, and he was often treated with confidence and generosity by each. The misunderstanding, which occasioned Edgar's retreat into Scotland,

---

[1] See the preceding Memoir, Life of Matilda of Flanders.
[2] See Dr. Lingard's learned note, p. 126, vol. ii. ed. 4.
[3] Eadmer.　　　　[4] Eadmer and Gemiticensis.

was productive of ultimate good to this country, as both Rufus and Malcolm joined in appointing him as arbiter of peace between England and Scotland, which were then engaged in a furious and devastating war.[1] Thus placed, in the most singular and romantic position that ever was sustained by a disinherited heir, Edgar conducted himself with such zeal and impartiality, as to give satisfaction to both parties, and the war terminated in a reasonable peace, which afforded a breathing time of two years to the harassed people of this island. After a reconciliation with William Rufus, which was never afterwards broken by the most trying circumstances, Edgar returned to the court of his favourite friend and companion, Robert of Normandy. The British kingdoms remained at peace till the dangerous illness of William Rufus, at Gloucester, tempted king Malcolm Canmore to invade his dominions, in the year 1093, for the purpose, as he said, of revenging the insults he had received from the Anglo-Norman sovereign; but in all probability his real object was to take advantage of Rufus's unpopularity with all classes, if his arms were crowned with success, and to set up the rival title of the descendants of the great Alfred, with whom he was now so closely united.

For the fifth time he now proceeded to ravage Northumberland. Hector Boethius and Buchanan insist that Malcolm was killed at the siege of Alnwick Castle, by the treachery of the besieged,[2] who, being reduced to the last extremity, offered to surrender, if the Scottish king would receive the keys in person. Malcolm of course acceded to this condition,[3] and coming to the gates, was there met by a knight bearing the keys on the point of a lance, which he offered to the king on his knee; but when Malcolm stooped to receive them, he treacherously thrust the point of the lance through the bars of his vizor, into his eye, and gave him a mortal wound, of the anguish of which he died.

This was heavy news to pour into the anxious ear of the widowed queen, who then lay on her death-bed, attended by her daughters, Matilda and Mary. The particulars of this sad scene are thus related by an eye-witness, the faithful Turgot.

During a short interval of ease, queen Margaret devoutly received the communion. Soon after, her anguish of body returned with redoubled violence; she stretched herself on the couch, and calmly awaited the moment of her dissolution. Cold, and in the agonies of death, she ceased not to put up her supplications to Heaven; these were some of her words :—

"Have mercy upon me, O God, according to the multitude of thy tender mercies; blot out mine iniquities; make me to hear joy and gladness, that the bones which thou hast broken may rejoice. Cast me not away from thy presence, and take not thy Holy Spirit from me; restore unto me the joy of thy salvation. The sacrifices of God are a broken spirit; a broken and a contrite heart, O God, thou wilt not despise."[4]

At that moment her young son, prince Edgar, returned from the disastrous English expedition, and approached her couch.

[1] Brompton. Hoveden. Y-Podigma of Neustria.
[2] Hector Boethius. Buchanan.   [3] Malmsbury.   [4] Turgot.

"How fares it with the king and my Edward?" asked the dying queen. The youthful prince stood mournfully silent.

"I know all—I know all," cried his mother; "yet, by this holy cross, I adjure you, speak out the worst." And Margaret presented to the view of her son that celebrated black cross which she had brought with her from England, as the most precious possession she derived from her royal Saxon ancestors.[1]

"Your husband and eldest son are both slain," replied the prince.

Lifting her eyes and hands towards heaven, she said, "Praise and blessing be to Thee, Almighty God, that thou hast been pleased to make me endure so bitter anguish in the hour of my departure, thereby, as I trust, to purify me in some measure from the corruption of my sins; and thou, O Lord Jesus Christ, who, through the will of the Father, hast given life to the world by thy death, O deliver me!"

While pronouncing the words "deliver me," she expired.

The reputation of her virtues, and the report that miracles had been wrought at her tomb, caused her name to be enrolled in the catalogue of saints, by the church of Rome. Whatever may be thought of the miracles, it is a pleasure to find the following enlightened passage, from the pen of a catholic ecclesiastic of the eleventh century :—

"Others," says Turgot, "may admire the indications of sanctity which miracles afford. I much more admire in Margaret the works of mercy. Such *signs* (namely, miracles) are common to the evil and the good; but the works of true piety and charity are peculiar to the good. With better reason, therefore, ought we to admire the deeds of Margaret which made her saintly, than her miracles, *had she performed any.*"

To this great and good man did the dying Margaret consign the spiritual guardianship of her two young daughters, the princesses Matilda and Mary, and her younger sons. Turgot has preserved the words with which she gave him this important charge; they will strike an answering chord on the heart of every mother.

"Farewell!" she said; "my life draws to a close, but you may survive me long. To you I commit the charge of my children. Teach them, above all things, to love and fear God; and if any of them should be permitted to attain to the height of earthly grandeur, O then, in an especial manner be to them a father and a guide. Admonish, and if need be, reprove them, lest they should be swelled with the pride of momentary glory, and through covetousness, or by reason of the prosperity of this world, offend their Creator, and forfeit eternal life. This, in the

---

[1] Carruthers' History of Scotland, vol. i. pp. 312—353.—The English viewed the possession of this jewel by the royal family of Scotland with great displeasure. It was enclosed in a black case, from whence it was called *the black cross.* The cross itself was of gold, and set with large diamonds. The figure of the Saviour was exquisitely carved in ivory. After the death of Margaret it was deposited on the high altar of Dunfermline. When Edward the First kept court there he seized on this cross as one of the English crown jewels, and carried it into England. Robert Bruce so vehemently insisted on its restoration, that queen Isabella yielded it, on the pacification, during her regency in 1327; but its surrender exasperated the English more than the most flagrant of her misdeeds.— See her Biography, vol. ii.

presence of Him who is now our only witness, I beseech you to promise and perform." [1]

Adversity was soon to try these youthful scions of royalty with her touchstone; and of the princess Matilda, as well as her saintly mother, it may justly be said,

> "Stern, rugged nurse, thy rigid lore
> With patience many a year she bore."

Soon after the disastrous defeat and death of her royal father and eldest brother, Donald Bane, the illegitimate brother of Malcolm Canmore, seized the throne of Scotland, and commanded all the English exiles, of whatsoever degree, to quit the kingdom, under pain of death.[2] Edgar Atheling, Matilda's uncle, then conveyed to England the orphan family of his sister, the queen of Scotland, consisting of five young princes, and two princesses.[3]

He supported Matilda, her sister and brothers, who were all minors, privately, from his own means. They were in considerable personal danger, from the accusation of one of the knights at the English court, who told William Rufus that the Saxon prince had brought into England, and was raising up, a family of competitors for the English crown. A friend of Edgar challenged and slew this mischievous talebearer; and William Rufus, supposing Providence had decided in favour of the innocent, treated Edgar and his adopted family with kindness and friendship.

The princesses Matilda and Mary were placed by their uncle in the nunnery of Rumsey, of which his surviving sister, Christina, was abbess; and for the princes, he sought and obtained an honourable reception for them at the court of William Rufus, who eventually sent him at the head of an army to Scotland, with which the Atheling succeeded in re-establishing his nephew, the elder brother of Matilda, on the throne of his ancestors.

Ordericus Vitalis confirms, in a great measure, the statements of

---

[1] Queen Margaret was buried at Dunfermline. Her body was disinterred at the Reformation, and the head is now preserved in a silver case at Douay, where the historian Carruthers declares he saw it at the Scotch college. It was in extraordinary preservation, with a quantity of fine hair, fair in colour, still upon it. This was in 1785.—Hist. of Scotland, vol. i. p. 313.

[2] Carruthers' Hist. of Scotland, vol. i. p. 316.

[3] Hardinge, in his rhyming chronicle, thus quaintly enumerates the posterity of Margaret Atheling (See Henry Ellis's edition):—

> "Edward, Dunkan, Edgar, Alixander the gay,
> And David also, (that kings were all they say,
> Eache after other of Scotlande throughout,)
> Whose mother is now St. Margarete without doubt.
> At Dunfermlyn shrined and canonised;
> By whom Malcolyn a daughter had also,
> King Henry's wife the first, full well avised
> Queen Maude, that's right well loved England through,
> Those crosses fair and royal, as men go,
> Through all England, she made at her expense,
> And divers good orders through her providence."

Turgot; and, after relating the death of queen Margaret, adds, " She had sent her two daughters, Edith (Matilda) and Mary, to Christina, her sister, who was a religieuse of the abbey of Rumsey, to be instructed by her in holy writ. These princesses were a long time pupils among the nuns. They were instructed by them, not only in the art of reading, but in the observance of good manners; and these devoted maidens, as they approached the age of womanhood, waited for the consolation of God. As we have said, they were orphans, deprived of both their parents, separated from their brothers, and far from the protecting care of kindred or friends. They had no home or hope but the cloister, and yet, by the mercy of God, they were not professed as nuns. They were destined by the Disposer of all earthly events for better things."

Camden proves that the abbey of Wilton, ever since the profession of the saintly princess Editha,[1] was the place of nurture and education for all the young princesses of the Anglo-Saxon royal family. This abbey of Black Benedictine nuns had been founded by king Alfred, and since his days had always received a lady of his royal line as its abbess,—a custom which does not seem to have been broken by the deposition of his family.

Wilton Abbey had been re-founded by queen Editha, consort to Edward the Confessor.[2] While that monarch was building Westminster Abbey, his queen was employing her revenues in changing the nunnery of Wilton, from a wooden edifice into one of stone.

The abbey of Rumsey was likewise a royal foundation, generally governed by an abbess of the family of Alfred. Christina is first mentioned as abbess of Rumsey in Hampshire, and afterwards as superior of the Wilton convent. As both belonged to the order of Black Benedictines, this transfer was not difficult; but chroniclers do not mention when it was effected, simply stating the fact, that the Scottish princess first dwelt at Rumsey, but that when she grew up she was resident at Wilton Abbey, under the superintendence of the abbess Christina, her aunt. Matilda thus became an inhabitant of the same abode where the royal virgins of her race had always received their education.[3]

It was the express desire of the queen, her mother, who survived that request but a few hours, that she should be placed under the care of the lady Christina at Rumsey.

While in these English convents, the royal maid was compelled to assume the thick black veil of a votaress,[4] as a protection from the insults of the lawless Norman nobles. The abbess Christina, her aunt, who was exceedingly desirous of seeing her beautiful niece become a nun professed, treated her very harshly, if she removed this cumbrous and inconvenient envelope, which was composed of coarse black cloth or serge; some say it was a tissue of horse-hair. The imposition of this veil was considered by Matilda as an intolerable grievance. She wore it,[5] as she herself acknowledged, with sighs and tears, in the pre-

---

[1] Daughter of Edgar the Peaceable.   [2] Camden.   [3] Orderious Vitalis.
[4] Eadmer.   [5] Ibid.

sence of her stern aunt; and the moment she found herself alone, she flung it on the ground, and stamped it under her feet.

During the seven years that Matilda resided in this dreary asylum, she was carefully instructed in all the learning of the age. Ordericus Vitalis says she was taught the "*litteratoriam artem*," of which she afterwards became, like her predecessor, Matilda of Flanders, a most munificent patroness. She was also greatly skilled in music, for which her love amounted almost to a passion. When queen, we shall find her sometimes censured, for the too great liberality she showed in rewarding, with costly presents, the monks who sang skilfully in the church service.[1]

The superior education which this illustrious princess received during these years of conventual seclusion, eminently fitted her to become the consort of so accomplished a prince as Henry le Beauclerc. Robert of Gloucester, and Piers of Langtoft, and, above all, Eadmer, a contemporary, assert that the royal pair had been lovers before circumstances admitted of their union. These are the words of quaint old Robin on the subject:—

> "Special love there had ere[2] been, as I understand,
> Between him and the king's fair daughter, Maud of Scotland.
> So that he willed her to wife, and the bishops also,
> And the high men of the land radde[3] him thereto."

Matilda received two proposals of marriage while she was in the nunnery at Rumsey; one from Alan duke of Bretagne, the mature suitor before mentioned, who demanded her in marriage of his brother-in-law, William Rufus, and obtained his consent, but he was prevented by death from fulfilling his engagement. Had it been otherwise, Matilda's only refuge from this ill-assorted union, would have been the irrevocable assumption of the black veil, of which she had testified such unqualified abhorrence.

The other candidate for the hand of the exiled princess, was the young and handsome William Warren, earl of Surrey, the son of the Conqueror's youngest daughter, Gundred, the favourite nephew of William Rufus, and one of the richest and most powerful of the baronage of England and Normandy.

The profession of Matilda was delayed for a time, by the addresses of these princes.[4] "But," continues the chronicler, "she was, by the grace of God, reserved for a higher destiny, and through his permission contracted a more illustrious marriage."[5] It is remarkable, that of the three lovers by whom Matilda was sought in marriage, one should have been the son-in-law, another the grandson, and the third the son, of that Norman conqueror who had established a rival dynasty on the throne of her ancestors.

Matilda pleaded her devotion to a religious life, as an excuse for declining the addresses of Warren, though, under existing circumstances, it seems strange that she should have preferred a lengthened sojourn in a

[1] Tyrrell.   [2] Ere means before, or formerly.   [3] Radde, advised.
[4] Ordericus Vitalis.   [5] Ibid.

gloomy cloister, to a union with a young, handsome, and wealthy peer
of the blood-royal of the reigning sovereign of England; and her refusal of Warren affords some reason for giving credence to the statements of Eadmer, Robert of Gloucester, and others of the ancient chroniclers, as to " the special love" that existed between Henry Beauclerc and
Matilda, during the season of their mutual adversity. Matilda was at
that time residing in the nunnery of Wilton, not far from Winchester,
the principal seat of the Norman sovereign. When we reflect on the
great intimacy which subsisted between Matilda's uncle, Edgar Atheling,
and the sons of the Conqueror, it appears by no means improbable that
prince Henry might have accompanied him in some of his visits to his
royal kinswomen, in the nunnery of Wilton, and perhaps been admitted,
under the sanction of his presence, to converse with the princesses, and
even to have enjoyed the opportunity of seeing Matilda without her
veil; which, we learn, from her own confession, she took every opportunity of throwing aside.

According to the testimony of the ancient chroniclers, especially the
chronicle of Normandy, this princess was remarkable for her beauty.[1]
Matthew Paris says she was " very fair, and elegant in person, as well as
learned, holy, and wise." These qualities, combined with her high
lineage, rendered her doubtless an object of attraction to the Norman
princes. Henry Beauclerc was ten years the senior of his nephew Warren, but his high mental acquirements and accomplishments were, to a
mind like that of Matilda of Scotland, far beyond the meretricious ad-
vantages which his more youthful rival could boast.

Robert of Gloucester, in his rhyming chronicle, gives this quaint
summary of the birth, education, and characteristics of Henry :—

> " In England was he born, Henri, this nobleman,
> In the third year that his father England wan;
> He was, of all his sons, best fitted king to be,
> Of fairest form and manners, and most gentle and free.
> For that he was the youngest to book his father him drew,
> And he became as it befel a good clerk enow.
> One time when he was young, his brother smote him, I wis,
> And he wept while his father stood by and beheld all this;
> 'Ne weep now,' he said, 'loving son, for it shall come to be,
> That thou shalt yet be king, and that thou shalt see.'
> His father made him, at Westminster, knight of his own hand,
> In the nineteenth year of his age, &c. &c.
> Taller he was some deal than his brethren were,
> Fair man and stout enow, with brown hair."

Henry was regarded by the people of the land with a greater degree
of complacency than the elder sons of the Conqueror, from the circumstance of his being an English-born prince. While yet a tender infant,
his mighty sire named him as a witness, (the only male witness,) of the
following curious charter to one of his followers, the founder of the
family of Hunter of Hopton :—

---

[1] The chronicle of Normandy says that Matilda was a lady of great beauty,
and much beloved by king Henry.

> " I, William, the king, the third year of my reign,
> Give to thee, Norman Hunter, to me that art both liefe (loving) and dear,
> The Hop and the Hopton, and all the bounds up and down,
> Under the earth to hell, above the earth to heaven.
> From me and mine to thee and thine,
> As good and as fair as ever they mine were.
> To witness that this is sooth,
> I bite the white wax with my tooth,
> Before Jugge,[1] Maude, and Margery.
> And my young sonne Henry,
> For a bowe and a broad arrowe,
> When I shall come to hunt on Yarrowe."[2]

The rhymes of this quaint feudal grant are undoubtedly far more agreeable to the year than the halting heroics of honest Robert of Gloucester, previously quoted, though compounded more than a century before his jingling chronicle was written. Several of the charters of William the Conqueror are in this form, and with the names of the same members of his family. It is probable that they were executed in the presence of his queen, " Maud ;" " Jugge," (sometimes used as an abbreviation for Judith,) must have been his niece Judith, afterwards the wife of Waltheof; and Margery, a daughter, who is sometimes enumerated in his family, by the chroniclers; and to these the name of that notable witness, the baby Henry, was doubtless added, as a joke, by the royal sire. Biting the white wax was supposed to give particular authenticity to conveyances from the crown, which were formerly each duly furnished with a proof impression of that primitive substitute for the great seal of England, the royal eye-tooth, sometimes familiarly specified by the monarch as his " fang-tooth." This custom, which took its rise from very remote antiquity, was needlessly adopted by the Anglo-Norman line of sovereigns, whose broad seals are peculiarly fine workmanship, bearing their veritable effigies crowned, sceptred, and in royal robes, seated on the king's stone bench; and on the reverse of the seal the same monarch is figured, armed cap-à-pié, and mounted on a war-charger, gallantly appointed.[3] Such are the impressions affixed to all their charters.

It is among the boasts of Cambridge[4] that Henry, so celebrated for his learning, received his education there. The ancient annals of St. Austin's, Canterbury, however, affirm " that he was instructed in philosophy beyond seas, where, for his knowledge in the liberal sciences, he was by the French surnamed Beauclerc."[5]

The following dialogue took place between Henry and his royal sire, when the latter lay on his death-bed at Hermentrude,[6] and was conclud-

---

[1] Pronounced Jucy, which rhymes to Margery; the rhymes, it will be observed, recur in the middle of the lines.　　　[2] Stowe ex Libro Richmond.
[3] Speed.　　　[4] J. Caius Cantabrig.
[5] St. Austin's Lib. MSS. A learned writer in the Archæologia supposes that this appellation was won by Henry's English Fables in the Esopian style; adding that the celebrated Troubadour poetess, Marie of France, who flourished in the reign of our Henry III., has translated the English monarch's work into Norman French.　　　[6] Speed.

8*

ing his elaborate confession of his past deeds of oppression and cruelty, with the verbal bequest of his dominions to his two eldest sons.

"And what do you give to me, father?" interrupted Henry, who stood weeping at the bedside, less touched, we fear, at the awful list of sins and wickednesses of which his dying sire had just disburthened his conscience, than at the tenour of a last will and testament in which he appeared to have no share.

" Five thousand pounds in silver, out of my treasury, do I give thee," replied the Conqueror.

" But what shall I do with treasure, if I have neither castle nor domain?" demanded the disappointed prince.

" Be patient, my son, and comfort thyself in God," rejoined the expiring monarch; " thy elder brothers do but go before thee: Robert shall have Normandy, and William England; but thou shalt be the inheritor of all my honours, and shalt excel both thy brethren in riches and power."

This oracular speech, though far enough from proving satisfactory at the time to the landless Henry, was afterwards magnified into a prophetic annunciation of his accession to the united dominions of England and Normandy.

Discontented as Henry was with the paternal legacy, he was in such haste to secure its payment, that he left the last duties to the remains of his royal sire to the care of strangers, while he flew to make his claim upon the treasury of the departed sovereign; rightly judging, that unless he forestalled his elder brethren in taking possession of the bequest, his chance of receiving it would be but small. In fact, Robert, whose extravagance had exhausted all his resources before he succeeded to the dukedom of Normandy, besought his youngest brother to assist him with a loan of at least part of the money. Henry, who had all the worldly wisdom of a premature statesman, complied, on condition of being put in possession of his mother's bequest of the Cotentin. Robert agreed; but, after he had been foiled in his attempt to dethrone Rufus, he returned to Normandy with exhausted coffers, and wrongfully repossessed himself of the Cotentin. Henry, greatly enraged at this treatment, was preparing to take up arms against Robert, when the latter, finding himself attacked by William, and abandoned by his false ally, Philip of France, thought proper to make the most earnest solicitations to Henry for assistance, and forgiveness for the late outrage of which he had been guilty.

Henry, being mollified by the submission of his elder brother, and understanding that a plot was in agitation to deliver Rouen to William, suddenly entered the city, and seizing Conon, the head of the conspirators, charged him with his treason to the duke, and caused him to be flung headlong from one of the highest towers. By this decisive step Henry preserved the capital for Robert.

Robert and William soon after came to an amicable agreement, and, conceiving a sudden affection for each other, they terminated their quarrel by making their wills in each other's favour, without any mention of Henry. Henry regarded this as a great affront, especially on the part

of Robert, to whom he had rendered such signal services, and demanded
of him either a restitution of his silver, or to be put in possession of the
Cotentin. On Robert's refusal, he seized on Mount St. Michael, where
he strongly entrenched himself.

The youthful adventurer maintained his rocky fortress with obstinate
valour, against the united efforts of his august brothers of England and
Normandy, till he was reduced to, the greatest straits for want of water.
He represented his distress to Robert, in a moving message, and obtained
leave to supply his, garrison with water, and a present of wine for his
own use. Rufus upbraided Robert with his compliance, which he called
" an act of folly."

" What !" replied Robert, with a sudden burst of that generous warmth
of feeling which formed the redeeming trait of his character, " is the
quarrel between us and our brother of that importance that we should
make him die of thirst? We may have occasion for a brother hereafter,
but where shall we find another if we destroy this ?"

After Robert had besieged St. Michael's Mount during the whole of
Lent, he brought Henry to terms; who, weary, perhaps, of keeping a
stricter fast than even the church of Rome enjoined at that season, surrendered the fortress; and having permission to go whither he pleased,
wandered about Germany and France for some time, forsaken of every
one save four faithful domestics, by whom he was attended.

In the year 1094, we find, from Matthew Paris, that Henry was in
England, and employed by William Rufus in assisting to quell the formidable rebellion of Robert Mowbray, the Lord of Northumberland. Prince
Henry's poverty, and dependence on the caprices of his brother, the Red
King, subjected him occasionally to the sneers of the wealthy Norman
barons, but more especially of his kinsman and rival, Warren,[1] who took
occasion, from his swiftness in pursuit of the forest game, " which ofttimes," says the chronicle of Normandy, " he, for lack of horse or dog,
followed on foot, to bestow the name of Deer's-foot on the landless
prince. This greatly troubled Henry, who hated Warren to the death,
but had no power to avenge himself, because the Red King loved Warren
greatly."[2] It is possible that Warren's courtship of Matilda of Scotland
was one cause of Henry's bitter animosity.[3] This courtship was sanctioned by Rufus, and some of the ancient chroniclers assert that Matilda
was contracted to him, but this appears without foundation.

Henry was in his thirty-second year, when the glancing aside of Wat
Tyrrel's arrow made him king of England. The chroniclers of that era
record that, from whatever cause, omens, dreams, and predictions of the
death of the Red King, were rife in the land, immediately preceding that
event.[4] Prince Henry was at this fatal hunting party;[5] and Wace, the
minstrel chronicler of the Norman line of princes, relates a most remarkable adventure that befell him on this occasion.[6] " Prince Henry
being separated from the royal party, while pursuing his game in an
adjoining glen of the forest, chanced to snap the string of his cross-bow,

[1] Wace.   [2] Ibid.   [3] Chronicle of Normandy by Wace.
[4] Malmsbury. Saxon Chron.   [5] Dunelm.   [6] Wace.

or arblast, and repairing to the hut of a forester, to get it mended or replaced, he was, the moment he entered this sylvan abode, saluted as king by an old woman whom he found there," whose description is somewhat similar to that of one of the witches in Macbeth.[1]   The following is a literal version of her address, from the Norman French rhymes of Wace :—

> "Hasty news to thee I bring,
> Henry, thou art now a king;
> Mark the words and heed them well,
> Which to thee in sooth I tell,
> And recall them in the hour
> Of thy regal state and power."

Before Henry had recovered from the surprise with which the weird woman's prediction had startled him, the cries of the Red King's attendants proclaimed the fatal accident that had befallen their royal master, and the hasty flight of the unlucky marksman by whose erring shaft he had died.   Prince Henry acted as Rufus doubtless would have done in his case; he sprang to his saddle, and made the best of his way to Winchester, without bestowing a moment's care or attention on the body of his deceased brother, which was irreverently thrown into the cart of one Purkiss, a Saxon charcoal-burner, that was passing through the forest, and, on no gentler bier, was ignobly borne back to the city which he had quitted that morning with such proud parade.[2]   Robert of Gloucester relates the circumstance, with his usual quaint minuteness; and among a number of his lame and tame lines, the following graphic couplet occurs, which we think our readers will consider worthy of quotation :—

> "To Winchester they bare him, all midst his green wound,
> And ever as he lay the blood well'd to ground."

William Breteuil,[3] the royal treasurer, was also at this memorable hunting party, and with him prince Henry actually rode a race to Winchester—ay, and won it too; for when Breteuil arrived at the door of the treasury, he found prince Henry standing before it, who greeted him with a demand of the keys.   Breteuil boldly declared, "That both treasure and crown belonged to the prince's eldest brother, duke Robert of Normandy, who was then absent in the Holy Land, and for that prince he would keep the treasures of the late king his master."   Then Henry drew his sword, and, backed by his powerful friend, Henry Bellomonte, afterwards earl of Leicester, and other nobles of his party, forced the keys from his kinsman Breteuil, and took possession of the treasure and regalia.   Breteuil loudly protested against the wrong that was done to duke Robert.

Some of the nobles who possessed large estates in Normandy, sided

---

[1] Wace.

[2] Saxon Chron. The lineal descendants of the said charcoal-maker, by name Purkiss, still live within the distance of a bow-shot from the spot where Rufus fell, and continue to exercise the trade of their ancestor.—Milner's Winchester.

[3] William Breteuil was the son of the Conqueror's great friend and counsellor, Fitz-Osborn, surnamed the Proud Spirit.—See the preceding memoir.

with Breteuil, in advocating the rights of the royal Crusader; and the debate growing very stormy, it was considered more expedient to argue the momentous question in the council-chamber. Thither the nobles and prelates adjourned; but while they were engaged in advocating, according as interest or passion swayed, the rival claims of Robert and Henry to the vacant throne, the majority being inclined for the elder brother, (the brave but proverbially *unready* Robert,) Henry had successfully pleaded his own cause to the populace, in the streets of Winchester; and they, strong in numbers, and animated with sudden affection for the English-born prince, who had promised to bestow upon them English laws and an English queen, gathered round the palace, and quickened the decision of the divided peers in council, by making the name of Henry resound in their ears; and Henry, thus elected by the voice of the people, was immediately proclaimed king, at Winchester. The remains of the luckless Rufus were hurried into the grave, with a sort of hunter's mass, the following morning, at an early hour, in Winchester Cathedral;[1] and Henry hastened to London, where, on Sunday, the 9th of August, the third day after his brother's death, he was crowned in Westminster Abbey, by Maurice, bishop of London. Before the regal circlet was placed on his brow, "Henry, at the high altar at Westminster, promised to God and the people," says the Saxon Chronicle, " to annul the unrighteous acts that took place in his brother's reign, and he was crowned on that condition."[2]

Henry promised everything that could reasonably be demanded of him, and set about reforming the abuses and corruptions that had prevailed during the licentious reign of the bachelor king, and completely secured his popularity with the English people, by declaring his resolution of wedding a princess of the blood of Alfred, who had been brought up and educated among them. Accordingly he demanded Matilda, the daughter of Malcolm, king of Scotland, and Margaret Atheling, of her brother Edgar, king of Scotland. The proposal was exceedingly agreeable to the Scottish monarch; but great difficulties were opposed to the completion of this marriage, by those who were of opinion that she had embraced a religious life.[3] The abbess Christina, Matilda's aunt, in particular, whose Saxon prejudices could not brook the idea that the throne of the Norman line of sovereigns should be strengthened by an alliance with the royal blood of Alfred, protested, "that her niece was a veiled nun, and that it would be an act of sacrilege to remove her from her convent."

Henry's heart was set upon the marriage, but he would not venture to outrage popular opinion, by wedding a consecrated nun. In this dilemma, he wrote a pressing letter to the learned Anselm, archbishop of Canterbury, who had been unjustly despoiled of his revenues by

---

[1] The monument that Henry I. raised for his brother Rufus, before the high altar at Winchester, is still to be seen there; he put himself to no great cost for funeral expenses, for it is a plain gravestone of black marble, of that shape called *dos d'ane*, to be seen, of brick or freestone, in country churchyards.

[2] Saxon Chronicle.   [3] Eadmer.

William Rufus, and was then in exile at Lyons, entreating him to
return, and render him his advice and assistance in this affair. When
Anselm heard the particulars of the case, he declared that it was too
mighty for his single decision, and therefore summoned a council of the
church at Lambeth, for the purpose of entering more fully into this important question.[1]

Matilda made her appearance before the synod, and was closely inter-
rogated by the primate Anselm, in the presence of the whole hierarchy
of England, as to the reality of her alleged devotion to a religious life.[2]

The particulars of her examination have been preserved by Eadmer,
who, as the secretary of the archbishop Anselm, was doubtless an eye-
witness of this interesting scene, and, in all probability, recorded the
very words uttered by the princess.

The archbishop commenced by stating the objections to her marriage,
grounded on the prevailing report that she had embraced a religious life,
and declared, " that no motive whatever would induce him to dispense
with her vow, if it had already been given to Almighty God."

The princess denied that there had been any such engagement on
her part.

She was asked " if she had embraced a religious life, either by her
own choice or the vow of her parents;" and she replied, " Neither."
Then she was examined as to the fact of her having worn the black veil
of a votaress in her father's court, and subsequently in the nunneries of
Rumsey and Wilton.

" I do not deny,"[3] said Matilda, " having worn the veil in my father's
court: for, when I was a child, my aunt Christina put a piece of black
cloth over my head; but when my father saw me with it, he snatched
it off in a great rage, and execrated the person who had put it on me.[4] I
afterwards made a pretence of wearing it, to excuse myself from unsuitable marriages; and, on one of these occasions, my father tore the veil
and threw it on the ground, observing to Alan earl of Bretagne, who
stood by, that it was his intention to give me in marriage, not to devote
me to the church."[5]

She also admitted that she had assumed the veil in the nunnery of
Rumsey, as a protection from the lawless violence of the Norman
nobles, and that she had continued to wear that badge of conventual
devotion, against her own inclination, through the harsh compulsion of
her aunt, the abbess Christina. " If I attempted to remove it," continued
Matilda, " she would torment me with harsh blows and sharp reproaches:
sighing and trembling, I wore it in her presence; but as soon as I withdrew from her sight, I always threw it off, and trampled upon it."[6]

This explanation was considered perfectly satisfactory by the council
at Lambeth, and they pronounced, that " Matilda, daughter of Malcolm,

[1] Not long after the return of Archbishop Anselm to England, the king, by the
advice of his friends, resolved to leave off his mistresses and marry; and he
having a very great affection for Matilda, daughter to Malcolm, late king of Scotland, resolved, if it might be lawful, to marry her.—Tyrrell.
[2] Eadmer. Malmsbury.   [3] Eadmer.   [4] Ibid.   [5] Ibid.   [6] Ibid.

king of Scotland, had proved that she had not embraced a religious life, either by her own choice or the vow of her parents, and she was therefore free to contract marriage with the king." The council, in addition to this declaration, thought proper to make public the most cogent reason which the Scottish princess had given for her assumption of the black veil, on her coming to England; which was done in the following remarkable words.[1]

" When the great king William conquered this land, many of his followers, elated by so great a victory, and thinking that everything ought to be subservient to their will and pleasure, not only seized the provisions of the conquered, but invaded the honour of their matrons and virgins whenever they had an opportunity. This obliged many young ladies, who dreaded their violence, to put on the veil, to preserve their honour."[2]

According to the Saxon chroniclers, Matilda, notwithstanding her repugnance to the consecrated veil, exhibited a very maidenly reluctance to enter the holy pale of matrimony with a royal husband. It is possible that the report of the immoral tenour of Henry's life before he ascended the throne, which was evidenced by his acknowledging the claims of twenty illegitimate children, might be regarded by a princess of her purity of mind and manners as a very serious objection; and if, as many of the early chroniclers intimate, there had been a previous engagement between Henry and herself, she of course felt both displeasure and disgust at his amours with the beautiful Nesta, daughter of the prince of Wales, and other ladies too numerous to particularize. It is certain that after the council at Lambeth had pronounced her free to marry, Matilda resisted for a time the entreaties of the king, and the commands of her royal brother and sovereign, to accept the brilliant destiny which she was offered.

All who were connected with the Saxon royal line importuned Matilda, meantime, with such words as these: " O most noble and most gracious of women, if thou wouldst, thou couldst raise up the ancient honour of England: thou wouldst be a sign of alliance, a pledge of reconciliation: but if thou persistest in thy refusal, the enmity between the Saxon and Norman races will be eternal; human blood will never cease to flow."[3]

Thus urged, the royal recluse ceased to object to a marriage, whereby she was to become the bond of peace to a divided nation, and the dove of the newly-sealed covenant between the Norman sovereign and her own people. Henry promised to confirm to the English nation their ancient laws and privileges, as established by Alfred, and ratified by Edward the Confessor — in short, to become a constitutional monarch; and on those conditions the daughter of the royal line of Alfred consented to share his throne.

Matthew Paris says positively that Matilda was a professed nun, and so averse to this marriage, that she invoked a curse upon all the descendants that might proceed from her union with the Norman king.

---

[1] Eadmer.　　　　[2] Ibid.　　　　[3] Saxon Chronicle.

But this is contradicted by all other historians; and if any foundation existed for the story, we think friend Matthew must, by a strange slip of the pen, have written down the name of the meek and saintly Matilda instead of that of the perverse virago, the abbess Christina, her aunt, who was so greatly opposed to those auspicious nuptials, and, for aught we know, might have been as much addicted to the evil habit of imprecation as she was to scolding and fighting.

Matilda's demurs, after all, occasioned little delay, for the archbishop Anselm did not return to England till October; the council at Lambeth was held in the latter end of that month, and her marriage and coronation took place on Sunday, November 11th, being St. Martin's day, just three months and six days after the inauguration of her royal lord at Westminster, August 5th, 1100; which we may consider quick work, for the despatch of such important business, and solemn ceremonials of state.

We give the singular scene of the marriage, in the very words of one who was a contemporary, and most likely an eye-witness.

" At the wedding of Matilda and Henry the First, there was a most prodigious concourse of nobility and people assembled in and about the church at Westminster, when, to prevent all calumny and ill report that the king was about to marry a nun, the archbishop Anselm mounted into a pulpit, and gave the multitude a history of the events proved before the synod, and its judgment, that the lady Matilda of Scotland was free from any religious vow, and might dispose of herself in marriage as she thought fit. The archbishop finished by asking the people in a loud voice, whether any one there objected to this decision, upon which they answered unanimously, with a loud shout, ' that the matter was rightly settled.' Accordingly the lady was immediately married to the king, and crowned before that vast assembly." [1]   A more simple yet majestic appeal to the sense of the people, in regard to a royal marriage, history records not.

To this auspicious union of the Anglo-Norman sovereign Henry I. with Matilda of Scotland, a princess of English lineage, English education, and an English heart, we may trace all the constitutional blessings which this free country at present enjoys. It was through the influence of this virtuous queen that Henry granted the important charter which formed the model and precedent of that great palladium of English liberty, Magna Charta; and we call upon our readers to observe, that it was the direct ancestress of our present sovereign-lady, who refused to quit her gloomy conventual prison, and to give her hand to the handsomest and most accomplished sovereign of his time, till she had obtained just and merciful laws for her suffering country, the repeal of the tyrannical imposition of the curfew, and, in some slight degree, a recognition of the rights of the commons.

When the marriage of Matilda of Scotland with Henry I. took place, a hundred copies of this digest of the righteous laws of Alfred and Edward the Confessor were made, and committed to the keeping of the

---

[1] William of Malmsbury.

principal bishoprics and menasteries in England; but when these were sought for, in the reign of John, to form a legal authority for the demands of the people, Rapin says, only one could be found, which was exhibited to the barons by Cardinal Langton. This was, in fact, the simple model on which Magna Charta was framed.

It is supposed that Henry I., after Matilda's death, destroyed all the copies (on which he could lay his hands) of a covenant which, in the latter years of his reign, he scrupled not to infringe whenever he felt disposed.

Hardinge, after recording the death of the Red King, relates the accession of Henry I., and his marriage with Matilda of Scotland, in the following rude stanzas :—

> "Henry his brother, the first king of that name,
> Was crowned with all the honour that might be;
> He reconciled St. Anselm who came home,
> And crowned Maude his wife full fair and free;
> That daughter was (full of benignite)
> To king Malcolyne and St. Margrete the queen
> Of Scotland, which afore that time had been;
>
> Of whom he gat William, Richard, and Molde,
> Whose goodness is yet spoken of full wide;
> If she were fair, her virtues many-fold
> Exceeded far—all vice she set aside;
> Debates that were engendered of pride
> She set at rest with all benevolence,
> And visited the sick and poor with diligence.
>
> The prisoners and women eke with child,
> Lying in abject misery ay about,
> Clothes, meat, and bedding new and undefiled,
> And wine and ale she gave withouten doubt,
> When she saw need in countries all throughout,
> Those crosses all that yet be most royal
> In the highways, with gold she made them all."[1]

MATILDA OF SCOTLAND,

QUEEN OF HENRY I.

CHAPTER II.

Popularity of Matilda's marriage—Called Matilda Atheling—Her charities—Her brother, king Alexander the Fierce—Her works of utility—Equitable laws of king Henry—Normans nickname the king and queen—Duke Robert's invasion —His consideration for Matilda—Matilda and archbishop's mediation— Henry's quarrels with archbishop Anselm—Duke Robert's visit—Presents his pension

---

[1] Sir Henry Ellis's version.

98   MATILDA OF SCOTLAND.

MATILDA's English ancestry, and English education, rendered the new king's marriage with her a most popular measure with the Anglo-Saxon people, of whom the great bulk of his subjects was composed. By them the royal bride was fondly styled Matilda Atheling, and regarded as the representative of their own regretted sovereigns. The allegiance which the mighty Norman conqueror, and his despotic son, the Red King, had never been able to obtain, except through the sternest measures of compulsion, and which, in defiance of the dreadful penalties of loss of eyes, limbs, and life, had been frequently withdrawn from these powerful monarchs, was freely and faithfully accorded to the husband of Matilda, Henry I., by the Saxon population. All the reforms effected by his enlightened government, and all the good laws which his enlarged views of political economy taught that wise monarch to adopt, were attributed, by his Anglo-Saxon subjects, to the beneficial influence of his young queen.

Robert of Gloucester was fully impressed with these ideas, as we may plainly perceive in the following lines in his rhyming chronicle, in which he speaks of Henry's marriage :—

" So that as soon as he was king, on St. Martyn's day I ween,
He spoused her that was called Maude the good queen,
That was *kind* [1] *heir of England*, as I have told before.
＊　　＊　　＊　　＊　　＊
Many were the good laws that were made in England,
Through Maude the good queen, as I understand."

Five-and-thirty years had elapsed since the metropolis had enjoyed the advantage of a resident court. Matilda of Flanders, during her brief visit to England, held her state at Westminster, the favourite abode of the two first Anglo-Norman monarchs; and the Londoners, whose prosperity had sensibly diminished in consequence of the entire absence of female royalty, beheld with unfeigned satisfaction the palace of Edward the Confessor, at Westminster, once more graced by the presence of a queen of the blood of Alfred, whose virtues, piety, and learning, rendered her a worthy successor of the last Saxon queen who had held her court there, Editha,

" That gracious rose of Godwin's thorny stem."

---

[1] *Kind* means, in ancient English, relationship; " next of kin," a familiar expression, is derived from it.

Those to whom the memory of that illustrious lady was justly dear, were probably not unmindful of the fact, that the youthful queen, on whom the hopes of England were so fondly fixed, had received that genuine Saxon name at the baptismal font; and though, in compliment to her Norman godfather, she was called Matilda, she was also Editha.

Like her saintly predecessor, Matilda fully verified the primitive title bestowed by the Saxon on their queens, Hlaffdige, or the giver of bread. Her charities were of a most extensive character, and her tender compassion for the sufferings of the sick poor carried her almost beyond the bounds of reason, to say nothing of the restraints imposed on royalty. She imitated the example of her mother, the saintly queen of Scotland, both in the strictness of her devotional exercises, and in her personal attentions to those who were labouring under bodily afflictions.[1] She went every day in Lent to Westminster Abbey, barefoot, and clothed in a garment of haircloth; and she would wash and kiss the feet of the poorest people, for which, according to Robert of Gloucester, she was once reproved, not without reason, by a courtier. He had his answer, however, as our readers will perceive from the following curious dialogue :—

> " ' Madam, for Godde's love is this well ado
> To handle such unclean limbs, and to kiss so?
> Foul would the king think if this thing he wist,
> And right well avile him ere he your lips kist.'
> ' Sir, sir !' quoth the queen, ' be still. Why say you so?
> Our Lord himself example gave for to do so.' "[2]

On another occasion, her brother, Alexander the Fierce, king of Scotland, when on a visit to the court of her royal husband, entering Matilda's apartments, found her on her knees, engaged in washing the feet of some aged mendicants; on which she entreated him to avail himself of the opportunity of performing a good and acceptable work of charity and humiliation, by assisting her in this labour of love, for the benefit of his soul.[3]

The warlike majesty of Scotland smiled, and left the room, without making any reply to this invitation. Perhaps he was conscious of his want of skill as an assistant at a pediluvium party; or it might be that he had seen too much of such scenes during the life of his pious mother queen Margaret, and feared that his sister would carry her works of benevolence to extremes that might prove displeasing to the tastes of so refined a prince as Henry Beauclerc.

But to do Matilda justice, her good works in general bore a character of more extended usefulness; so much so, that we even feel the benefit of them to this day, in the ancient bridge she built over " my Lady Lea." Once being, with her train on horseback, in danger of perishing while fording the river Lea, at Oldford, during *a high flood*, in gratitude for her preservation, she built the first arched bridge ever known in England, a little higher up the stream, called by the Saxons Bow[4] Bridge, still to

---

[1] Weever.   [2] Robert of Gloucester.   [3] M. Paris.

[4] Bow, from *bogen*, an arch, a word in the German language, pronounced with the *g* sounded like *y*, which brings it close to the Anglo-Saxon.

he seen at Stratford-le-Bow, " though the ancient and mighty London Bridge has been broken down."

Bow Bridge she built at the head of the town of Stratford; likewise Channel's Bridge, over a tributary stream of the Lea, the way between them being well paved with gravel. She gave certain manors, and a mill called Wiggin Mill, for ever, towards keeping in repair the said bridges and way.[1]

Matilda founded the hospital at St. Giles in the Fields, and also Christ Church,[2] which stood on the very spot now called Duke's Place, noted as the resort of a low class of Jews.

This excellent queen also directed her attention to the important object of making new roads, and repairing the ancient highways, that had fallen into decay during the stormy years which had succeeded the peaceful and prosperous reign of her great uncle, Edward the Confessor. By this means, travellers and itinerant merchants were greatly facilitated, in their journeys through the then wild and perilous country, which, with the exception of the four great Roman ways,[3] was only intersected by a few scattered cart-tracks, through desolate moors, heaths, and uncultivated wastes and woodlands. These public benefits, which Matilda the Good conferred upon the people from whose patriotic monarchs she derived her descent, were in all probability the fruits of her regency, during the absence of her royal husband in Normandy; for it is scarcely to be supposed that such stupendous undertakings could have been effected, by the limited power and revenues of a mere queen-consort.

Henry the First, be it remembered, was placed on the throne by the Saxon division of his subjects, who were the commons of England, and by them he was supported in his regal authority against the Norman aristocracy, who formed a powerful party, in favour of his elder brother's pretensions to the crown of England. The moral and political reforms with which Henry commenced his reign, and, above all, the even-handed measure of justice which he caused to be observed towards all who presumed to infringe the laws, gave great offence to many of those haughty nobles who had been accustomed to commit the most flagrant crimes with impunity, and to oppress their humbler neighbours, without fear of being arraigned for their misdeeds. The establishment of the equitable laws which protected the wives and daughters of Englishmen from insult, the honest trader from wrong and robbery, and the poor from violence, were attributed to the influence of Matilda, whom they insultingly styled " the Saxon woman,"[4] and murmured at the virtuous restraints which her presence and authority imposed upon the court.[5] The conjugal affection which subsisted between the royal pair, excited, withal, the ridicule of those who had been the profligate associates of

[1] Hayward's Three Norman Kings.   [2] Pennant.
[3] Which mighty works were of infinite use to our ancestors in ages later than the Norman era. Robert of Gloucester speaks of their utility in his day, and says,
" Thilk ways by mony a town do wend."
[4] Thierry.   [5] Eadmer.

the bachelor king, William Rufus; and it was universally displeasing to the haughty Norman peers, to see the king's gracious demeanour towards the hitherto oppressed and dispirited English portion of his subjects, for whom his amiable consort was constantly labouring to procure a recognition of their rights. "The malice of certain evil-minded men," says Eadmer, "busied itself in inventing the most cutting railleries on king Henry and his wife of English blood. They nicknamed them Leofric and Godiva, and always called them so when not in the royal presence."[1] It is probable that Warren, the disappointed suitor of Matilda, and his kinsman Mortimer, with others of the audacious Norman *quens*, who had previously exercised their wit in bestowing an offensive *sobriquet* on Henry before his accession to the throne, were among the foremost of those invidious detractors, who could not endure to witness the wedded happiness of their sovereign, and the virtuous influence of his youthful queen.

The invasion of duke Robert, Henry's eldest brother, on his return from the Holy Land, took place in the second year of Matilda's marriage. King Henry's fleet being manned with Norman seamen, and, of course, under the influence of Norman chiefs, revolted, and, instead of guarding the coasts of England from the threatened invasion of the duke, swept across the narrow seas, and brought him and his armament in triumph to Portsmouth, where he was joined by the majority of the Anglo-Norman baronage.[2] Robert had also his partisans among the English; for Edgar Atheling so far forgot the interests of his royal niece, queen Matilda, as to espouse the cause of his friend Robert against the king her husband.

Robert landed at Portsmouth, and marched direct to Winchester, where queen Matilda then lay in with her first-born child, William the Atheling. When this circumstance was related to the duke, he relinquished his purpose of storming the city, with the observation, "that it never should be said he commenced the war by an assault on a woman in childbed, for that would be a base action."[3]

Matilda duly appreciated this generous consideration, on the part of her royal brother-in-law and godfather, and exerted all her influence to negotiate a peace between him and her lord, in which she was assisted by the good offices of the archbishop Anselm; and this formidable crisis passed over without the effusion of a drop of blood.[4] These are Hardinge's words on the subject:

> "But Anselm archbishop of Canterbury,
> And queen Matilda, made them well accord;
> The king to pay three thousand marks yearly
> To duke Robert, withouten more discord."

After this happy pacification, Henry invited Robert to become his guest at the court, where the easy-tempered duke was feasted and entertained, greatly to his satisfaction, by his royal god-daughter Matilda,[5] who, in her love of music, and the encouragement she bestowed on

---

[1] Eadmer. Thierry.   [2] Saxon Annals, A.D. 1101.
[3] Chronique de Normandie.   [4] Ibid.   [5] M. Paris.

9 *

minstrels, or *trouvieres*, quite coincided with the tastes of her sponsor and brother-in-law; "for," says Malmsbury, " every poet hastened to the court of Matilda to read his verses to that queen, and to partake of her bounty." [1]   So much did Robert enjoy his sojourn at Henry's court, that he stayed there upwards of six months, though his presence was greatly required in his own dominions.[2]

An unfortunate misunderstanding took place between Henry and the archbishop Anselm, early in the year 1103.   This quarrel originated in an attempt made by the archbishop, to deprive the king of a privilege, which had been claimed by the Saxon monarchs, of appointing his own bishops.   Anselm wished to restore the nomination to the chapters, which Henry resolutely opposed.   Both appealed to the pope, but Anselm went to Rome, to plead his own cause against the king's three advocates, and remained in exile.

The following year Robert revisited England, either to demand payment of his pension, or to raise a revolt.   He was, however, attended by only twelve gentlemen.   Henry, having speedy information of his landing, declared, if he fell into his hands, he would keep him so closely imprisoned, that he should never give him any more trouble.   " Not so, sire," replied the count de Mellent, " he is your brother, and God forbid[3] that you should do so great a villany; let me meet and talk with him, and I will take care that he shall return quietly into Normandy, and give you acquittance of his pension withal."

" By my faith," replied the king, " I will make you do what you say."

The count then mounted his horse, and encountering duke Robert on the road to Southampton, greeted him with these words: " St. Mary! what brings you into this country?   Who has given you such fatal counsel?   You know you have hitherto compelled the king to pay you four thousand marks a-year, and for this cause you will be taken and put to death, or detained in prison for life.   He is determined to be avenged on you, I promise you."   When the duke heard this he was greatly disturbed, and asked " if he could not return to Southampton?" " No," replied Mellent, " the king will cause you to be intercepted; but even if you could reach that place, the wind is contrary for your escape by sea."

" Counsel me," cried the duke, " what I ought to do."

" Sire," replied the count, " the queen is apprised of the news, and you know that you showed her great kindness when you gave up the assault on Winchester, because she lay in childbed there.   Hasten to her, and commit yourself and your people to her care, and I am sure she will guard you from all harm."   Then duke Robert went to the queen, and she received and reassured him very amiably, and by the sweet words she said to him, and the fear he was in of being taken, he was

---

[1] Matilda was so generous a patron of poets and minstrels, that the chroniclers declare they crowded her court from all parts of Europe, and sang her praises, and presented her with their panegyrics; and the only fault left on her memory is, that she sometimes oppressed her tenants, and spent her revenues too closely, in providing rewards for these gentry.—William of Malmsbury.

[2] Will. Gemiticensis.   [3] Chronique de Normandie.

induced to sacrifice those pecuniary claims on the king his brother, for which he had resigned the realm of England.

When Henry heard that his brother had granted an acquittance for this money to the queen, he sent to the queen, to come to him with duke Robert. Matilda brought the duke to the king, and the duke thus addressed him:

"Fair sire, I am come to see you out of affection, and not to injure either you or yours. We are brothers, born of one father and one mother. If I am the eldest, you have the honour of a crown, which is a much better thing. I love you well, and thus it ought to be. Money and rents I seek not of you, nor ever will. I have quitted to the queen all you owe me for this kingdom. Enter we now together into perfect amity. We will exchange gifts of jewels, dogs, and birds, with such things as ought to be between brothers and friends."

"We will do as you say," replied the king, "and thanks for what you have said."[1]

The Saxon chronicler and some other historians affirm, indeed, that he invaded England; "but it is plain," says Sir John Hayward, "that he only came for disport and play," that is, to recreate himself at the court of Henry Beauclerc, and to enjoy the agreeable society of the queen his god-daughter, with the music and minstrelsy in which they both so greatly delighted.

Well would it have been for the luckless Robert, if all his tastes had been equally harmless and refined; but he had propensities disgraceful to his character as an individual, and ruinous to his fortunes as a prince. The chroniclers relate that he indulged in such excess of revelry, while he was at the English court, that he was often in a state of inebriation for days together.[2]

According to some historians, Robert resigned his pension to Matilda at a carouse, and when he became aware of the folly of which he had been guilty, he was greatly exasperated, and bitterly reproached his brother Henry "with having cheated and despoiled him, by employing the queen to beguile him with fair words out of his pension, when he was under the influence of wine."[3]

There was nothing but animosity between the royal brothers, after this affair. Robert's indignation at the trick he had been played, led him to make use, not only of reproaches, but menaces, against Henry, who availed himself of that excuse to make war upon him. In the year 1104, Henry left the government of England in the prudent hands of Matilda, and embarked for Normandy. While there, he consented to meet Anselm, the archbishop, at the castle of l'Aigle, where, through the mediation of his sister Adela, countess of Blois, a reconciliation was happily effected. Anselm then returned to England, where he was met at Dover by the queen Matilda, who received and welcomed him with the greatest demonstrations of satisfaction.[4] As the venerable primate

---

[1] Chronique de Normandie, 248–9.   [2] Eadmer.   [3] Ibid. Gemiticensis.

[4] Pascal II. admitted Anselm, the favourite priest and prelate of Matilda, to a seat near his right foot, saying, "We admit this prelate into our circle, he being, as it were, the pope of the farther hemisphere."—Godwin de Praes.

was in feeble health, the queen took the precaution of preceding him on the road from Dover to the metropolis, providing, as she went, for his comforts and accommodation.[1]

Matilda, independently of the feeling of political expediency which rendered this public testimonial of respect to the archbishop desirable, after the unpopular schism between him and her royal husband, was, in all probability, naturally inclined to testify her regard for a person who had been so actively instrumental in raising her to the exalted station which she then enjoyed.

Yet the return of Anselm was attended with circumstances which gave great pain to Matilda, as an English queen. Both the king and archbishop, after their reconciliation, united in enforcing inexorably the celibacy of the Anglo-Saxon clergy, whose lower orders had previously been able to obtain licenses to marry. Anselm now excommunicated all the married clergy.

Two hundred of these unfortunate Saxons, barefoot, but clad in their clerical robes, encountered the king and queen in the streets of London. They implored the king's compassion; he turned from them with words of insult. They then supplicated the queen to intercede for them, but Matilda, with tears in her eyes, assured them "that she dared not interfere."[2]

The year 1104 was marked by the birth of a princess, who was first named Alice, or Adelais,[3] but whose name the king afterwards changed to that of his beloved and popular queen, Matilda. This princess was afterwards the celebrated empress Matilda. Some writers, on the authority of Gervasius, the monk of Canterbury, assert that she was the first-born child of Henry and Matilda; but the fact that prince William was eighteen at the time when the fatal loss of the white ship deprived England of her heir apparent, in the year 1120, makes it evident that he was the eldest of the two. It has been said that Matilda placed her little daughter, for education and nurture, in the Royal Abbey of Wilton, where she had herself completed her studies.

The profound tranquillity that subsisted in her husband's dominions, during his frequent absences in Normandy, is a proof that Matilda understood the art of domestic government, and practised it with a happier effect than the two first Anglo-Norman sovereigns, whose reigns were so greatly disturbed by insurrections.

Henry, after his successful campaign in Normandy, returned to England—in his personal appearance, at least, an altered man. The Anglo-Normans had adopted the picturesque Saxon fashion—which, however, was confined to persons of high rank—of wearing their hair long, and flowing in ringlets on their shoulders; and the king was remarkable for the luxuriance and beauty of his love-locks, which he cherished with peculiar care, no doubt out of a laudable desire to conform to the tastes of his queen, the daughter of a Saxon princess. His courtiers imitated the royal example, which gave great scandal to the Norman clergy. One day, while the king was in Normandy, he and his train entered a

---

[1] Eadmer.   [2] Lingard.   [3] Ibid.

church, where an ecclesiastic of the name of Serlo, bishop of Seez, took up his parable on the sinfulness of this new fashion,[1] " which," he protested, " was a device of the evil one to bring souls into everlasting perdition; compared the moustached, bearded, and long-haired men of that age to filthy goats;" and, in short, made so moving a discourse on the unloveliness of their present appearance, that the king of England and his courtiers melted into tears; on which Serlo, perceiving the impression which his eloquence had made, drew a pair of scissors out of his sleeve, and, instead of permitting their penitence to evaporate in a few unmeaning drops, persuaded his royal and noble auditors to prove the sincerity of their repentance, by submitting their ringlets to his discretion, and brought his triumph to a climax, by polling the king and congregation with his own hands.[2]

Henry was then courting popularity, in the duchy of Normandy, and well knew that the readiest way to effect his object, was to win the good report of the monks. He had previously scandalized all piously disposed persons, by choosing for his private chaplain a priest whose only merit consisted in being able to hurry over matins and mass in half an hour. This was Roger le Poer,[3] afterwards the rich and potent bishop of Salisbury, whose hasty despatch of the morning service so charmed Henry, that he swore aloud in the church, " that he had at length met with a priest fit for a soldier." Roger, when he received this flattering commendation from the lips of royalty, was only a poor curate at Caen, but was advanced by Henry to the highest preferment in the church and state.

After Henry had submitted his flowing ringlets to the reforming shears of Serlo, he published an edict, compelling his lieges to relinquish these sinful adornments also.

Queen Matilda did not long enjoy the society of her royal husband in England, and during the brief period he spent with her at Northampton, in the winter season, his whole time and thoughts were employed in raising the means for pursuing the war in Normandy. His unfortunate brother, Robert, finding himself sorely pressed on every side, and left, by his own improvident folly, without resources for continuing the contest, came over to England unattended, and, repairing to the court at Northampton, forced an interview with Henry[4] (who was reluctant to admit him into his presence), and earnestly besought his compassion, telling him at the same time, " he was ready to submit everything to his brotherly love, if he would only permit him to retain the appearance of a sovereign." As it by no means suited Henry's policy to yield to the dictates of natural affection, he coldly turned away, muttering something to himself, that was unintelligible to the by-standers, and which he could not be induced to explain.

Robert's quick temper could not brook this contemptuous usage, and, in a paroxysm of rage, he indignantly assailed his younger brother with a storm of reproaches, mingled with abuse and menaces; and without waiting to employ the good offices of queen Matilda, through whose

---

[1] Orderious Vitalis.   [2] Ibid.   [3] Godwin de Praes.   [4] M. Paris.

kindly influence it is possible he might have obtained reasonable conditions of peace, he departed from Northampton the same hour.

In the spring, Henry once more committed the domestic affairs of his kingdom to the care of Matilda, and having levied an enormous tax on his subjects, to support the expenses of the war, embarked for Normandy.

Matilda was principally employed, during the king's absence, in superintending the magnificent buildings at New Windsor, which were founded by Henry, and in the completion of the royal apartments in the Tower of London. She, as well as Henry, patronised Gundulph, the episcopal architect, to whom England is indebted for the most magnificent and lasting of her public buildings. Many useful public works, to which we have before alluded, furnished, under her auspices, employment for the working classes, and improved the general condition of the people.

While civilization and the arts of peace were rapidly progressing, through the beneficial influence of Matilda, at home, the arms of her royal consort were universally triumphant in Normandy. The unfortunate Robert Courthose, with his young son William, (who was called Clito, or royal heir,) with the earl of Montaigne and all the nobles of their party, were taken prisoners, at the decisive battle of Tinchebray, which was fought on the vigil of St. Michael, exactly forty years after the famous battle of Hastings. The English were much elated at this circumstance, whereby they flattered their national pride with the idea, that the husband of their beloved queen, of Saxon lineage, had wiped away the dishonour of the Norman conquest, by subjugating Normandy to the yoke of England.[1] Edgar Atheling, Matilda's uncle, was taken fighting for his friend Robert of Normandy, besides four hundred valiant knights.[2] Henry instantly released the aged prince, for love of the queen his niece, say some of the chroniclers of that period, and at her intercession settled a pension upon him for life.

Henry, now at the summit of his ambition, having verified the death-bed prediction of his father, the Conqueror, that he should unite in his own person the inheritance of both his brothers, returned triumphantly to England with his unfortunate captives. Robert he sent to Cardiff Castle, where for a time his confinement was only a sort of honourable restraint—at least, if we may credit the account which Henry himself gives of it, in a letter to the pope; as follows:

"I have not," says he, "imprisoned him as an enemy; but I have placed him in a royal castle, as a noble stranger broke down with many troubles, and I supply him abundantly with every delicacy and enjoyment."

Henry and Matilda kept their Easter this year at Bath, and, during the summer, introduced the popular custom of making a royal progress through different parts of England.[3]

The following year Henry and Matilda kept court, for the first time, at New Windsor, then called, from the picturesque winding of the river Thames, Windlesore.

[1] Saxon Annals.   [2] W. Malmsbury.   [3] Saxon Chronicle.

This beautiful retreat was originally used as a hunting-seat by William the Conqueror, who, for better security of his person, converted it into a fortress or castle; but the extensive alterations and improvements which the elegant tastes of the Beauclerc sovereign and his accomplished consort Matilda of Scotland effected, first gave to Windsor Castle the magnificent and august character, as a royal residence, which has rendered it ever since a favourite abode with succeeding sovereigns.

In the year 1108, the affairs of Normandy requiring the presence of the king, another temporary separation took place between Matilda and her royal lord. Indeed, from the time that the duchy of Normandy was subjected to his sway, it became a matter of necessity, in order to preserve his popularity with his continental subjects, to pass a considerable portion of his time among them. Meanwhile the peace and integral prosperity of England were best promoted by the presence of Matilda, who formed the bond of union between Henry of Normandy and the Saxon race. Therefore it appears to have been a measure of political expediency for her to remain, with her splendid court, at Westminster or London, endearing herself daily more and more to the people, by her works of princely charity, and the public benefits which she was constantly labouring to promote. Thus we see, on accurate examination, that, contrary to the assertions of one or two paradoxical writers, who have assumed that Matilda was not treated with the affection and respect that were her due in wedded life, she enjoyed a degree of power and influence in the state, perfectly unknown to the Saxon queens.

Matilda was so nobly dowered withal, that in after reigns the highest demand ever made on the part of a queen-consort was, that she should be endowed with a dower equal to that of Matilda of Scotland.[1]

By close examination of the earliest authorities, we find, that the first parliaments held by the Anglo-Norman dynasty, were the fruits of the virtuous influence of this excellent queen over the mind of her husband. But as the fact that parliaments were ever held before the reigns of Henry III. and Edward I. has been a point of great contest among modern historians, we feel it indispensable to bring forward our proofs, first, that parliaments were held; and next, that they were held through the influence of Matilda. The earliest historian who wrote in English, Robert of Gloucester, declares of Henry I.[2]

> " When his daughter was ten years old, to council there he drew,
>   On a Whitsunday, a great parliament he *name* (held)
>   At Westminster noble enow, that much folk came." [3]

The other fact is proved by Piers of Langtoft, a parallel historian, who wrote in French, and, with the most minute detail, points out the classes of whom Matilda advised Henry to take counsel—viz., barons, lords of towns, and burgesses. Here are the lines:

---

[1] Tyrrell. [2] Vol. ii., p. 430. The edition is royal octavo.
[3] Robert of Gloucester died before he completed the reign of Henry III.; consequently, if the first parliaments were held in that of Edward I., he could not even have mentioned such legislative assemblies without possessing the gift of prophecy.

> " Mald the good queen gave him in council.
> To love all his folks and leave all his *turpeils*, (disputing,)
> To bear him with his barons that held of him their fees, (feofs,)
> And to lords of towns and burgesses of cities :
> Through council of Dame Mald, a kind woman and true,
> Instead of hatred old, there now was love all new;
> Now love they full well the barons and the king,
> The king does ilk a deal at their bidding."

Robert of Gloucester, from first to last, speaks of queen Matilda as an active agent in the government of England, and the restorer and upholder of the Saxon form of legislature, whose system was that of a representative constitution. He says,

> " The goodness that king Henry and the good queen Mold
> Did to this land ne may never be told."

The year 1109 must have been an era of eventful interest to Matilda. Her royal husband, having spent the winter and spring in Normandy,[1] returned to England in the summer, to visit her and their infant family, and kept court with uncommon splendour, in his new palace at Windsor, which had been completed in his absence. It was there that he received the ambassadors who came to solicit the hand of the princess Matilda for the emperor Henry V.[2] The proposal was eagerly accepted by Henry Beauclerc; and the princess, then just turned of five years old, was solemnly espoused, by proxy, to her royal suitor, who was forty years her senior; but, on account of her tender age, the infant bride was allowed for the present to remain under the care of the queen her mother.[3]

About the same period Alexander the Fierce of Scotland, Matilda's brother, condescended to wed Isabella, the youngest illegitimate daughter of his sister's husband. His motives for contracting this alliance are difficult to imagine, since the young lady was remarkable for the plainness of her person and the impropriety of her conduct.[4]

The fact that Henry's numerous illegitimate children were many of them adults at this period, proves that they were born in his youth, and at all events before his marriage with Matilda of Scotland.

In the year 1109, the mighty Norman chief Fitz-Haymon, lord of Glamorgan, dying without sons, left the lady Aimabel, his young heiress, to the guardianship of the king. Henry, wishing to secure so rich a prize for his eldest natural son Robert, proposed him to his fair ward, as a suitable husband for her. But the haughty Norman damsel, though only sixteen, intrepidly replied, " That the ladies of her house were not accustomed to wed nameless persons."

Then the king answered, " Neither shalt thou, damsel; for I will give my son a fair name, by which he and his sons shall be called. Robert Fitzroy shall be his name henceforth."

" But," objected the prudent heiress of Glamorgan, " a name so given is nothing. Where are the lands, and what the lordship, of the man you will me to wed, sire?"

---

[1] Saxon Annals.　　[2] M. Paris. Huntingdon.　　[3] M. Paris.　　[4] W. Malmsbury.

"Truly," responded the king, with a smile, " thy question is a shrewd one, damsel : I will endow my son Robert with the lands and honours of Gloucester, and by that title shall he henceforth be called."

The lady Aimabel made no further demur, we are told, but wedded the king's son without delay. The fact was, the king was generously bestowing upon his son Robert the lands and honours which had been granted or sold to Fitz-Haymon, her deceased father, by William Rufus, once the patrimony of the luckless Brihtric Meaw,[1] and the young lady, who seems to have been gifted with no ordinary share of worldly wisdom, thought, no doubt, that she had better hold the lands and honours of Gloucester on the tenure of wife-service to the king's son, than lose them altogether. Such were the dealings of the Anglo-Norman sovereigns with their wards. The high-spirited heiress of Fitz-Haymon was, however, fortunate in the marriage that was thus arranged for her by her royal guardian. Robert Fitzroy was the princely earl of Gloucester who so valiantly upheld the title of his half-sister, the empress Matilda, to the English crown, in the succeeding reign.

The following year, an enormous tax, of three shillings on every hide of land, was levied, to pay the portion of the princess Matilda, by which the sum of 824,000*l.* was raised ; and the princess was sent over to her imperial husband with a magnificent retinue: she was espoused to him in the cathedral of Mentz,[2] and solemnly crowned by the archbishop of Cologne.

Queen Matilda was in the next year left to keep court alone, in consequence of a formidable insurrection in Normandy, in favour of William Clito, son of the unfortunate Robert Courthose, which was privately fomented by the earl of Flanders. King Henry, perceiving that all classes of his continental subjects were averse to the yoke of an absent sovereign, considered it expedient to forego the society of his queen and their children, for a period of nearly two years, while he held his separate state in Normandy.

In the year 1112, we find the king and queen[3] were together at Winchester, with their court, where they personally assisted at the removal of the bodies of Alfred the Great, and his queen Alswitha, from the ruinous chapel of Newminster, close to Winchester Cathedral, to the magnificent abbey of Hyde,[4] founded and endowed by Henry and Matilda, as a more suitable shrine for the relics of their illustrious progenitor,—from whom, be it remembered, Henry, as well as his Saxon queen, was descended in the eighth generation, through the marriage of Elstrith, the daughter of Alfred, with an earl of Flanders, his maternal ancestor.

Here, too, the bones of Edward the Elder, and his queen, the immediate ancestors of Matilda, were at the same time translated.[5]

---

[1] See the preceding Biography, and Domesday-book.
[2] Simeon of Durham.   [3] Archæologia.
[4] Henry VIII. brutally desecrated the place where reposed the remains of these patriot sovereigns. Englishmen of the eighteenth century, more barbarous still, converted the holy fane into a bridewell, and the bones of Alfred were by felon hands exhumed.   [5] Archæologia.

The following year Henry was again in Normandy, where he entered into an amicable treaty with one of his most troublesome enemies, Fulk earl of Anjou, by a matrimonial alliance between his heir, prince William, and Alice, the daughter of that earl.

The education of Matilda's eldest daughter being considered as completed in 1114, the marriage was fully solemnized between her and the emperor Henry V., and they were both crowned a second time, with great pomp, in the cathedral at Mentz. The young empress was then only in her twelfth year. Notwithstanding this great disparity in age, it appears that the youthful bride enjoyed a reasonable share of happiness with her mature consort, by whom she was treated with the greatest indulgence, while her great beauty and majestic carriage won the hearts of the German princes, and obtained for her unbounded popularity.

Matilda's eldest son, prince William, (or the Atheling, as he was more generally styled by the English,) was, in the year 1115, conducted by the king his father with great pomp into Normandy, where he was presented to the states as the heir of the duchy, and fealty was sworn to him by the barons and freemen. This prince was then only twelve years old. He returned with his royal father to England in July, and the following year Henry summoned that memorable parliament mentioned by Holinshed, as the first held since the Norman conquest, to meet at Salisbury, and there appointed the young prince as his successor. William of Malmsbury says, " Every freeman of England and Normandy, of whatsoever degree, or to whatsoever lord his vassal service was due, was made to perform homage, and swear fealty to William, son of king Henry and queen Matilda." The Easter festival was kept this year by the royal family at Odiham Castle, in Hampshire.

Matilda passed the Christmas festival of the same year, in the company of her royal husband, at the abbey of St. Alban's.[1] They were the guests of abbot Richard, who had then brought to a happy conclusion the building of that magnificent fabric. He invited the queen, who was one of its benefactresses, the king, and the archbishop of Rouen, and many prelates and nobles, to assist at the consecration of the abbey, which took place Christmas-day, 1115. The royal pair, with their suite of nobles and ladies, were lodged in the abbey, and entertained from December 25th to January 6th. The queen, sanctioned by Henry, gave, by charter, two manors to St. Alban's. The existence of a portrait of queen Matilda is certainly owing to this visit; for in a rich illuminated volume, called the Golden Book of St. Alban's, (now in the British Museum,) may still be seen a miniature of the royal benefactress.[2] The queen is attired in the royal mantle of scarlet, lined with

---

[1] Newcome's History of St. Alban's, pp. 52, 93.

[2] Cottonian MSS. Nero D. 7. A beautiful and accurate copy from the original has been drawn by M. Kearney at the expense of Henry Howard, Esq., of Corby, the descendant of Matilda, and presented by him to the authors of this work. It corrects, in many particulars, the errors of an engraving published by Strutt. We have the opportunity, in this second edition, of describing Matilda's portrait, from an examination of the Golden Book itself. The Golden Book of

white fur; it covers the knees, and is very long. The mantle is square to the bust. A cordon of scarlet and gold, with a large tassel, passes through two gold knobs: she holds the cordon in her left hand. She wears a tight kirtle of dark blue, buttoned down the front with gold. Her sleeves fit close to the arms, and are scarlet like the mantle. A white veil is arranged in a square form on the brow, and is surmounted by a gold crown, formed of three large trefoils, and gold *oreillettes* appear beneath the veil, on each side of the cheeks. The veil flows behind her shoulders with lappets. Matilda is very fair in complexion: she has a long throat, and elegant form, of tall proportions. She displays with her right hand the charter she gave the abbey, from which hangs a very large red seal, whereon, without doubt, was impressed her effigy in grand relief. She sits on a carved stone bench, on which is a scarlet cushion figured with gold leaves. This cushion is in the form of a woolpack, but has four tassels of gold and scarlet. A piece of figured cloth is hung at the back of her seat. There are no armorial bearings — one proof of the authenticity of the portrait. "Queen Matildis gave us Bellwick and Lilleburn," is the notation appended by the monks of St. Alban's to this portrait.

About this period, the stately new palace at Woodstock being completed, and the noble park, reckoned the finest at that time in England, having been walled round, Henry stocked it with a curious menagerie of wild beasts, the first zoological collection ever seen in this country. It is described in very quaint terms by Stowe, who says, "The king craved from other kings lions, leopards, lynxes, and camels, and other curious beasts, of which England hath none. Among others, there was a strange animal called a stryx, or porcupine, sent him by William of Montpelier; which beast," says the worthy chronicler, "is, among the Africans, counted as a kind of hedgehog, covered with pricking bristles, which they shoot out naturally on the dogs that pursue them."

Unbounded hospitality was one of the social virtues of this peaceful

---

St. Alban's is a sort of conventual album, in which were entered the portraits of all the benefactors of the abbey, together with an abstract of their donations. Five different artists, of various degrees of merit, may be traced in this collection. Some of the miniatures are exquisitely designed and coloured, others are barbarous and puerile in their execution; some of the portraits are represented holding well-filled purses, others displaying the charters, with large pendent seals, which secured broad lands to church and poor. It is true, that Matilda's portrait was not entered till the fourteenth century, when the book was first commenced; but the style of dress, together with the form of the throne on which the queen is seated, prove that the original design was drawn in the queen's own day; for the artists of the middle ages drew only what they saw; and had the limner been inclined to give a supposititious portrait of queen Matilda, he would have designed her figure clad in the costume of Edward the Third's era, and seated in the high-backed Gothic chair of state on which royal persons were enthroned since the days of Edward the First, as may be seen by reference to any collection of engravings from regal seals; instead of which, Matilda is seen seated on the primitive stone bench of Anglo-Saxon royalty, represented on the seals of the Anglo-Norman and early Plantagenet monarchs.

reign,[1] especially at this peculiar era, when the benignant example of the good queen had, for a period of nearly seventeen years, produced the happiest effect in softening the manners of the haughty and powerful Norman families, who were at that time the magnates of the land.

The Norman families, at this period, were beginning to practise some of the peaceful pursuits of the Anglo-Saxons, and ladies of high rank considered it no infringement on the dignity of their station to attend to the profitable concerns of the poultry-yard and the dairy. The countess Constance of Chester, though the wife of Hugh Lupus, the king's first cousin, kept a herd of kine, and made good Cheshire cheeses, three of which she presented to the archbishop of Canterbury. Giraldus Cambriensis bears honourable testimony to the excellence of the produce of the cheese-shire in that day.

A fresh revolt in Normandy[2] deprived Matilda of the society of her husband and son in 1117. The king, according to Eadmer, returned and spent Christmas with her, as she was at that time in a declining state of health;[3] leaving prince William with his Norman baronage, as a pledge for his return.[4] His sojourn was, of necessity, very brief. He was compelled, by the distracted state of affairs in Normandy, to rejoin his army there, and Matilda never saw either her husband or her son again.

Resigned and perfect in all the duties of her high calling, the dying queen remained, during this trying season, in her palace at Westminster,[5] lonely, though surrounded with all the splendour of royalty; enduring with complacency and patience the separation from her beloved consort and children, and affording, to the last hour of her life, a beautiful example of piety and self-denial.

She expired on the 1st of May, 1118,[6] passionately lamented by every class of the people, to whom her virtues and wisdom had rendered her inexpressibly dear.

According to the most ancient chroniclers, the king her husband was much afflicted when the intelligence of Matilda's death reached him, amidst the turmoil of battle and siege in Normandy.[7]

Piers of Langtoft alludes to the grief felt by the royal widower, at the loss of his amiable consort, in terms of the most homely simplicity :—

"Now is the king sorry, her death doth him *gram*" (grieve).

Hardinge's rhyming chronicle produces the following quaint stanzas on the death of Matilda, and the sorrow of king Henry for her loss :—

---

[1] The following verses from an ancient MS., quoted by Collins, afford an interesting witness of this fact. They were inscribed by sir William Fitz-William, the lord of Sprotborough, on an ancient cross which was demolished at the Reformation:—

> "Whoso is hungry, and lists well to eat,
> Let him come to Sprotborough to his meat,
> And for a night and a day
> His horse shall have both corn and hay,
> And no one shall ask him: 'when he goeth away?'"

[2] Ordericus Vitalis.　　　　　　　　　　[3] Saxon Annals.
[4] Eadmer, p. 118; see Rapin, vol. i. 199.　　[5] William of Malmsbury.
[6] Saxon Annals.　　　　　　　　　　　　[7] Robert Gloucester.

> "The year of Christ a thousand was full clear,
> One hundred eke and therewithal eighteen,
> When good queen Maude was dead and laid on bier,
> At Westminster buryed, as well was seen;
> For heaviness of which, the king I ween,
> To Normandy then went with his son,
> The duke William, and there with him did won."

Hardinge is, however, mistaken in supposing that Henry was with his beloved consort at the time of her decease.

The same chronicler gives us another stanza on the death of Henry, in which he, in yet more positive terms, speaks of the conjugal affection which united the Norman sovereign to his Saxon queen:

> "Of Christe's date was there a thousand year,
> One hundred also, and nine and thirty mo,
> Buryed at Redynge, as well it doth appear,
> In the abbye which there he founded so,
> Of monkes black, whenever they ride or go,
> That pray for him and queen Maude his wife,
> Who either other loved withouten strife."

Another chronicler says, "Nothing happened to trouble the king, save the death of his queen Matilda, the very mirror of piety, humility, and princely bounty." [1]

The same causes that had withheld the king from attending Matilda in her dying illness prevented him from honouring her obsequies with his presence. Matilda was buried on St. Philip's day in Westminster abbey, on the right side of her royal uncle, Edward the Confessor.[2] Great disputes, however, have existed as to the place of her interment,[3] which has been contested with almost as much zeal as was displayed by the seven cities of Greece, in claiming the honour of having given birth to Homer. The monks of Reading averred that their royal patroness was buried in her own stately abbey there, where her illustrious consort was afterwards interred. The rhyming chroniclers insist that she was buried in St. Paul's cathedral, and that her epitaph was placed in Westminster abbey. These are the words of Piers of Langtoft :—

> "At London, in St, Paul's, in tomb she is laid,
> Christ, then, of her soul have mercie.
> If any one will *witten* (know) of her storie,
> At Westminster it is written *readily*."

That is to say, so that it may be plainly read.

Tyrrell declares that she was buried at Winchester, but that tablets to her memory were set up in many churches,—an honour, which she shares with queen Elizabeth.

The following passage from the learned and faithful antiquary, Weever, expressly indicates that it was his opinion that the mortal remains of Matilda, "the Good Queen," repose near the relics of her royal uncle, Edward the Confessor, in the solemn temple founded by

---

[1] Florence of Worcester.   [2] Pennant's London.   Robert of Gloucester.
[3] According to Stowe, her grave was in the vestry of the abbey.

that last Saxon monarch, and which had been completed under her careful superintendence. "Here lieth in Westminster abbey, without any tomb, Matilda or Maud, daughter of Malcolm Canmore, king of Scots, and wife of Henry I. of England, who brought to him children, William, Richard, and Mary, who perished by shipwreck, and likewise Maud, who was wife to Henry, the fifth emperor. She died the first day of May, 1118."[1] She had an excellent epigram made to her commendation, whereof these four verses only remain:

> " Prospera non laetam fecere, nec aspera tristem,
>   Aspera risus erant, prospera terror erant;
> Non decor efficit fragilem, non sceptra superbam,
>   Sola potens humilis, sola pudica decens."

Henry of Huntingdon, the chronicler, no mean poet, was the author of these Latin lines. From the numerous translations extant of this beautiful epitaph, we select the following exquisite lines, which come very close to the original, and afford a lovely portrait of the feminine graces of this admirable queen.

> "Success ne'er sat exulting in her eye,
>   Nor disappointment caused the frequent sigh;
> Beauty nor made her vain, nor sceptre proud,
>   Nor titles taught to scorn the meaner crowd;
> Supreme humility was awful grace,
>   And her best charm a bashfulness of face."

Matilda died in the eighteenth year of her marriage, and about the forty-first of her age. Her favourite residence was the royal palace of the Saxon kings at Westminster, where, with occasional visits to New Windsor, Winchester, and Woodstock, and other places in which the king her husband thought proper to hold his courts, she passed the greater portion of her wedded life.

Many curious remains still exist of the old palace in Westminster, where Matilda kept state as queen, and ended her life. This venerable abode of our early sovereigns, was originally built by Canute, and, being devastated by fire, was rebuilt by Edward the Confessor, with such enduring solidity, that antiquaries still point out different portions, which were indubitably the work of the royal Saxon, and therefore must have formed part of the residence of his great niece. Part of the old palace of Westminster is still to be seen, in the buildings near Cotton-garden, and the lancet-shaped windows about Old Palace Yard are declared to appertain to it.[2] Cotton-garden was the private garden of the ancient palace, and therefore belonged especially to queen Matilda. It would be idle to dwell on Westminster Hall and Westminster Abbey, though the original sites of both were included in the precincts of this palace, because one was rebuilt from the ground by Richard II., and the other by Henry III. Great devastation was made in the royal abode of the Anglo-Saxon queen, by the late disastrous conflagration of the House of Lords and its adjacent apartments, which all belonged to it.

---

[1] Weever's Funeral Monuments.   [2] Pennant.

The House of Lords was an antique oblong room; it was the hall of state of Matilda's palace; it was called *the* white-hall, but without any reference to the vast palace of Whitehall, to which the seat of English royalty was transferred in the reign of Henry VIII. As the Painted Chamber, still entire, is well known to have been the bedchamber of Edward the Confessor, and the apartment in which he expired,[1] there can be no doubt but that it was the state bedchamber of his niece. A curious room in Cotton House was the private oratory of the Confessor, and was assuredly used by Matilda for the same purpose; while at the south end of the Court of Requests are to be seen two mighty Saxon arches, the zig-zag work of which indicates that its architecture is the most ancient in our country. This was once a deserted state-chamber[2] of the royal Saxon palace; but it has been used lately by the House of Commons.

There is a statue of Matilda in Rochester cathedral, which forms the pilaster to the west door; that of king Henry, her husband, forms another. The hair of the queen depends over either shoulder, in two long plaits, below the knees. Her garments are long and flowing, and she holds an open scroll of parchment in her hand.

King Henry proved the sincerity of his regard for Matilda, by confirming all her charters after her death. Madox, in his History of the Exchequer, quotes one of that monarch's charters, reciting " that he had confirmed to the Priory of the Holy Trinity in London the grant of his queen Matilda, for the good of her soul, of 25*l.*, on the farm of the city of Exeter, and commands his chief justiciar and the barons of his exchequer to constrain the sheriff of Devonshire to pay the same to the said canons."[3]

Matilda's household was chiefly composed of Saxon ladies, if we may trust the evidence of Christian names. The maids of honour were Emma, Gunilda, and Christina, pious ladies, and full of alms-deeds, like their royal mistress. After the death of the queen, these ladies retired to the hermitage of Kilburn, near London, where there was a holy well, or medicinal spring. This was changed into a priory[4] in 1128, as the deed says, " for the reception of these three virgins of God, sacred damsels who had belonged to the chamber of Matilda, the good queen-consort to Henry I."[5]

History only particularizes two surviving children of Matilda of Scot-

---

[1] Howell.

[2] The appellation of Court of Requests has no reference to modern legal proceedings. It was the feudal court of the High Steward of England. It is used by the House of Commons since the destruction of St. Stephen's Chapel, while the Lords have taken possession of the Painted Chamber.

[3] Charter Antiq. N. n. 16.

[4] On its site are a public-house and tea-gardens, now called Kilburn Wells.

[5] The original deed, preserved in the Cottonian MSS., Claudius A. says of these maids of honour—" Tres virgines Deo sacratas domicellas, videlicit, camere Matildis bone regine Consortis regis Henrici primi." The term *domicella* proves their rank was noble, as this term will be seen applied even to the daughters of emperors.

land and Henry I.; but Gervase, the monk of Canterbury, says she had, besides William and the empress Matilda, a son named Richard. Hector Boethius mentions a daughter of hers, named Euphemia. The Saxon Chronicle and Robert of Gloucester both speak of her second son Richard. Piers of Langtoft says, "The two princes, her sons, were both in Normandy when Matilda died;" and Hardinge says she had two sons, William and Richard.

Prince William never returned to England after the death of his royal mother. During the remainder of the year 1118, he was fighting by his father's side, against the invading force of the king of France, and the partisans of his cousin William Clito. On one occasion, when the noble war-horse and its rich caparisons, belonging to that gallant but unfortunate prince, having been abandoned during a hasty retreat, were captured, and Henry presented this prize to his darling heir, the noble youth generously sent them back, with a courteous message, to his rival kinsman and namesake.[1]

His royal father, king Henry, did not disdain to imitate the magnanimous conduct of his youthful son, after the memorable battle in which the standard of France was taken: when the favourite charger of Louis le Gros fell into his hands, he returned it to the French monarch the next day.

The king of France, as *suzerain* of Normandy, at the general pacification, required of Henry the customary homage for his feof. This the victorious monarch considered derogatory to the dignity of a king of England to perform, and therefore deputed the office to prince William, who was then invested with the duchy, and received the oath of fealty from the states.[2] The prince solemnly espoused his betrothed bride Alice, the daughter of Fulk, earl of Anjou, June 1119. King Henry called her Matilda, out of respect, it is said, for the memory of his mother, but more probably from a tender regard for his deceased consort, Matilda of Scotland, the love of his youth, and the mother of his children. The marriage was celebrated at Lisieux,[3] in the county of Burgundy; and the prince remained in Normandy with his young bride, attended by all the youthful nobility of England and the duchy, passing the time gaily with feasts and pageants, till the 25th of November, in the year 1120; when king Henry (who had been nearly two years absent from his kingdom) conducted prince William, with his retinue, to Barfleur,[4] for the purpose of embarking for England. The king and his train set sail the same night, leaving the prince to follow in another ship.

Fitz-Stephen, the captain of the *Blanche Nef* (the finest vessel in the Norman navy) demanded the honour of conveying the heir of England home; because his father had commanded the Mora, the ship which brought William the Conqueror to the shores of England. His petition was granted; and the prince, with his gay and splendid company, entered the fatal bark with light hearts, and commenced their voyage with mirth and minstrelsy. The prince incautiously ordered three casks of wine to

[1] Holinshed.   [2] Orderious Vitalis.   Tyrrell.
[3] Saxon Annals.   [4] Orderious Vitalis.

be given to the ship's crew; and the sailors were, in consequence, for the most part, intoxicated, when they sailed, about the close of day.

Prince William, who was desirous of overtaking the rest of the fleet, pressed Fitz-Stephen to crowd his sails, and put out his sweeps. Fitz-Stephen, having named the white ship as the swiftest vessel in the world, to make good his boast, and oblige his royal passenger, caused his men to stretch with all their might to the oars, and did everything to accelerate the speed of his light bark. While the *Blanche Nef* was rushing through the water with the most dangerous velocity, she suddenly struck on a rock called the *Catte-raze* with such impetuosity, that she started several planks, and began to sink. All was instant horror, and confusion. The boat was, however, let down; and the young heir of England, with several of his youthful companions, got into it, and having cleared the ship, might have reached the Norman shore in safety; but the cries of his illegitimate sister, Matilda countess of Perche, who distinctly called on him, by name, for succour, occasioning a tender impulse of compassion, he commanded the boat back, to take her in. Unfortunately, the moment it neared the ship, such numbers sprang into it, that it instantly sank with its precious freight, and all on board perished; and of the three hundred persons who embarked in the white ship, but one soul escaped to tell the dismal tale. This person was a poor butcher of Rouen, named Berthould, who climbed to the top of the mast, and was the next morning rescued by some fishermen. Fitz-Stephen, the master of the luckless white ship, was a strong mariner, and stoutly supported himself for some hours in the water, till he saw Berthould on the mast, and calling to him, asked if the boat with the heir of England had escaped; but when the butcher, who had witnessed the whole catastrophe, replied, " that all were drowned and dead," the strong man's force failed him; he ceased to battle with the waves, and sank to rise no more.[1]

The report of this disaster reached England the next day. Theobald of Blois, the king's nephew, was the first who heard it; but he dared not inform his uncle of the calamity which had rendered his house desolate. Besides the heir-apparent of England, prince William, the Saxon chronicler says, there was another son of Henry and Matilda, named Richard, and also Richard, a natural son of the king; Matilda, his natural daughter, countess of Perche; Richard earl of Chester, his cousin, with his bride, the young lady Lucy of Blois, daughter of Henry's sister Adela, and the flower of the juvenile nobility, who are mentioned by the Saxon chronicler as a multitude of " incomparable folk."

King Henry had reached England with his fleet in safety, and for three days was permitted to remain in a state of the most agonizing suspense and uncertainty respecting the fate of his children. No one choosing to become the bearer of such evil tidings, at length Theobald de Blois, finding it could no longer be concealed, instructed a favourite little page to communicate the mournful news to the bereaved father; and the child, entering the royal presence with a sorrowful step, knelt down at

---

[1] Thierry's Anglo-Normans.

Henry's feet, and told him that the prince and all on board the white ship were lost. The great Henry was so thunderstruck with this dreadful news, that he staggered and sank upon the floor in a deep swoon, in which state he remained for many hours. When he recovered, he broke into the bitterest lamentations, magnifying at the same time the great qualities of his heir and the loss he had sustained; and the chroniclers all agree that he was never again seen to smile.

It is Henry of Huntingdon who exults so uncharitably over the catastrophe of the white ship, in the following burst of poetic eloquence:—

"The proud youth; he thought of his future reign, when he said he would yoke the Saxons like oxen. But God said, ' It shall not be, thou impious one, it shall not be:' and so it has come to pass; that brow has worn no crown of gold, but has been dashed against the rocks of the ocean. It was God himself who would not that the son of the Norman should again see England."

Brompton also speaks unfavourably of this unfortunate young prince; but it should be remembered that England was a divided nation at that period, and that the Saxon chroniclers wrote in the very gall of bitterness against those whom the Norman historians commended. Implicit credence is not to be given to the assertions of either. It is only by reading both, and carefully weighing and collating facts, that the truth is to be elicited.

In the last act of his life, William Atheling manifested a spirit so noble, so tenderly compassionate, and forgetful of selfish considerations, that we can only say it was worthy of the son of Matilda, the good queen.

The young wife of prince William was left a widow at the early age of twelve years. She was not among the devoted company who sailed in the white ship.[1] Henry I. was much attached to her, but she returned to her father, the earl of Anjou, and remaining constant to the memory of her princely consort, she was veiled a nun at Fontevraud. The body of prince William was never found.

Queen Matilda's only surviving child, the empress Matilda, thus became king Henry's heiress presumptive. She was the first female who claimed the royal office in England. The events of her life are so closely interwoven with those of the two succeeding queens, Adelicia, and Matilda of Boulogne, her contemporaries, that to avoid the tedium of repetition, and also to preserve the chronological stream of history in unbroken unity, which is an important object, we must refer our readers to the Lives and Times of those queens, for the personal history of this princess, from whom her present majesty queen Victoria derives her title to the crown of England.

---

[1] She was with king Henry in his ship.

ADELICIA OF LOUVAINE,

SURNAMED THE FAIR MAID OF BRABANT;

SECOND QUEEN OF HENRY I.

Adelicia's beauty—Imperial descent from Charlemagne—Standard embroidered by Adelicia—Preserved at Liege—Adelicia sought in marriage by Henry I.—Richly dowered—Embarks for England with Henry—King and queen parishioners of archbishop of Canterbury—Violence of archbishop—He crowns Adelicia—Eulogies on her beauty—Her prudence—Encouragement of literature—Empress Matilda—Adelicia childless—Empress Matilda kept in Adelicia's chamber—Difficult position of the queen—Friendship with her step-daughter—Second marriage of the empress—Adelicia's conjugal virtues—Matilda returns to England—Remains with the queen—Birth of prince Henry—Death of king Henry—Adelicia's respect for his memory—Her troubadour writes king Henry's life—Her second marriage—William Albini—Her dowry—Palace—Receives empress Matilda—Message to king Stephen—Conjugal happiness of Adelicia—Her children—Charitable foundations at Arundel—Her younger brother abbot of Affligham—Adelicia retires to Affligham nunnery, in Flanders—Dies there—Record of her death—Buried—Her issue by Albini—Adelicia ancestor of two of our queens.

THIS princess, to whom contemporary chroniclers have given the name of "the fair maid of Brabant," is one of the most obscure characters in the illustrious catalogue of English queens. Tradition, and her handmaid Poetry, have, however, spoken bright things of her; and the surviving historical records of her life, though brief, are all of a nature tending to confirm the good report which the verses of the Provençals have preserved of her virtues and accomplishments.

Descended, through both her parents, from the imperial Carlovingian line,[1] Adelicia boasted the most illustrious blood in Christendom. She was the eldest daughter of Godfrey of Louvaine, duke of Brabant and Lotheir (or Lower Lorraine), and Ida, countess of Namur.[2] Her father, as the great-grandson of Charles, brother to Lothaire of France, was the lawful representative of Charlemagne. The male posterity of the unfortunate Charles having been cut off by Hugh Capet, the rights of his house became vested in the descendants of his eldest daughter, Gerberga.[3] Lambert, the son of Gerberga, by her marriage with Robert of Louvaine, was the father of Godfrey. Ermengarde, the second daughter of Charles, married Albert, the third count of Namur; and their sole daughter and heiress, Ida, (the mother of Adelicia,) became the wife of her cousin, Godfrey of Louvaine, surnamed Barbatus, or the Bearded, because he had made a vow never to shave his beard till he had recovered Lower

---

[1] Howard Memorials.
[2] Betham's Genealogical Tables. Bucknet's Trophies of Brabant. Howard's Memorials of the Howard Family. [3] Ibid.

Lorraine, the patrimony of his ancestors. In this he succeeded in the year 1107, after which he triumphantly displayed a smooth chin, in token that he had fulfilled his obligation, and finally obtained from his subjects and contemporaries the more honourable appellation of Godfrey the Great.[1] The dominions of this prince were somewhat more extensive than the modern kingdom of Belgium, and were governed by him with the greatest wisdom and ability.

From this illustrious lineage Adelicia appears to have inherited the distinguished beauty and fine talents for which the Lorraine branch of the house of Charlemagne has ever been celebrated. She was also remarkable for her proficiency in feminine acquirements. A standard which she embroidered in silk and gold for her father, during the arduous contest in which he was engaged for the recovery of his patrimony, was celebrated throughout Europe for the exquisite taste and skill displayed by the royal Adelicia in the design and execution of her patriotic achievement.[2] This standard was unfortunately captured at a battle near the castle of Duras, in the year 1129, by the bishop of Liege and the earl of Limbourg, the old competitor of Godfrey for Lower Lorraine, placed by them, as a memorial of their triumph, in the great church of St. Lambert, at Liege, and was for centuries carried in procession, on Rogation days, through the streets of that city. The church of St. Lambert was destroyed during the French Revolution; yet the learned editor of the Howard Memorials fondly indulges in the hope that this interesting relic of his royal ancestress's feminine skill and patriotic feelings may be still in existence, and destined, perhaps, hereafter to be brought to light, like the long-forgotten Bayeux tapestry. The plain, where this memorable trophy was taken, is still called the field of the Standard.[3]

The fame of the fair maid of Brabant's charms and accomplishments, it is said, induced the confidential advisers of Henry 1. of England to recommend their sorrow-stricken lord to wed her, in hopes of dissipating that corroding melancholy which, since the loss of his children in the fatal white ship, had become constitutional to him. The temper of this monarch had, in fact, grown so irascible, that his greatest nobles feared to enter his presence, and it is said that, in his causeless transports of rage, he indulged himself in the use of the most unkingly terms of vituperation to all who approached him;[4] which made his peers the more earnest in their counsels for him to take a second wife. Adelicia of Louvaine was the object of his choice. Henry's ostensible motive in contracting this marriage was the hope of male posterity, to inherit the united realms of England and Normandy. He had been a widower two years, when he entered into a treaty with Godfrey of Louvaine for the hand of his beautiful daughter.

Robert of Gloucester, when recording the fact in his rhyming chronicle, says,

> "He knew no woman so fair as she
> Was seen on middle earth."

[1] Bucknet's Trophies. Howard Memorials.
[2] Memoirs of the Howard Family. Bucknet's Trophies of Brabant.
[3] Brutsholme.   [4] Speed. Rapin.

The name of this princess has been variously written by the chroniclers of England, Normandy, Germany, and Brabant, as Adeliza, Alicia, Adelaide, Aleyda or Adelheite, which means most noble. In the Saxon Chronicle she is called Æthelice, or Alice.

Mr. Howard of Corby Castle, the immediate descendant of this queen, in his "Memorials of the Howard Family,"[1] calls her Adelicia for the best of reasons—her name is so written in an original charter of the 31st of Henry I., confirming her grant of lands for the foundation of an hospital of lepers at Fugglestone, near Wilton, dedicated to St. Giles; which deed, with part of the seal appendant, is still preserved in the corporation chest at Wilton.

The Provençal and Walloon poets, of whom this queen was a munificent patroness, style her *Alix la Belle*, Adelais, and Alise, varying the syllables according to the structure of the verses which they composed in her honour—a licence always allowed to poetical writers; therefore, the rhymes of the troubadours ought not to be regarded as the slightest authority in settling the point. Modern historians generally speak of this princess by her Latinized name of Adeliza, but her learned descendant's version of her name is that which ought to be adopted by her biographer.

There is no authentic record of the date of Adelicia's birth. Mr. Howard supposes she was about eighteen years old at the period of her marriage with Henry I., and it is certain that she was in the bloom of her beauty at the time he sought her hand.

In proportion to the estimation in which the charms of Adelicia were held, did Henry fix her dower, which was so munificent that the duke of Louvaine, her father, scrupled not to consign her to her affianced lord, as soon as the contract of marriage was signed.

This ceremony took place on the 16th of April, 1120, but the nuptials were not celebrated till some months after this period. King Henry, in person, conducted his betrothed bride to England, in the autumn of this year.[2] They landed about Michaelmas, and, according to some historians, the royal pair were married at Ely, soon after their arrival; but if so, it must have been a private arrangement, for the nuptials were publicly solemnized at Windsor, on the 24th of January, 1121;[3] having been delayed in consequence of a singular dispute between the archbishop of Canterbury and the bishop of Salisbury, which established a point too important to be omitted in a history, embracing, in a peculiar manner, the habits and customs of royalty.

Roger le Poer, the bishop of Salisbury, that notable preacher of short sermons, claimed the right to marry the royal pair, because the fortress of Windsor was within his diocese. This right was disputed by the aged Ralph, archbishop of Canterbury, who was a great stickler for the prerogatives of his office; and an ecclesiastical council was called, in

---

[1] Through the courtesy of his grace the duke of Norfolk, I have been favoured with a copy of this inestimable volume, which, as it is printed for private use, is inaccessible to the public, but is most important as a book of reference to the writers of royal and noble biographies.

[2] Henry of Huntingdon. White Kennet.   [3] Eadmer.

which it was decided, that wherever the king and queen might be within the realm of England, they were the parishioners of the archbishop of Canterbury. Accordingly, the ceremony was triumphantly performed by the venerable primate, though bowed down by so many infirmities, that he appeared like one tottering on the verge of the grave.

This afforded Henry an excuse for deputing the honour of crowning him and his fair young bride on the following day, at Westminster, to his favourite prelate, Roger le Poer, the bishop of Salisbury, above named, to console him for his disappointment with regard to the hymeneal office. But the archbishop was not thus to be put off. The right of crowning the king and queen he considered a still more important branch of his archiepiscopal prerogatives than that of marrying them, and, *malgré* his age and paralysis, he hastened to the abbey, where the ceremonial had commenced at an unusually early hour. Roger le Poer having, according to his old custom, made unprecedented expedition in the performance of his office, had already placed the royal diadem on the monarch's brow, when archbishop Ralph sternly approached the royal chair, and asked Henry, "Who had put the crown on his head?"[1]

The king evasively replied, "If the ceremony had not been properly performed, it could be done again." On which, as some chroniclers assert, the choleric old primate gave the king such a smart blow with his crosier, that he smote the crown from his head;[2] but Eadmer says, he only raised it up by the strap which passed under the chin, and so turned it off his head. He then proceeded to replace it with all due form, and afterwards crowned the fair young queen. This most extraordinary coronation took place on Sunday, January 30th, 1121.

The beauty of the royal bride, whom Piers of Langtoft calls

"The May withouten vice,"

made a great impression on the minds of the people, which the sweetness of her manners, her prudence, and mild virtues, strengthened in no slight degree. It was on the occasion of her bridal coronation that Henry of Huntingdon, the chronicler, addressed to Adelicia those celebrated Latin verses, of which Camden has given us the following translation:—[3]

"When Adeliza's name should grace my song,
A sudden wonder stops the muse's tongue;
Your crown and jewels, when compared to you,
How poor your crown, how pale your jewels show!

---

[1] Eadmer. Speed.   [2] Speed.
[3] "Anglerum regina, tuos Adeliza, decores,
Ipsa referre parans musa stupore regit.
Quid diadema tibi pulcherrima? Quid tibi gemma?
Pallet gemma tibi, nec diadema nitet.
De me tibi cultus, cultum natura ministrat:
Non esornari forma beata potest,
Ornamenta cava, nec quicquam luminis inde
Accipis; illa micant lumine clara tuo;
Non puduit modicas de magnis dicere laudes,
Nec pudeat Dominum, te precor, esse meam."

> Take off your robes, your rich attire remove;
> Such pomps may load you, but can ne'er improve;
> In vain your costly ornaments are worn,
> You they obscure, while others they adorn.
> Ah! what new lustres can these trifles give,
> Which all their beauty from your charms receive?
> Thus I your lofty praise, your vast renown,
> In lowly verse am not ashamed to have shown,
> Oh, be you not ashamed my services to own!"

The wisdom of this lovely girl-queen early manifested itself in the graceful manner by which she endeavoured to conform herself to the tastes of her royal lord, in the encouragement of the polished arts, and the patronage of literature. Henry's love for animals had induced him to create an extensive menagerie at Woodstock, as we have seen, during the life of his first queen, Matilda of Scotland, who was probably well acquainted with natural history. The youthful Adelicia evidently knew nothing of zoology previously to her marriage with Henry Beauclerc; but, like a good wife, in order to adapt herself to his pursuits, she turned her attention to that study; for we find Philippe de Thuan wrote a work on the nature of animals for her special instruction. The poetical naturalist did not forget to allude to the personal charms of his royal patroness in his courtier-like dedication.

> "Philippe de Thuan, en franceise raisun,
> Ad estrait bestaire un livre de grammaire,
> Pour lour d'une feme ki mult est belle,
> Alix est namée, reine est corunée,
> Reine est d'Engleterre, sa ame nait ja guere."

> "Philippe de Thuan, in plain French,
> Has written an elementary book of animals,
> For the praise and instruction of a good and beauteous woman,
> Who is the crowned queen of England, and named Alix."

One of the most approved historians of her day, the author of the Waltham Abbey Manuscripts,[1] states of himself, that he was appointed a canon of Waltham Abbey, through the patronage of queen Adelicia. This chronicler is the same person who has so eloquently described the dismal search made for Harold's body, after the battle of Hastings.

Adelicia was deprived of the society of her royal husband a few weeks after their marriage, in consequence of a formidable inbreak of the Welsh, who had entered Cheshire, and committed great ravages. Henry went in person to the defence of his border counties, and having defeated the invaders, pursued them far into the country.

During this campaign his life was in some peril, while separated from the main body of his troops, in a narrow defile among the mountains, where he fell into an ambush, and at the same time an arrow, which was aimed at him from the heights above, struck him on the breast, but rebounded from his armour of proof. Henry, who probably did not give his Cambrian foes credit for that skill in archery for which his

---

[1] See Cottonian MSS. Julius D. S. See note, p. 50.

Norman followers were famed, intimated his suspicions of treachery among his own people, by exclaiming, "By our Lord's death, it was no Welsh hand that shot that arrow!"[1]

This narrow escape, or, perhaps, a wish of returning to Adelicia at Westminster, induced the king to conclude a peace with the Welsh. A very brief season of domestic intercourse was, however, permitted to the royal pair. Fulk, earl of Anjou, having espoused his younger daughter, Sybil, to William Clito, the earls of Mellent and Montfort, with a considerable party of the baronage of Normandy, openly declared themselves in favour of that prince, the heir of their lawful duke, Robert Courthose.

Henry I. was keeping the Easter festival, with his beautiful young queen, at Winchester, when the news that Fulk of Anjou had joined this formidable confederacy reached him. He sailed for Normandy in April 1123; and Adelicia was left, as her predecessor, Matilda of Scotland, had often been before her, to hold her lonely courts during the protracted absence of her royal consort, and to exert herself for the preservation of the internal peace of England, while war or state policy detained the king in Normandy.

Adelicia, following the example of her popular predecessor Matilda, " the good queen," in all that was deserving of imitation, conducted herself in a manner calculated to win the esteem and love of the nation; using her queenly influence for the establishment of good order, religion, and refinement, and the encouragement of learning and the arts. The king was absent from England three years and a half, before the expiration of which time Adelicia joined him in Normandy. Henry had defeated his enemies at the battle of Terroude, near Rouen, and taken a merciless vengeance on the revolted vassals of Normandy, who were so unfortunate as to fall into his hands. His treatment of the luckless troubadour knight, Luke de Barré,[2] though the circumstances are almost too dreadful for repetition, bears too strongly on the manners and customs of the twelfth century to be omitted. Luke de Barré had, according to the testimony of Ordericus Vitalis, been on terms of the greatest familiarity with Henry Beauclerc in the days of their youth, but, from some cause, had joined the revolt of the earl of Mellent in the late insurrection; and the said earl, and all the confederate peers allied against Henry's government in Normandy, had been wonderfully comforted and encouraged by the *sirventes*, or war-songs, of Luke.

These songs were provokingly satirical; and, being personally levelled against Henry, contained, we should suppose, some passages, which involved a betrayal of confidence; for Henry was so bitterly incensed, that when the luckless poet was made prisoner at the battle of Terroude, he barbarously condemned his former friend to lose his eyes on a scaffold, by the hands of the public executioner. This sentence was greatly lamented by the court; for Luke de Barré was not only a pleasant and jocose companion, but a gentleman of courage and honour. The earl of Flanders interceded for the wretched victim.[3]

---

[1] Chron. Walli.   [2] Sismondi.   Ordericus Vitalis.

"No, sir, no," replied Henry; "for this man being a wit, a bard, and a minstrel, forsooth! hath composed many ribald songs against me, and sung them to raise the horse-laughs of mine enemies. Now it hath pleased God to deliver him into mine hands, punished he shall be, to deter others from the like petulance."[1]

The sentence therefore took place, and the hapless poet died of the wounds he received in struggling with the executioner.[2] The Provençal annalists, however, declare that the gallant troubadour avoided the execution of Henry's sentence, by dashing his head against the wall, which caused his death. So much for the punishment of libels in the twelfth century.

The Saxon Chronicle specifies that queen Adelicia returned to England, September, 1126, accompanied by king Henry and his daughter, the empress Matilda, the heiress presumptive of England, then a widow, in her twenty-fourth year.

According to Malmsbury and other several contemporary historians, strange and mysterious reports were in circulation throughout Europe, connected with the death, or rather we should say the disappearance of Matilda's imperial spouse; for it was affirmed that he was not dead, though his obsequies had been performed with all due solemnity, and a stately monument was raised to his memory, in the cathedral of Spires.

Ever since the miserable death of his unhappy father, Henry IV., the emperor Henry V. had been subject to great mental disquiet, from the remorse which perpetually deprived him of rest. "One night," says William of Malmsbury, "he rose up from the side of the empress, and taking his staff in hand, with naked feet he wandered forth into the darkness, clad only in a woollen garment, and was never again seen in his own palace." This wild tale is repeated by Hoveden, Giraldus, and Higden, and is confirmed by various ancient manuscript chronicles, besides Trevisa, who adds, by way of sequel to the legend, that "the conscience-stricken emperor fled to England, where at Westchester he became a hermit, changing his name to God's-call, or the called of God. He lived in daily penance for the space of ten years, and was buried in the cathedral church of St. Werburga the Virgin."

The empress Matilda, after the funeral of her august spouse at Spires in 1125, took possession of his imperial diadem, which she brought to England, together with a treasure which, in those days, was by some considered of even greater importance—the hand of St. James. Matilda was reluctant to leave Germany, where she was splendidly dowered, and enjoyed a remarkable share of popularity. The princes of the empire were so much charmed with her prudent conduct and stately demeanour, that they entreated the king, her father, to permit her to choose a second consort from among their august body, promising to elect for their emperor the person on whom her choice might fall.[3]

King Henry, however, despairing of a male heir, as he had been married to Adelicia six years, reclaimed his widowed daughter from the

---

[1] Ordericus Vitalis.   [2] Ibid. Sismondi.
[3] W. Gemiticensis.   W. Malmsbury.   Sir John Haward.   Speed.
10*

admiring subjects of her late consort, and carried her with him to England. Soon after their arrival, Henry summoned a parliament for the
purpose of causing the empress Matilda to be acknowledged as the
heiress presumptive to the crown. This was the first instance that had
occurred, since the consolidation of the Heptarchy under one supreme
head, of a female standing in that important position with regard to the
succession of the English crown. There was, however, neither law nor
precept to forbid a female from holding the regal office, and Henry failed
not to set forth to the representatives of the great body of the people,
who had been summoned on this important business, his daughter's
descent from their ancient line of sovereigns; telling them, " That
through her, who was now his only heir, they should come to be
governed again by the royal English blood, if they would make oath to
secure to her, after his death, the succession as queen of England, in
case of his decease without a male heir." [1]

It is, doubtless, on the authority of this remarkable passage in Henry's
speech, that historians have called his first wife, Matilda of Scotland,
the heiress of the Saxon line. This is worthy of observation.

The people of England joyfully acceded to Henry's proposition; and
the nobles and prelates of the Norman aristocracy, then assembled in
council on this occasion, swore fealty to the high and mighty lady Matilda as their future sovereign.

Stephen earl of Mortagne, the king's favourite nephew, (being the third
son of the Conqueror's fourth daughter, Adela, countess of Blois,) was
the first who bent his knee in homage to the daughter of his liege lord,
as the heiress of England, and swore to maintain her righteous title to
the throne of her royal father.

Stephen was the handsomest man in Europe, and remarkable for his
fine carriage and knightly prowess. He bore great sway in the councils
of his royal uncle, and was a general favourite of the nobles of England
and Normandy. It has been said withal, that his fine person and graceful manners made a deep impression on the heart of the widowed heiress
of England.

The royal family kept their Christmas this year at Windsor,[2] but the
empress Matilda did not grace the festivities by her presence, but remained in the deepest seclusion, " abiding continually," says Matthew
Paris, " in the chamber of Adelicia;"— by which it appears, that notwithstanding her high rank and matronly dignity as the widow of an
emperor, the heiress of England had no establishment of her own.
This retirement, lasting for several months, gave rise to many myste-.
rious reports as to the cause of her being hidden from the people, who
had so recently been required to swear fealty to her as their future sovereign. By some it was said, " that the king, her father, suspected her
of having accelerated the death of her late husband, the emperor, or of
causing him to be spirited away from his palace." But that was evidently a groundless surmise; for Gemiticensis, a contemporary chronicler, bears testimony to " her prudent and gracious behaviour to her

---

[1] Henry of Huntingdon. W. Malmsbury. W. Gemiticensis.   [2] Saxon Annals

imperial spouse, which," he observes, " was one of the causes which won the esteem of the German princes, who were urgent in their entreaties to her royal father for her restoration." This Henry pertinaciously refused, repeating, " that she was his only heir, and must dwell among her own people."[1] Yet, early in the following year, he again bestowed her in marriage, without the consent of his peers of parliament, and decidedly against her own inclination, on a foreign prince, whom she regarded with the most ineffable scorn, as her inferior in every point of view.

We have seen that, in her tender infancy, Matilda was used as a political puppet, by her parent, to advance his own interest, without the slightest consideration for her happiness. *Then* the victim was led a smiling sacrifice to the altar, unconscious of the joyless destiny to which parental ambition had doomed her. *Now* the case was different; it was no meek infant, but a royal matron, who had shared the imperial throne of a Kaiser, and received for years the homage of vassal princes. Moreover, she whom Henry endeavoured to compel to an abhorrent marriage of state, possessed a mind, as inflexible as his own. The disputes between the king and his daughter must have arisen to a very serious height, before he took the unpopular step of subjecting her to personal restraint, by confining her to the apartment of his queen.

Matthew Paris, indeed, labours to convince us that there was nothing unreasonable in this circumstance. " Where," says he, " should an empress live rather than with a queen, a daughter than with a mother, a fair lady, a widow, and the heir of a great nation, than where her person might be safest from danger, and her conduct from suspicion?" The historian, however, forgets that Matilda was the step-daughter of the queen; that Adelicia was not older than herself, and, from the acknowledged gentleness of her disposition, unlikely to assume the slightest maternal control over the haughty heiress of England. Adelicia must have felt herself very delicately situated in this business; and it appears probable that she acted as a mediator between the contending parties, conducting herself rather as a loving sister than an ambitious step-dame. The accomplished editor of the Howard Memorials infers that a very tender friendship existed between the empress Matilda and Adelicia through life, which probably had commenced before the fair maid of Brabant was selected from among the princesses of Europe to share the crown of England with Henry I.; for Matilda's imperial spouse, the emperor Henry V., had been actively instrumental in assisting Godfrey Barbatus, the father of Adelicia, in the recovery of Lower Louvaine— an obligation which the Louvaine princess certainly endeavoured to repay to his widow.[2]

Adelicia's uncle, Wido of Louvaine, afterwards Pope Calixtus II., was at one period bishop of Vienna, and it is even possible that Henry's attention was first attracted to the fair maid of Brabant at the court of his daughter; and the previous intimacy between the ladies may account for the fact that the haughty Matilda lived on such good terms with her

---

[1] W. Gemiticensis.   [2] Howard Memorials. Chronicles of Brabant.

step-mother; for Adelicia appears to have been the only person with whom she did not quarrel.

The prince to whom Henry I. had pledged the hand of his perverse heiress, was Geoffrey Plantagenet, the eldest son of his old antagonist, Fulk, earl of Anjou, and brother to the widowed princess, who had been espoused to Matilda's brother, William the Atheling.

Geoffrey Plantagenet, the heir of Anjou, had been the favourite companion of king Henry I. when on the continent. His fine person, his elegant manners, great bravery, and, above all, his learning, made his society very agreeable to the monarch who still possessed these excellencies in great perfection.[1] He chose to become the sponsor of Geoffrey in chivalry, and, at his own expense, had had that high ceremony performed at Rouen. After the bath into which, according to the ancient custom, the young chevalier was plunged, Henry gave him, as his godson in arms, a Spanish steed, a steel coat of mail, and cuisses of double proof against both lance and arrow, spurs of gold, a scutcheon, adorned with golden lions, a helmet, enriched with jewels, a lance of ash, with a Poictiers[2] head, and a sword made by Gallard, the most famous of the ancient armorers. Some of the French chroniclers declare this Geoffrey to be the first person that bore the name of Plantagenet, from putting in his helmet a plume of the flowering broom, when he went to hunt in the woods.

The king of England did not confine himself to this chivalric adoption; he was resolved that his accomplished favourite should become his son-in-law. There were, moreover, strong political reasons, in Henry's opinion, for this union. Fulk of Anjou, who had hitherto supported the claims of his gallant young son-in-law, William Clito, to the dukedom, was willing to abandon his cause, provided Henry would marry Matilda to his heir. This Henry had engaged to do, without the slightest attention to his daughter's feelings. His favourite nephew, Stephen of Blois, who is said to have rendered himself only too dear to the imperial widow, was, unfortunately for them both, a married man at that time, or the long and ruinous civil wars that desolated England during his usurpation might have been averted by a matrimonial alliance. The ceremony of betrothment between the reluctant Matilda and Geoffrey of Anjou took place on Whitsunday, 1127, and she was, after the festivities of Whitsuntide were over, conducted into Normandy by her half-brother, Robert earl of Gloucester, and Brian, son of Alan Fergeant, earl of Richmond, with great pomp.

The feasts and pageants that attended her arrival in Normandy were prolonged during three weeks. On the first day, heralds in grand costume went through the streets and squares of Rouen, shouting at every crossway this singular proclamation :—

" Thus saith king Henry !

" Let no man here present, whether native or foreigner, rich or poor,

---

[1] 1126 to 1127. Chron. de Normand. and Script. Rer. France.
[2] Poictiers probably derives its name from these lance-heads.

high or low, warrior or rustic, be so bold as to stay away from the royal rejoicings; for whosoever shall not take a part in the games and diversions, shall be considered guilty of an offence to our lord the king."[1]

King Henry had given positive commands to Matilda and her illustrious escort, that the nuptials should be solemnized by the archbishop of Rouen immediately on her arrival;[2] but he was himself compelled to undertake a voyage to Normandy, in August, to see the marriage concluded, which did not take place till the 26th of that month;[3] from which we may reasonably infer that the reluctant bride paid very little attention to his directions. The affair was at length, however, accomplished to Henry's satisfaction, more especially as Fulk of Anjou, being called to the throne of Jerusalem, by the death of Baldwin II., his father-in-law, resigned his patrimonial territories to his heir. Yet there were many circumstances that rendered this alliance a fruitful source of annoyance to Henry. The Anglo-Norman barons and prelates were highly offended, in the first place, that the king should have presumed to marry the heiress out of the realm without consulting them on the subject; and the people of England were no less displeased, at the open violence that had been put on the inclinations of the descendant of their ancient sovereigns in this foreign marriage. As for Matilda, it should seem that she did not consider herself by any means bound to practise the duty of obedience, or even of common courtesy, to a husband who had thus been forced upon her against her own will; and while she exacted the most unqualified submissions from her luckless helpmate, she perpetually wearied her father with her complaints of his conduct.

Queen Adelicia was rejoined by king Henry, in the autumn, and they kept their Christmas together in London. Early in the following spring, 1128, he was again compelled to embark for Normandy, to defeat the enterprising designs of his nephew, William Clito, who, having succeeded to the earldom of Flanders, in right of his grandmother Matilda, the wife of William the Conqueror, was enabled to assume a more formidable attitude than he had yet done. But this gallant and unfortunate prince met with his death in consequence of a slight wound in the thumb, which he took in disarming a mutinous soldier of his lance. He died six days after,[4] in the monastery of St. Bertin, July 27, 1128.

This formidable rival being now removed, Henry appeared at the summit of his ambition, and was considered the mightiest monarch of the West. He was the husband withal of one of the most beautiful and amiable princesses in Europe.

Whether the fair Adelicia loved her royal spouse, history has not recorded; but her conduct as a wife, a queen, and even as a step-mother, was irreproachable. When all circumstances are considered, it can

[1] Brompton. Malmsbury. Script. Rer. Fran.
[2] Saxon Annals. S. Dunelm. Malmsbury. Huntingdon. [3] Saxon Annals.
[4] His captive father, Robert Courthose, it is said, one morning surprised his attendants by weeping piteously, and exclaiming, "My son is dead! my son is dead!" and related, "that he had in his dreams, that night, seen him mortally wounded with a lance."—Ordericus Vitalis.

I

scarcely be imagined, however, that her splendid marriage was productive of happiness to the youthful wife of Henry I. To say nothing of
the disparity in years between this illustrious pair, the morbid sorrow
of which Henry was the perpetual prey after the loss of his children in
the white ship, the irascibility of temper to which he gave way in his
old age, and his bitter disappointment at the want of offspring from his
second marriage, must have been most distressing to the feelings of his
gentle consort. Then the stormy disputes between Henry and his only
daughter Matilda could not have been otherwise than very painful to
her. Whatever, however, were the trials with which Adelicia had to
contend, she evidently supported them with silent magnanimity, and at
the same time endeavoured to soothe and cheer the gloom of her way-
ward lord by attracting to the court the most distinguished poets and
minstrels of the age, who repaid her liberal patronage by celebrating
her virtues and her charms.

Adelicia frequently attended her royal husband on his progresses.
Her presence was, doubtless, of medicinal influence in those fearful
hours when the pangs of troubled conscience brought the visitations of
an evil spirit upon Henry, and sleep either forsook his pillow or brought
visionary horrors in its train. " In the year 1130, the king complained
to Grimbald, his Saxon physician, that he was sore disquieted of nights,
and that he seemed to see a great number of husbandmen with their
rustical tools stand about him, threatening him for wrongs done against
them. Sometimes he appeared to see his knights and soldiers threatening him; which sight so feared him in his sleep, that ofttimes he rose
undrest out of his bed, took weapon in hand, and sought to kill them
he could not find. Grimbald, his physician, being a notably wise man,
expounded his dreams by true conjecture, and willed him to reform
himself by alms and prayer, as Nebuchadnezzar did by the counsel of
Daniel." [1]

It is probable that the unfortunate troubadour knight, Luke de Barré,
was not forgotten by the conscience-stricken monarch, though historians have not recorded that his mangled form was among the ghastly
dramatis personæ that, in his latter years, made king Henry's nights
horrible; — no enviable state of companionship, we should imagine, for
the young and innocent being whose fate was indissolubly linked with
his. It must have been a relief at all times to Adelicia when her royal
husband's presence was required in Normandy.

On the death of Adelicia's uncle, pope Calixtus II., a dispute occurring in the election of two rival pontiffs as successors to the papal chair,
Henry proceeded to the continent, in the year 1130, in the hope of reap-
ing some political advantage from the candidate whose cause he espoused.
His arrangements were perfectly satisfactory as to that matter, but he was,
to the last degree, harassed by the quarrels between his daughter and her
unbeloved spouse, Geoffrey of Anjou. After he had thrice adjusted their
differences, Matilda, on some fresh offence which she either gave or took,
abjured her husband's company, departed from his court, and claimed

[1] Stowe. H. Huntingdon.

the protection of the king her father, with whom she once more returned to England,[1] having, by the eloquence of tears and complaints, succeeded in exciting his indignation against her husband, and persuading him that she was an injured person.

Soon after their arrival in England, a parliament was summoned to meet at Northampton, September, 1131, where the oath of fealty to Matilda, as the heiress of England, was again renewed by the general estates of the nation.[2]

It was a subject of the greatest disappointment, both to the sovereign and the people, that there was no prospect of either the queen Adelicia, or the empress Matilda (though both were still young and beautiful women) bringing heirs to the crown. So desirable was the possibility of the royal line being continued through Matilda considered, that when the count of Anjou sent an humble entreaty to his haughty consort to return to him, the king and parliament seconded his request; and all due submissions having been made by Geoffrey, Matilda was at length induced to return to him.[3]

A passage from Mezerai casts some light on the mysterious separation that took place between the widowed empress and her new spouse. After the nuptials of this pair, a monk came to Matilda, and declared that her late lord, the emperor Henry, had not died at Utrecht, as she and all the world supposed, but that he finished his days as a servant in an hospital, which severe penance he had sworn to inflict on himself for his heavy sins. When dying at Angers, the disguised emperor discovered himself to this monk, his confessor, who came to Matilda with the news. In conclusion it is said, the empress attended the death-bed of Henry V., and recognised and acknowledged him, as the emperor, her first husband.

This is a fine tragic tale, whether it be true or false.

The following year was remarkable for a destructive fire, which consumed the greatest part of London;[4] but soon after this national calamity, the joyful news that the empress Matilda had given birth to a prince,[5] diverted the attention of the royal family from the contemplation of this misfortune, and cast the last gleam of brightness on the declining years of the king.

The young prince was named Henry, after his royal grandfather, the king of England. The Normans called him Fitz-Empress, but king Henry proudly styled the boy Fitz-Conqueror, in token of his illustrious descent from the mightiest monarch of the line of Rollo.[6]

King Henry summoned his last parliament in 1133, for the purpose of causing this precious child to be included in the oath of fealty, by which the succession to the throne was, for the third time, secured to his daughter, the empress Matilda. If his queen Adelicia had brought him a son, after these repeated acts in favour of his daughter by a princess who was regarded by the majority of the people as the heiress of the royal English line, in all probability, a civil war respecting the

[1] Roger Hoveden. H. Huntingdon. [2] Malmsbury. H. Huntingdon.
[3] M. Paris. [4] H. Huntingdon. [5] R. Diceto. M. Paris. [6] M. Westminster.

succession, would have occurred on the death of king Henry. The barrenness of the beautiful young queen, however, though so deeply lamented by her royal husband, was at that time, no doubt, a providential dispensation, and one of the causes of the amity and confidence that subsisted between her and her haughty step-daughter.

Towards the latter end of this summer, king Henry embarked on his last voyage for Normandy. The day was remarkable for a total eclipse of the sun, accompanied with storms and violent commotions of the deep.[1] It was so dark, say the annalists of that era, " that on board the royal ship no man might see another's face for some hours." The eclipse was followed by an earthquake; and these two phenomena were, according to the spirit of the age, regarded as portents of horror and woe, and it was predicted that the king would never return from Normandy.[2]

On a former occasion, when Henry had embarked for England, in June 1131, he was so dismayed by the bursting of a water-spout over the vessel, and the fury of the wind and waves, that, believing his last hour was at hand, he made a penitent acknowledgment of his sins, promising to lead a new life if it should please God to preserve him from the peril of death, and, above all, he vowed to repeal the oppressive impost of danegelt for seven years, if he were permitted to reach the English shore in safety.[3] From this incident we may infer that Henry I. was by no means impressed with his brother Rufus's bold idea, of the security of a king of England from a watery grave; but the catastrophe of his children in the fatal white ship had no doubt some effect on his mind, during these perils on the deep.

The summer of 1133 he spent in Normandy, in feasts and rejoicings, for the birth of his infant grandson. That event was, however, only the precursor of fresh dissensions between that ill-assorted pair, the empress Matilda and her husband, Geoffrey Plantagenet. Her late visit to England had renewed the scandalous reports respecting her partiality for her cousin, Stephen of Blois; and the birth of a son in the sixth year of their marriage to the long childless pair proved anything but a bond of union between them.[4]

There is no reason to suppose that Adelicia was with the king her husband at the time of his death, which took place in Normandy, in the year 1135, at the Castle of Lyons near Rouen, a place in which he much delighted. It is said, that having over-fatigued himself in hunting in the forest of Lyons, he returned much heated, and, contrary to the advice of his courtiers and physicians, made too full a meal on a dish of stewed lampreys, his favourite food, which brought on a violent fit of indigestion (called by the chroniclers a surfeit), ending in a fever, of which he died, after an illness of seven days, at midnight, December 1st, in the sixty-seventh year of his age. He appears to have been perfectly conscious of his approaching dissolution, for he gave particular directions respecting his obsequies to his natural son, Robert earl of Gloucester, whom he charged to take 60,000 marks out of his treasure-chest at

[1] Saxon Annals.   [2] W. Malmsbury.   [3] Saxon Annals.   [4] Saxon Chronicle.

Falaise, for the expenses of his funeral, and the payment of his merce-nary troops.[1] He solemnly bequeathed his dominions to his daughter the empress, not without some indignant mention of her luckless spouse, Geoffrey of Anjou, his former *élève* and *bel ami.* He absolutely ex-cluded him from any share in his bequests, and with much earnestness constituted his beloved son, earl Robert, the protector of his daughter's rights.

His nephews, Warren earl of Surrey, and Stephen de Blois earl of Mortagne, with Robert earl of Leicester, were standing round the bed of the expiring monarch, and were witnesses of his charge to his son, the earl of Gloucester.[2]

Robert of Gloucester gives the following serio-comic account of the royal wilfulness, in partaking of the interdicted food which caused his death :

"When he came home he willed him a lamprey to eat.
Though his leeches him forbade, for it was a feeble meat;
But he would not them believe, for he loved it well enow,
And eat in evil case, for the lamprey it him slew,
For right soon after it into anguish him drew,
And he died for his lamprey unto his own woe."

The noble earls who surrounded the death-bed of king Henry, and listened to his last instructions respecting his funeral, attended his remains from the town of St. Denis le Forment (where he breathed his last) to Rouen; and when they entered that city, they reverently bore the bier, on which the royal corpse was laid, on their shoulders by turns.[3]

At Rouen, the remains of this mighty sovereign, in preparation for removal to England, underwent the process of embalming, as it was called, according to the barbarous fashion described by the chroniclers : the body was sliced and powdered with much salt, and wrapped in a bull's hide.

The remains of king Henry were interred with great pomp on Christ-mas-day, at the abbey of Reading, which he had built and magnificently endowed for that purpose. On the anniversary of the death of her royal lord, queen Adelicia, to testify her respect for his memory, gave by charter the manor of Eton in Hertfordshire to the abbey of Reading, for prayers to be said for his soul; and, by a second charter, she also gave the manor of Stanton Harcourt, in Oxfordshire, and the churches of Cham, Eslingham, and others, for the expenses of his anniversary—a solemn service for the repose of his soul,—which was yearly to be cele-brated there.[4] The royal widow also gave one hundred shillings, out of the hythe, or wharf (Queen hythe), belonging to her in London, to be applied to the expenses of a lamp, to burn perpetually before his tomb.[5] In these charters and deeds she styles herself "Adalid the queen,

---

[1] Ordericus Vitalis. W. Malmsbury.   Ibid.   [2] Henry Huntingdon.
[4] Howard Memorials. Monasticon, Charter 7. art. Reading.   [5] Ibid.

wife of the most noble king Henry, and daughter of Godfrey, duke of Lotharingia." [1]

The chroniclers of that reign, several of whom were well acquainted with him, have given the following lively description of the person of Adelicia's royal lord. " He was, for personage, of reasonable stature, broad-breasted, well-jointed, and full of flesh, amiable of countenance, with fine and penetrating eyes, and black hair, carelessly hanging about his forehead." [2] It is to be remarked, that after he had been induced, by the eloquent preaching of friar Serlo, to submit this natural ornament to the shears of that priestly reformer, he was very strict in his prohibitions to his subjects against long hair.

Two illuminated portraits of Henry I. are in existence: both represent him as advanced in life, and in a melancholy attitude; supposed to be after the loss of his children. His face is handsome, with high and regular features, his hair curling, but not long; his figure is emaciated, he is clad in a very close dress, the shoe and stocking all of a piece, and the toe pointed; he wears a mantle wrapped about him. His crown is ornamented with three trefoils; his sceptre is a staff with an ornamented head. He is seated on a stone bench, carved in an architectural design. He is represented in the coronation robes he wore at the crowning of Adelicia. [3]

Henry received from his subjects the title of the Lion of Justice. This appellation was drawn from the prophecies of Merlin, then very popular in England. On the accession of every sovereign to the English throne, all his subjects consulted these rigmaroles, as naturally as we consult an almanac, to know when there is a new moon.

" After two dragons," says Merlin, " the Lion of Justice shall come, at whose roaring the Gallic towers and island serpents shall tremble."

This Lion of Justice certainly suffered no one to break the laws but himself, if he is accountable for the villanies of his purveyors, his standard of justice was not very high: " the king's servants, and a multitude following the royal retinue, took and spoiled everything the way the king went, there being no discipline or good order taken.[4] When they could not consume what they found in the house they had broken into, they made the owners carry it to market and sell it for them; they burned the provisions, or washed their horses' feet with the ale or mead, or poured the drink on the ground, or otherwise wasted it, so that every

[1] Ego Adalid Regina, uxor nobilissimi Regis Henrici, et filia Godfridi ducis Lotharingiæ.   [2] Cottonian MSS. Vitellius.
[3] These portraits exactly agree with the descriptions of the costume from the monastic chronicles. " They wore close breeches and stockings, all of a piece, made of fine cloth;" the pointed shoes were brought in by William Rufus, but were first invented by Folque le Rechin (whose surname means the quarreller), count of Anjou, to hide his corns and bunions. The queen and women of rank wore gowns and mantles trailing on the ground. The married women wore an additional robe over the gown, not unlike the sacerdotal garment; to the girdle a large pouch or purse was suspended, called an *aumonière*. The men wore their hair in long curls, unless seized with sudden fits of fanaticism. The married women braided theirs very closely to the side of the face, or hid it.
[4] Eadmer.

one hearing of the king's coming would run away from their houses."
Whenever Henry I. was under any apprehensions from his brother
Robert, he regulated his household somewhat better, and kept the law-
lessness of his purveyors within bounds.[1]

Henry carried the art of dissimulation to such a pitch that his grand
justiciary started when he heard the king had praised him, and exclaimed,
" God defend me! the king praises no one but him whom he means to
destroy."[2]

The result proved the deep knowledge which the minister had of his
royal master's character, as Henry of Huntingdon, his archdeacon, details at length.

What degree of happiness Adelicia the Fair enjoyed during the fifteen
years of queenly splendour which she passed as the consort of Henry
Beauclerc, no surviving records tell; but that she was very proud of his
achievements and brilliant talents, we have the testimony of the poetical
chronicler, who continued the history of Brut, from William the Conqueror, through the reign of William Rufus. It appears, moreover, that
the royal dowager employed herself during her widowhood in collecting
materials for the history of her mighty lord; for Gaimar, the author of
the history of the Angles, observes, " that if he had chosen to have
written of king Henry, he had a thousand things to say, which the
troubadour called David, employed by queen Adelicia, knew nought
about; neither had he written, nor was the Louvaine queen herself in
possession of them."

If the collection of queen Adelicia should ever be brought to light, it
would no doubt afford a curious specimen of the biographical powers of
the illustrious widow, and her assistant, Troubadour David, whose name
has only been rescued from oblivion by the jealousy of a disappointed
rival in the art of historical poetry.

During the life of the king her husband, Adelicia had founded and
endowed the hospital and conventual establishment of St. Giles, near
Wilton;[3] and, according to a Wiltshire tradition, she resided there during some part of her widowhood, in the house which is still called by
her name.[4] She was likewise dowered by her late husband, king Henry,
in the fair domain of Arundel Castle, and its rich dependencies, the forfeit inheritance[5] of the brutal Robert earl of Belesme; and here, no doubt,
the royal widow held her state at the expiration of the first year of
cloistered seclusion, after the death of her illustrious spouse.

Camden thus describes the spot which the magnificent taste of the
late duke of Norfolk has, within the last century, rendered one of the
most splendid objects of attraction in England:—" Beyond Selsey, the
shore breaks, and makes way for a river that runs out of St. Leonard's
forest, and then by Arundel, seated on a hill, over a vale, of the river
Arun." At this Saxon castle, built and strengthened on the hill above
the waters, Adelicia was residing when she consented to become the
wife of William de Albini, of the Strong Hand, the lord of Buckenham
in Norfolk, and one of the most chivalrous peers in Europe.

---

[1] Malmsbury.   [2] Henry of Huntingdon.   [3] Howard Memorials.
[4] Sir Richard Hoare's Modern Wiltshire.   [5] Tierney's Arundel.

According to Mr. Howard's computation, Adelicia was in her thirty-second year at the time of king Henry's death, in the very pride of her beauty; and she contracted her second marriage in the third year of her widowhood, A.D. 1138.[1]

Her second spouse, William de Albini, with the Strong Arm, was the son of William de Albini, who was called Pincerna,[2] being the chief butler or cup-bearer of the duchy of Normandy. William the Conqueror appointed him to the same office in England at his coronation in Westminster Abbey; which honour has descended by hereditary custom to the duke of Norfolk, his rightful representative and heir; and when there is a coronation banquet, the golden cup out of which the sovereign drinks to the health of his or her loving subjects becomes his perquisite.[3]

It appears that Adelicia and Albini were affianced some time previous to their marriage; for when he won the prize at the tournament held at Bourges in 1137, in honour of the nuptials of Louis VII. of France and Eleanora of Aquitaine, Adelaide, the gay queen-dowager of France, fell passionately in love with him, and wooed him to become her husband, but he replied, "that his troth was pledged to Adelicia, the queen of England."[4]

Although it may be considered somewhat remarkable that two queen-dowagers of similar names should have fixed their affections on the same gentleman, there is every reason to believe that such was the fact; but the marvellous legend so gravely related by Dugdale,[5] containing the sequel of the tale, namely, the unlady-like conduct of the rejected dowager of France, in pushing the strong-handed Albini into a cave in her garden, where she had secreted a fierce lion to become the minister of her jealous vengeance, together with the knight's redoubtable exploit in tearing out the lion's heart, which he must have found conveniently situated at the bottom of his throat, a place where no anatomist would have thought of feeling for it, must be regarded as one of the popular romances of the age of chivalry.

We have seen another version of the story, in which the hero is said to have deprived the lion, not of his heart, but his tongue; and this is doubtless the tradition relating to William of the Strong Hand, since the Albini-lion on the ancient armorial bearings of that house is tongueless, and is, by-the-bye, one of the most good-tempered looking beasts ever seen.

Romance and ideality out of the question, William de Albini was not only a knight *sans peur et sans reproche*, stout in combat, and constant in loyalty and love, but history proves him to have been one of the greatest and best men of that age. His virtues and talents sufficiently justified the widow of the mighty sovereign of England and Normandy in bestowing her hand upon him; nor was Adelicia's second marriage in the slightest degree offensive to the subjects of her late husband, or considered derogatory to the dignity of a queen-dowager of England.

[1] Howard Memorials.　　　　　　[2] Ibid.　　　　　　[3] Ibid.
[4] Howard Memorials. Dugdale.　　[5] Dugdale's Baronage.

Adelicia, by her union with Albini, conveyed to him a life interest in her rich dowry of Arundel, and he accordingly assumed the title of earl of Arundel, in her right, as the possessor of Arundel Castle.[1] It was at this feudal fortress, on the then solitary coast of Sussex, that the royal beauty, who had for fifteen years presided over the splendid court of Henry Beauclerc, voluntarily resided with her second husband — the husband, doubtless, of her heart—in the peaceful obscurity of domestic happiness, far remote from the scenes of her former greatness.

Adelicia's wisdom in avoiding all the snares of party, by retiring from public life at a period so full of perilous excitement as the early part of Stephen's reign, cannot be disputed. Her gentle disposition, her good taste, and feminine feelings, fitted her for the enjoyments of private life, and she made them her choice.

There was, however, nothing of a selfish character in the conduct of the royal matron in declining to exert such influence as she possessed in advocating the claims of her step-daughter Matilda to the throne of England. As a queen-dowager, Adelicia had no voice in the choice of a sovereign; as a female, she would have departed from her province, had she intermeddled with intrigues of state, even for the purpose of assisting the lawful heir to the crown. She left the question to be decided by the peers and people of England; and as they did not oppose the coronation of Stephen, she had no pretence for interfering; but she never sanctioned the usurpation of the successful rival of her step-daughter's right, by appearing at his court. And when the empress Matilda landed in England, to dispute the crown with Stephen, the gates of Arundel Castle were thrown open to receive her and her train, by the royal Adelicia and her high-minded husband Albini.[2] It was in the year 1139 when this perilous guest claimed the hospitality, and finally the protection, of the noble pair, whose wedded happiness had been rendered more perfect by the birth of a son, probably very little before that period, for it was only in the second year of their marriage. And she, over whose barrenness as the consort of the mightiest monarch of the West, both sovereign and people had lamented for nearly fifteen years, became, when the wife of a subject, the mother of a numerous progeny, the ancestress of an illustrious line of English nobles, in whose veins her royal blood has been preserved in uninterrupted course to the present day.

According to Malmsbury, and many other historians, the empress Matilda was only attended by her brother, the earl of Gloucester, and a hundred and forty followers, when she landed at Portsmouth, in the latter end of September. Gervase and Brompton aver that she came with a numerous army; but the general bearings of history prove that this was not the fact, since Matilda was evidently in a state of absolute peril when her generous step-mother afforded her an asylum within the walls of Arundel Castle, for we find that her devoted friend and brother, Robert earl of Gloucester, when he saw that she was honoura-

---

[1] Howard Memorials. Tierney's Hist. Arundel.
[2] Malmsbury. Speed. Rapin.

bly received there, considered her in a place of safety, and, attended by only twelve persons, proceeded to Bristol.

No sooner was Stephen informed that the empress Matilda was in Arundel Castle, than he raised the siege of Marlborough, and commenced a rapid march towards Arundel, in order to attack her in her retreat. The spirit with which he pushed his operations alarmed the royal ladies.[1] Adelicia dreaded the destruction of her castle, the loss of her beloved husband, and the breaking up of all the domestic happiness she had enjoyed since her retirement from public life. The empress Matilda suffered some apprehension lest her gentle step-mother should be induced to deliver her into the hands of her foe. There was, however, no less firmness than gentleness in the character of Adelicia; and the moment Stephen approached her walls, she sent messengers to entreat his forbearance, assuring him " that she had admitted Matilda not as *his* enemy, but as her daughter-in-law and early friend, who had claimed her hospitality, which respect for the memory of her late royal lord, king Henry, forbade her to refuse; the same considerations would compel her to protect her, while she remained beneath the shelter of her roof."[2] Adelicia added, " that if he came in hostile array against her castle of Arundel, with intent to make Matilda his prisoner, she must frankly say, that she was resolved to defend her to the last extremity, not only because she was the daughter of her late dear lord, king Henry, but as the widow of the emperor Henry and her guest;" and she besought Stephen, " by all the laws of courtesy and the ties of kindred, not to place her in such a painful strait as to compel her to do anything against her conscience." In conclusion, she requested with much earnestness " that Matilda might be allowed to leave the castle, and retire to her brother."

Stephen acceded to the proposal, the siege was raised, and the empress proceeded to join her adherents at Bristol. Malmsbury assures us, that the impolitic conduct of Stephen on this occasion was nothing more than what the laws of chivalry demanded from every true knight.

We are inclined to regard Stephen's courteous compliance with the somewhat unreasonable prayer of the queen-dowager, as a proof of the high respect in which she was held, and the great influence over the minds of her royal husband's kindred, which her virtues and winning qualities had obtained while she wore the crown-matrimonial of England. Adelicia conducted herself with equal prudence and magnanimity in the defence and deliverance of her step-daughter, exhibiting a very laudable mixture of the wisdom of the serpent with the innocence of the dove and the courage of the lion. The lion was the cognizance of the royal house of Louvaine; and Mr. Howard is of opinion, that this proud bearing was assumed by the family of Albini, in token of descent from the fair maid of Brabant, rather than with any reference to the fabled exploit of her second husband, related in Dugdale's baronage.[3]

A grateful remembrance of the generous conduct of Stephen, in all

[1] Malmsbury. Gervase. M. Paris. H. Huntingdon.
[2] Gervase. Malmsbury. Rapin.   [3] Howard's Memorials.

probability withheld Adelicia and Albini from taking part with the empress Matilda against him, in the long and disastrous civil war which desolated the ravaged plains of England with kindred blood, during so many years of that inauspicious reign. They appear to have maintained a strict neutrality, and to have preserved their vassals and neighbours from the evils attendant upon the contest between the empress and the king.

Adelicia, after her happy marriage with the husband of her choice, was not forgetful of the respect which she considered due to the memory of her late royal lord, king Henry; for, by a third charter, she granted to his favourite abbey of Reading the church of Berkeley Harness in Gloucestershire,[1] with suitable endowments, " to pray for the soul of king Henry and duke Godfrey her father, and also for the health of her present lord," whom she styles, " William earl of Chichester, and for her own health, and the health of her children." Thus we observe that this amiable princess unites the departed objects of her veneration in the devotional offices which she fondly caused the monks of Reading to offer up, for the welfare of her living husband, her beloved children, and herself. To her third son, Adelicia gave the name of her deceased lord, king Henry. Her fourth was named Godfrey, after her father and elder brother, the reigning duke of Brabant.

Adelicia chiefly resided at Arundel Castle, after her marriage with William de Albini, but there is also traditional evidence, that she occasionally lived with him in the noble feudal castle, which he built, after his marriage with her, at Buckenham in Norfolk. It is still designated in that county, as *New* Buckenham, though the mound, part of the moat, and a few mouldering fragments of the walls, are all that remain of the once stately hall, that was at times graced with the dowager court of *Alix la Belle.*

The priory of St. Bartholomew, likewise called the priory of the Causeway, in the parish of Lyminster, near Arundel, was established by queen Adelicia, after her marriage with William de Albini, as a convent of Augustinian canons.[2] It was situated at the foot of the hill which overlooks the town from the south side of the river.

The number of inmates appears originally to have been limited by the royal foundress to two persons, whose principal business was to take charge of the bridge, and to preserve the passage of the river. All her gifts and charters were solemnly confirmed by her husband, William Albini, who appears to have cherished the deepest respect for his royal spouse, always speaking of her as " *eximia regina,*"—that is, inestimable or surpassingly excellent queen.[3]

We find, from the Monasticon, that Adelicia gave in trust to the bishop of Chichester certain lands in Arundel, to provide salaries for the payment of two chaplains to celebrate divine service in that castle. The last recorded act of Adelicia was the grant of the prebend of West Dean to the cathedral of Chichester, in 1150.

---

[1] Monasticon, Charter 9. Howard Memorials.
[2] Dugdale's Monasticon. Lib. Epist. B. vol. xviii.   [3] Ibid.

In the year 1149, a younger brother of Adelicia, Henry of Louvaine, was professed a monk in the monastery of Affligham, near Alost in Flanders, which had been founded by their father Godfrey, and his brother Henry of Louvaine; and soon after, the royal Adelicia herself,[1] stimulated no doubt by his example, withdrew not only from the pomps and parade of earthly grandeur, but from the endearments of her adoring husband and youthful progeny, and, crossing the sea, retired to the nunnery in the same foundation, where she ended her days,[2] and was likewise buried.[3]

Mr. Howard, in his interesting sketch of the life of his royal ancestress, states it to be his opinion, that Adelicia did not take this important step without the full consent of her husband. Strange as it appears to us, that any one who was at the very summit of earthly felicity should have broken through such fond ties of conjugal and maternal love as those by which Adelicia was surrounded, to bury herself in cloistered seclusion, there is indubitable evidence that such was the fact.

Sanderus, in his Account of the Abbeys and Churches of Brabant, relates that "Fulgentius, the abbot of Affligham, visited queen Adelicia at the court of her royal husband, Henry I.; where he was received with especial honours." The same author expressly states, that Adelicia died in the convent of Affligham, and was interred there on the 9th of the calends of April. He does not give the date of the year. From the mortuary of the abbey, he quotes the following Latin record of the death of this queen;[4]

"Aleidem genuit cum barba dux Godefredus,
Que fuit Anglorum regina piissima morum."

The annals of Margan date this event in the year 1151.

There is a charter in Affligham, granted by Henry of Louvaine, on condition that prayers may be said, for the welfare of his brother Godfrey, the reigning duke, his sister Aleyda the queen, and Ida, the countess of Cleves, and their parents.[5]

Adelicia must have been about forty-eight years old at the time of her death. She had been married eleven years, or thereabouts, to William de Albini, Lord of Buckenham. At his paternal domain of New Buckenham in Norfolk, a foundation was granted by William de Albini of the Strong Arm, enjoining that prayers might be said for the departed spirit of his *eximia regina*. He survived her long enough to be the happy means of composing, by an amicable treaty, the death-strife which had convulsed England for fifteen years, in consequence of the bloody succession war between Stephen and the empress Matilda.[6]

This great and good man is buried in Wymondham Abbey, near the tomb of his father, the Pincerna of England and Normandy.

By her marriage with Albini, Adelicia became the mother of seven surviving children. William earl of Arundel, who succeeded to the estates and honours; Reyner; Henry; Godfrey; Alice, married to the

[1] Butken's trophies du Brabant.   [2] Ibid.
[3] Sanderus's Abbeys and Churches in Brabant.   [4] Ibid.
[5] Howard Memorials.   [6] This will be detailed in the succeeding biography.

count d'Eu; Olivia; Agatha. The two latter were buried at Boxgrove, near Arundel.

Though Adelicia had so many children by her second marriage, her tender affection for her father's family caused her to send for her younger brother, Joceline of Louvaine, to share in her prosperity and happiness; and the munificent earl, her husband, to enable this landless prince to marry advantageously, gave him the fair domain of Petworth, on his wedding Agnes, the heiress of the Percies: " since which," says Camden, " the posterity of that Joceline, who took the name of Percy, have ever possessed it—a family certainly very ancient and noble, the male representatives of Charlemagne, more direct than the dukes of Guise, who pride themselves on that account. Joceline, in a donation of his which I have seen, uses this title: ' Joceline of Louvaine, brother to queen Adelicia, Castellaine of Arundel.' "

Two ducal peers of England are now the representatives of the imperial Carlovingian line—namely, the duke of Norfolk, the heir of queen Adelicia; and the duke of Northumberland, the lineal descendant of her brother Joceline of Louvaine.

The two most unfortunate of all the queens of England, Anna Boleyn and Katharine Howard, were the lineal descendants of Adelicia, by her second marriage with William de Albini.

MATILDA OF BOULOGNE,

QUEEN OF STEPHEN.

Matilda's descent from Saxon kings—Her mother a Saxon princess—Her father
—Matilda espoused to Stephen of Blois—Residence at Tower-Royal—Matil-
da's popularity in London—Stephen seizes the throne—Birth of prince Eustace
—Coronation of Matilda—Queen left regent—Disasters—Queen besieges Dover
Castle—Mediates peace with her uncle—Empress Matilda lands in England
—Henry of Blois—Civil war—Queen goes to France—Marriage of her young
heir—Raises an army—Stephen captured—Arrogance of empress—Queen's
grief—Exertions in Stephen's cause—Queen Matilda writes to bishop Blois—
Her supplication for Stephen's liberty—Obduracy of empress—Queen appeals
to arms—Empress in Winchester—Her seal—Insults Londoners—Driven from
London—Successes of the queen—Takes Winchester—Escape of empress—
Earl of Gloucester taken—Exchanged for Stephen—Illness of king Stephen—
Empress escapes from Oxford—Her son—Decline of empress's cause—Queen
Matilda founds St. Katherine by the Tower—Death of the queen—Burial—
Tomb—Epitaph—Children—Eustace—Death of king Stephen—Burial by his
queen—Exhumation of their bodies.

MATILDA of Boulogne, the last of our Anglo-Norman queens, was a
princess of the ancient royal line of English monarchs. Her mother,
Mary of Scotland, was the second daughter of Malcolm Canmore and
Margaret Atheling, and sister to Matilda the Good, the first queen of
Henry Beauclerc. Mary of Scotland was educated with her elder sister,
in the royal monasteries of Wilton and Rumsey, under the stern tutelage
of their aunt Christina; and was doubtless, like the princess Matilda,
compelled to assume the habit of a votaress. Whether the youthful
Mary testified the same lively antipathy to the consecrated black veil,
that was exhibited by her elder sister, no gossiping monastic chronicler
has recorded; but she certainly forsook the cloister, for the court of
England, on Matilda's auspicious nuptials with Henry I., and exchanged
the badge of celibacy for the nuptial ring soon afterwards, when her
royal brother-in-law gave her in marriage to Eustace, count of Boulogne.

The father of this nobleman was brother-in-law to Edward the Confessor, having married Goda, the widowed countess of Mantes, sister to
that monarch; both himself and his son Eustace had been powerful
supporters of the Saxon cause. The enterprising spirit of the counts
of Boulogne, and the contiguity of their dominions to the English
shores, had rendered them troublesome neighbours to William the Conqueror and his sons, till the chivalric spirit of crusading attracted their
energies to a different channel, and converted these pirates of the narrow
seas into heroes of the cross, and liberators of the holy city.

Godfrey of Boulogne, the hero of Tasso's *Gierusaleme Liberata,* and
his brother Baldwin, who successively wore the crown of Jerusalem,

were the uncles of Matilda, Stephen's queen. Her father, Eustace count of Boulogne, was also a distinguished crusader. He must have been a mature husband for Mary of Scotland, since he was the companion in arms of Robert of Normandy, and her uncle Edgar Atheling. Matilda, or, as she is sometimes called for brevity, Maud of Boulogne, was the sole offspring of this marriage, and the heiress of this illustrious house.

There is every reason to believe Matilda was educated in the abbey of Bermondsey, to which the countess of Boulogne, her mother, was a munificent benefactress. The countess died in this abbey while on a visit to England, in the year 1115, and was buried there. We gather from the Latin verses on her tomb, that she was a lady of very noble qualities, and that her death was very painful and unexpected.[1]

Young as Matilda was, she was certainly espoused to Stephen de Blois before her mother's decease; for this plain reason, that the charter by which the countess of Boulogne, in the year 1114, grants to the Clugniac monks of Bermondsey her manor of Kynewardstone, is, in the year she died, confirmed by Eustace her husband, and Stephen her son-in-law.[2] Stephen, the third son of a vassal peer of France, obtained this great match through the favour of his royal uncle, Henry I. He inherited from the royal Adela, his mother, the splendid talents, fine person, and enterprising spirit of the mighty Norman line of sovereigns. A very tender friendship had subsisted between Adela, countess of Blois, and her brother, Henry Beauclerc, who at different periods of his life had been under important obligations to her; and when Adela sent her landless boy to seek his fortunes at the court of England, Henry returned the friendly offices which he had received from this faithful sister, by lavishing wealth and honour on her son.

Stephen received the spurs of knighthood from his uncle king Henry, previous to the battle of Tinchebraye, where he took the count of Mortagne prisoner, and received the investiture of his lands. He was farther rewarded by his royal kinsman with the hand of Matilda, the heiress of Boulogne.[3]

"When Stephen was but an earl," says William of Malmsbury, "he gained the affections of the people, to a degree that can scarcely be imagined, by the affability of his manners, and the wit and pleasantry of his conversation, condescending to chat and joke with persons in the humblest stations, as well as with the nobles, who delighted in his company, and attached themselves to his cause from personal regard."[4]

Stephen was count of Boulogne in Matilda's right, when, as count of Mortagne, he swore fealty in 1126 to the empress Matilda, as heiress to the Norman dominions of Henry I.

The London residence of Stephen and Matilda was Tower-Royal, a palace built by king Henry, and presented by him to his favoured nephew, on the occasion of his wedding the niece of his queen Matilda Atheling. The spot to which this regal-sounding name is still appended, is a close lane between Cheapside and Watling Street. Tower-Royal was a fortress

---

[1] Hist. Bermondsey Abbey.   [2] Annales Abbatæ Bermondsey.
[3] Ordericus Vitalis.   [4] W. Malmsbury. Ordericus Vitalis

of prodigious strength; for more than once, when the Tower of London itself fell into the hands of the rebels, this embattled palace of Stephen remained in security.[1]

It is a remarkable fact, that Stephen had embarked on board the *Blanche Nef*, with his royal cousin, William the Atheling, and the rest of her fated crew; but with two knights of his train, and a few others who prudently followed his example, he left the vessel with the remark that "she was too much crowded with foolish, headstrong young people."[2]

After the death of prince William, Stephen's influence with his royal uncle became unbounded, and he was his constant companion in all his voyages to Normandy.

There are evidences of conjugal infidelity on the part of this gay and gallant young prince, about this period, proving that Matilda's cup of happiness was not without some alloy of bitterness. How far her peace was affected by the scandalous reports of the passion which her haughty cousin the empress Matilda, the acknowledged heiress of England and Normandy, was said to cherish for her aspiring husband, we cannot presume to say; but there was an angel-like spirit in this princess, which supported her under every trial, and rendered her a beautiful example to every royal female in the married state.

Two children, a son and a daughter, were born to the young earl and countess of Boulogne, during king Henry's reign. The boy was named Baldwin, after Matilda's uncle, the king of Jerusalem;—a Saxon name withal, and therefore likely to sound pleasantly to the ears of the English, who, no doubt, looked with complacency on the infant heir of Boulogne, as the son of a princess of the royal Atheling blood, born among them, and educated by his amiable mother to venerate their ancient laws, and to speak their language. Prince Baldwin, however, died in early childhood, and was interred in the priory of the Holy Trinity, without Aldgate, founded by his royal aunt, Matilda of Scotland. The second child of Stephen and Matilda, a daughter named Maud, born also in the reign of Henry I., died young, and was buried in the same church. Some historians aver that Maud survived long enough to be espoused to the earl of Milan.

So dear was the memory of these, her buried hopes, to the heart of Matilda, that after she became queen of England, and her loss was supplied by the birth of another son and daughter, she continued to lament for them; and the Church and Hospital of St. Katherine by the Tower were founded and endowed by her, that prayers might be perpetually said by the pious sisterhood for the repose of the souls of her first-born children.

In the latter days of king Henry, while Stephen was engaged in stealing the hearts of the men of England, after the fashion of Absalom, the mild virtues of his amiable consort recalled to their remembrance her royal aunt and namesake, Henry's first queen, and inspired them with a trembling hope of seeing her place filled eventually by a princess so

---

[1] Stowe's Survey. Pennant's London.   [2] Ordericus Vitalis.

much more resembling her than the haughty wife of Geoffrey of Anjou. The Norman woman looked upon her mother's people with scorn, and from her they had nothing to expect but the iron yoke which her grandfather, the Conqueror, had laid upon their necks, with, perhaps, an aggravation of their miseries. But Stephen, the husband of her gentle cousin, the English-hearted Matilda, had whispered in their ears of the confirmation of the great charter of their liberties, which Henry of Normandy had granted when he became the husband of the descendant of their ancient kings, and broken, when her influence was destroyed by death and a foreign marriage.

King Henry's daughter, the empress Matilda,[1] was the wife of a foreign prince residing on the Continent. Stephen and his amiable princess were living in London, and daily endearing themselves to the people, by the most popular and affable behaviour. The public mind was certainly predisposed in favour of Stephen's designs, when the sudden death of king Henry in Normandy left the right of succession for the first time to a female heir. Piers of Langtoft thus describes the perplexity of the nation respecting the choice of the sovereign:—

> "On bier lay king Henry,
> On bier beyond the sea;
> And no man might rightly know
> Who his heir suld be."

Stephen, following the example of the deceased monarch's conduct at the time of his brother Rufus's death,[2] left his royal uncle and benefactor's obsequies to the care of Robert earl of Gloucester, and the other peers who were witnesses to his last words; and embarking at Whitesand, a small port in Matilda's dominions, in a light vessel, on a wintry sea, he landed at Dover, in the midst of such a storm of thunder and lightning, that, according to William of Malmsbury, every one imagined the world was coming to an end. As soon as he arrived in London, he convened an assembly of the Anglo-Norman barons before whom his confederate and friend, Hugh Bigod, the steward of king Henry's household, swore on the holy Evangelists, "that the deceased sovereign had disinherited the empress Matilda on his death-bed, and adopted his most dear nephew Stephen for his heir."[3]

On this bold affirmation, the Archbishop of Canterbury absolved the peers of the oaths of fealty they had twice sworn to the daughter of their late sovereign—and declared "that those oaths were null and void, and contrary, moreover, to the laws and customs of the English, who had never permitted a woman to reign over them."

This was a futile argument, as no female had ever stood in that important position, with regard to the succession to the crown of England, in which the empress Matilda was now placed; therefore no precedent had occurred for the establishment of a salique law in England.

Stephen was crowned on the 26th of December, his name-day, the feast of St. Stephen.[4] He swore to establish the righteous laws of

---

[1] The Biography of the empress Matilda is continued through this life.
[2] Malmsbury. [3] Malmsbury. Rapin. [4] Sir Harris Nicol. Chronolog of History.

Edward the confessor, for the general happiness of all classes of his subjects.[1]   The English regarded Stephen's union with a princess of their
race as the best pledge of the sincerity of his professions in regard to the
amelioration of their condition.   These hopes were, of course, increased
by the birth of prince Eustace, whom Matilda brought into the world
very soon after her husband's accession to the throne of England.   It
was, perhaps, this auspicious event that prevented Matilda from being
associated in the coronation of her lord on St. Stephen's day, in Westminster Abbey.   Her own coronation, according to Gervase, took place
March 22d, 1136, being Easter Sunday, not quite three months afterwards. Stephen was better enabled to support the expenses of a splendid
ceremonial in honour of his beloved queen, having, immediately after
his own hasty inauguration, posted to Winchester and made himself
master of the treasury of his deceased uncle king Henry; which contained, says Malmsbury, " one hundred thousand pounds, besides stores
of plate and jewels."

The empress Matilda was in Anjou at the time of her father's sudden
demise.   She was entirely occupied by the grievous sickness of her
husband, who was supposed to be on his death-bed.[2] After the convales-
cence of her lord, as none of her partisans in England made the slightest
movement in her favour, she remained quiescent for a season, well know-
ing that the excessive popularity of a new monarch is seldom of long
continuance in England.   Stephen had begun well by abolishing dane-
gelt, and leaving the game in the woods, forests, and uncultivated wastes,
common to all his subjects; but after awhile he repented of his liberal
policy, and called courts of inquiry to make men give account of the
damage and loss he had sustained in his fallow deer and other wild
game; he likewise enforced the offensive system of the other Norman
monarchs for their preservation.

Next he obtained the enmity of the clergy, by seizing the revenues
of the see of Canterbury; and lastly, to the great alarm and detriment
of the peacefully disposed, he imprudently permitted his nobles to build
or fortify upwards of a thousand of those strongholds of wrong and robbery called castles, which rendered their owners in a great measure
independent of the crown.

Baldwin de Redvers, earl of Devonshire, was the first to give Stephen
a practical proof of his want of foresight in this matter, by telling him,
on some slight cause of offence, " that he was not king of right, and he
would obey him no longer."   Stephen proceeded in person to chastise
him; in the meantime David, king of Scotland, invaded the northern
counties, under pretence of revenging the wrong that had been done to
his niece, the empress Matilda, by Stephen's usurpation and perjury.

Matilda of Boulogne, Stephen's consort, stood in the same degree of
relationship to the king of Scotland, as the empress Matilda, since her
mother, Mary of Scotland, was his sister, no less than Matilda, the queen
of Henry I.

Stephen concluded a hasty peace with the Welsh princes, and advanced

---

[1] Malmsbury. Brompton.   [2] Carruthers' Hist. of Scotland, pp. 327, 328.

to repel the invasion of king David; but when the hostile armies met near Carlisle, he succeeded in adjusting all differences by means of an amicable treaty, perhaps through the intreaties or mediation of his queen.

Easter was kept at Westminster this year, 1137, by Stephen and Matilda, with greater splendour than had ever been seen in the court of Henry Beauclerc, to celebrate the happy termination of the storm that had so lately darkened the political horizon; but the rejoicings of the queen were fearfully interrupted by the alarming illness which suddenly attacked the king, in the midst of the festivities for his safe return from the Welsh and northern expeditions.

This illness, the effect no doubt of the preternatural exertions of both mental and corporeal powers, which Stephen had compelled himself to use, during the recent momentous crisis of his fortunes, was a sort of stupor, or lethargy so nearly resembling death, that it was reported in Normandy that he had breathed his last; on which the party of the empress began to take active measures, both on the continent and in England, for the recognition of her rights.[1] The count of Anjou entered Normandy at the head of an army, to assert the claims of his wife and son; which were, however, disputed by Stephen's elder brother, Theobald count of Blois, not in behalf of Stephen, but himself; and the earl of Gloucester openly declared himself in favour of his sister the empress, and delivered the keys of Falaise to her husband, Geoffrey of Anjou.[2]

When Stephen recovered from his death-like sickness, he found everything in confusion,—the attention of his faithful queen, Matilda, having doubtless been absorbed in anxious watchings by his sick-bed, during the protracted period of his strange and alarming malady. She was now left to take care of his interests in England as best she might; for Stephen, rousing himself from the pause of exhausted nature, hastened to the continent with his infant heir Eustace, to whom queen Matilda had resigned the earldom of Boulogne, her own fair inheritance. Stephen, by the strong eloquence of an immense bribe, prevailed on Louis VII. of France, as suzerain of Normandy, to invest the unconscious babe with the duchy, and to receive his liege homage for the same.[3]

Meantime some portentous events occurred during Matilda's government. Sudden and mysterious conflagrations then, as now, indicated the sullen discontent of the very lower order of the English people. On the 3d of June, 1137, Rochester cathedral was destroyed by fire; the following day, the whole city of York, with its cathedral and thirty churches, was burnt to the ground; soon after, the city of Bath shared the same fate. Then conspiracies began to be formed in favour of the empress Matilda, in various parts of England; and lastly, her uncle, David king of Scotland, once more entered Northumberland, with banners displayed, in support of his supplanted kinswoman's superior title to the crown.[4] Queen Matilda, with courage and energy suited to this

---

[1] Hoveden. Brompton. Ordericus Vitalis.   [2] M. Paris, &c. &c.
[3] Ordericus Vitalis. Henry of Huntingdon. Brompton. M. Paris. Rapin. Speed.
[4] Brompton. Rapin. Ordericus Vitalis.

alarming crisis, went in person, and besieged the insurgents, who had seized Dover castle; and she sent orders to the men of Boulogne, her loyal subjects, to attack the rebels by sea.

The Boulonnois obeyed the commands of their beloved princess with alacrity, and to such good purpose, by covering the Channel with their light-armed vessels, that the besieged, not being able to receive the slightest succour by sea, were forced to submit to the queen.[1] At this juncture Stephen arrived, and succeeded in chastising the leaders of the revolt, and drove the Scottish king over his own border. Nevertheless the empress Matilda's party, in the year 1138, began to assume a formidable aspect. Every day brought tidings to the court of Stephen of some fresh revolt. William of Malmsbury relates, that when Stephen was informed of these desertions, he passionately exclaimed, " Why did they make me king, if they forsake me thus? By the birth of God,[2] I will never be called an abdicated king !"

The invasion of queen Matilda's uncle, David of Scotland, for the third time increased the distraction of her royal husband's affairs, especially as Stephen was too much occupied with the internal troubles of his kingdom, to be able to proceed, in person, against him. David, and his army, were, however, defeated with immense slaughter, by the warlike Thurstan, archbishop of York, at Cuton Moor. The particulars of this engagement, called the battle of the Standard, where the church militant performed such notable service for the crown, belong to general history, and are besides too well known to require repetition in the biography of Stephen's queen.

Matilda[3] was mainly instrumental in negotiating the peace which was concluded this year between her uncle and her lord. Prince Henry, the heir of Scotland, having, at the same time, renewed his homage to Stephen for the earldom of Huntingdon, was invited by the king to his court. The attention with which the young prince was treated by the king and queen was viewed with invidious eyes by their ill-mannered courtiers; and Ranulph, earl of Chester, took such great offence at the royal stranger being seated above him at dinner, that he made it an excuse for joining the revolted barons, and persuaded a knot of equally uncivilized nobles to follow his example on the same pretence.[4]

The empress Matilda, taking advantage of the fierce contention between Stephen and the hierarchy of England, made her tardy appearance, in pursuance of her claims to the crown, in the autumn of 1140. Like her uncle, Robert the Unready, the empress allowed the critical moment to slip, when, by prompt and energetic measures, she might have gained the prize for which she contended. But she did not arrive till Stephen had made himself master of the castles, and, what was of more importance to him, the great wealth of his three refractory prelates, the bishops of Salisbury, Ely, and Lincoln.

---

[1] Ordericus Vitalis.   [2] This was Stephen's usual oath.   Malmsbury.
[3] " Through the mediation of Matilda, the wife of Stephen, and niece of David, a peace was concluded at Durham between these two kings, equitable in itself and useful to both parties."—Carruthers' Hist. of Scotland, vol. i. p. 339.
[4] Speed.

When the empress was shut up within the walls of Arundel castle, Stephen might, by one bold stroke, have made her his prisoner; but he was prevailed upon to respect the ties of consanguinity, and the high rank of the widow, and of the daughter of his benefactor king Henry. It is possible, too, that recollections of a tenderer nature, with regard to his cousin the empress, might deter him from imperilling her person, by pushing the siege. According to some of the chroniclers, the empress sent, with queen Adelicia's request that she might be permitted to retire to Bristol, a guileful letter or message to Stephen,[1] which induced him to promise, on his word of honour, that he would grant her safe conduct to that city. Though the empress knew that Stephen had violated the most solemn oaths which he had taken in regard to her succession to the crown, she relied upon his honour, and put herself under his protection, and was safely conducted to the castle of Bristol. King Stephen gave to his brother, Henry of Blois, bishop of Winchester, and to Walleran, earl of Mellent, the charge of conducting the empress to Bristol castle. This bright trait of chivalry contrasts beautifully with the selfishness and perfidy too prevalent at the era.

It was during this journey, in all probability, that Henry de Blois arranged his plans with the empress Matilda, for making her mistress of the royal city of Winchester, which was entirely under his influence.

While the earl of Gloucester, on behalf of his sister the empress, was contesting with king Stephen the realm of England at the sword's point, queen Matilda proceeded to France, with her son Eustace, to endeavour to strengthen her husband's cause by the aid of her foreign connexions; and, while at the court of France, successfully exerted her diplomatic powers in negotiating a marriage between the princess Constance, sister of Louis VII., and prince Eustace, then about four years old. The queen presided at this infant marriage, which was celebrated with great splendour.

Instead of receiving a dowry with a princess, queen Matilda paid a large sum to purchase her son the bride; Louis VII. in return solemnly invested his young brother-in-law with the duchy of Normandy, and lent his powerful aid to maintain him there as the nominal sovereign, under the direction of the queen his mother. This alliance, which took place in the year 1140,[2] greatly raised the hopes of Stephen's party; but the bands of foreign mercenaries, which his queen Matilda sent over from Boulogne and the ports of Normandy to his succour, had an injurious effect on his cause, and were beheld with jealous alarm by the people of the land; " whose miseries were in no slight degree aggravated," says the chronicler Gervase, " by the arrival of these hunger-starved wolves, who completed the destruction of the land's felicity."

It was during the absence of queen Matilda and her son, prince Eustace, that the battle, so disastrous to her husband's cause, was fought, beneath the walls of Lincoln, on Candlemas-day, 1141. Stephen had shut up a great many of the empress Matilda's partisans and their families in the city of Lincoln, which he had been for some time besieging.

---

[1] Gervase.   Henry of Huntingdon.   [2] Florence of Worcester.   Tyrrell.
13*

The earl of Gloucester's youngest daughter, lately married to her cousin Ranulph, earl of Chester, was among the besieged; and so determined were the two earls, her father and her husband, for her deliverance, that they encouraged their followers to swim, or ford, the deep cold waters of the river Trent,[1] behind which Stephen and his army were encamped, and fiercely attacked him in their dripping garments; and all for the relief of the fair ladies who were trembling within the walls of Lincoln, and beginning to suffer from lack of provisions. These were the days of chivalry, be it remembered.[2] Speed gives us a descriptive catalogue of some of the leading characters among our valiant king Stephen's knights *sans peur*, which, if space were allowed us, we would abstract from the animated harangue with which the earl of Gloucester endeavoured to warm his shivering followers into a virtuous blaze of indignation, after they had emerged from their cold bath.[3]

His satirical eloquence was received by the partisans of the empress with a tremendous shout of applause; and Stephen, not to be behind-hand with his foes in bandying personal abuse as a prelude to the fight, as his own powers of articulation happened to be defective, deputed one Baldwin Fitz-Gilbert, a knight who was blessed with a Stentorian voice, to thunder forth his recrimination on the earl of Gloucester and his host, in the ears of both armies. Fitz-Gilbert, in his speech, laid scornful stress on the illegitimacy of the empress's champion, whom he designated, " Robert, the base-born general."[4]

The battle, for which both parties had prepared themselves with such a sharp encounter of keen words, was, to use the expression of contemporary chroniclers, " a very sore one;" but it seems as if Stephen had fought better than his followers that day. "A very strange sight it was," says Matthew Paris, " there to behold king Stephen, left almost alone in the field, yet no man daring to approach him, while, grinding his teeth and foaming like a furious wild boar, he drove back with his battle-axe the assailing squadrons, slaying the foremost of them, to the eternal renown of his courage. If but a hundred like himself had been with him, a whole army had never been able to capture his person; yet, single-handed as he was, he held out till first his battle-axe brake, and afterwards his sword shivered in his grasp, with the force of his own resistless blows; though he was borne backward to his knees by a great stone, which by some ignoble person was flung at him. A stout knight, William of Kames, then seized him by the helmet, and holding the point of his sword to his throat, called upon him to surrender."[5]

Even in that extremity Stephen refused to give up the fragment of his sword to any one but the earl of Gloucester, his valiant kinsman, who, coming up, bade his infuriated troops refrain from further violence, and conducted his royal captive to the empress Matilda, at Gloucester. The earl of Gloucester, it is said, treated Stephen with some degree of courtesy; but the empress Matilda, whose hatred appears to have emanated

[1] Malmsbury. Rapin. Speed.		[2] Polydore Vergil. Speed. Malmsbury.
[3] Roger Hoveden. H. Huntingdon. Polychronicon.
[4] Roger Hoveden. H. Huntingdon. Speed.		[5] H. Huntingdon. Speed. Rapin.

from a deeper root of bitterness than mere rivalry of power, loaded him with indignities, and ordered him into the most rigorous confinement, in Bristol castle. According to general historians, she caused him to be heavily ironed, and used the royal captive as ignominiously as if he had been the lowest felon; but William of Malmsbury says, "this was not till after Stephen had attempted to make his escape, or it was reported that he had been seen several times beyond the bounds prescribed for air and exercise."

The empress Matilda made her public and triumphant entry into the city of Winchester, February 7, where she was received with great state by Stephen's equally haughty brother, Henry de Blois, bishop of Winchester, and cardinal legate. He appeared at the head of all the clergy and monks of the diocese; and even the nuns of Winchester[1] (a thing before unheard of) walked unveiled in the procession, to receive and welcome the rightful heiress of the realm, the daughter of the great and learned Henry Fitz-Conqueror, and of Matilda, the descendant of the Atheling. The English had also the satisfaction of seeing the male representative of their ancient monarchs on that occasion within the walls of Winchester; for David of Scotland, the son of Margaret of Atheling, was present, to do honour to his niece,—the victorious rival of Stephen's crown. Henry de Blois resigned the regal ornaments, and the paltry residue of her father's treasure, into the hands of the empress. The next day he received her with great pomp in his cathedral church, where he excommunicated all the adherents of his unfortunate brother, and promised absolution to all who should abandon his cause and join the empress.[2]

In this melancholy position did queen Matilda find her husband's cause, when she returned from her successful negotiation, of the marriage between the French king's sister, and her son the young count of Boulogne, whom she had left, for the present, established as duke of Normandy. The peers and clergy had alike abandoned the luckless[3] Stephen in his adversity; and the archbishop of Canterbury, being a man of tender conscience, had actually visited Stephen in prison, to request his permission to transfer his oath of allegiance to his victorious rival, the empress Matilda.

In this predicament, the faithful consort of the fallen monarch applied herself to the citizens of London, with whom she had ever maintained a great share of popularity. They knew her virtues, for she had lived among them; and her tender affection for her royal spouse in his adversity, was well pleasing to those who had witnessed the domestic happiness of the princely pair, while they lived in Tower-Royal, as count and countess of Boulogne; and the remembrance of Stephen's free and pleasant conduct, and affable association with all sorts and conditions of men, before he wore the thorny diadem of a doubtful title to the sovereignty of England, disposed the magistracy of London to render every

---

[1] Rudborne's Hist. of Winchester.
[2] Gesta Stephani. Gervase. Malmsbury. Rapin.
[3] Malmsbury. Huntingdon, Ger. Dor.

assistance in their power to their unfortunate king.[1] So powerfully, indeed, had the personal influence of queen Matilda operated in that quarter, that when the magistrates of London were summoned to send their deputies to a synod at Winchester, held by Henry de Blois, which had predetermined the election of the empress Matilda to the throne, they instructed them to demand the liberation of the king in the name of the barons and citizens of London, as a preliminary to entering into any discussion with the partisans of his enemy. Henry de Blois replied, " that it did not become the Londoners to side with the adherents of Stephen, whose object was to embroil the kingdom in fresh troubles."[2]

Queen Matilda, finding that the trusty citizens of London were baffled by the priestly subtlety of her husband's brother, Henry de Blois, took the decided, but at that time unprecedented, step, of writing, in her own name, an eloquent letter to the synod, earnestly entreating those in whose hands the government of England was vested, to restore the king, her husband, to liberty.

This letter the queen's faithful chaplain, Christian, delivered, in full synod, to the legate Henry de Blois. The prelate, after he had perused the touching appeal of his royal sister-in-law, refused to communicate its purport to the assembly; on which Christian boldly took the queen's letter out of his hand, and read it aloud to the astonished conclave, courageously disregarding the anger and opposition of the legate, who was at that time virtually the sovereign of the realm.[2] Henry de Blois effectually prevented any good effect resulting from the persuasive address of the high-minded consort of his unfortunate brother, by dissolving the synod, and declaring " that the empress Matilda was lawfully elected as the domina or sovereign lady of England." The following are the words of the formula in which the declaration was delivered:

" Having first, as is fit, invoked the aid of Almighty God, we elect as lady of England and Normandy the daughter of the glorious, the rich, the good, the peaceful king Henry, and to her we promise fealty and support."[3]

No word is here of the good old laws — the laws of Alfred and St. Edward, or of the great charter which Henry I. agreed to observe. The empress was the leader of the Norman party, and the head of Norman feudality, which, in many instances, was incompatible with the Saxon constitution.

Arrogant and disdainful as her imperial education had rendered her, she bore those new honours with anything but meekness; she refused to listen to the counsel of her friends, and treated those of her adversaries whom misfortune drove to seek her clemency with insolence and cruelty, stripping them of their possessions, and rendering them perfectly desperate. The friends who had contributed to her elevation frequently met with a harsh refusal when they asked favours; " and," says an old historian, " when they bowed themselves down before her, she did not rise in return."[5]

[1] Malmsbury. Rapin.   [2] Ibid.   [3] Ibid.   [4] Gesta Stephani Regis.
[5] Gesta Stephani Regis. Thierry.

Meantime the sorrowful queen Matilda was unremitting in her exertions for the liberation of her unfortunate lord, who was at this time heavily ironed, and ignominiously treated, by order of the empress.[1] Not only England, but Normandy, was now lost to the captive monarch her husband, and their young heir, prince Eustace; for Geoffrey of Anjou, as soon as he received intelligence of the decisive battle of Lincoln, persuaded the Norman baronage to withdraw their allegiance from their recently invested duke, and to transfer it to his wife the empress, and her son Henry, certainly the rightful heirs of William the Conqueror. The loss of regal state and sovereign power was, however, regarded by the queen of Stephen as a matter of little moment. In the season of adversity, it was not the king, but the man, the husband of her youth, and the father of her children, to whom the tender-hearted Matilda of Boulogne clung, with a devotion not often to be met with in the personal history of royalty. It was for his sake that she condescended to humble herself, by addressing the most lowly entreaties to her haughty cousin, the empress Matilda — to her, who, if the report of some contemporary chroniclers is to be credited, had betrayed her husband into a breach of his marriage vow. The insulting scorn with which the empress rejected every petition which the wedded wife of Stephen presented to her, in behalf of her fallen foe, looks like the vindictive spirit of a jealous woman; especially, when we reflect, that not only the virtues of Matilda of Boulogne, but the closeness of her consanguinity to herself, required her to be treated with some degree of consideration and respect.

There appears even to be a covert reference to the former position in which these princesses had stood, as rivals in Stephen's love, by the proposal made by his fond queen. She proposed, if his life were but spared, to relinquish his society, and that he should not only for ever forego all claims upon the crown and succession of England and Normandy, but, taking upon himself the vows and habit of a monk, devote himself to a religious life, either as a pilgrim or a cloistered anchorite,[2] on condition that their son, prince Eustace, might be permitted to enjoy, in her right, the earldom of Boulogne, and his father's earldom of Mortagne, the grant of Henry I. This petition was rejected by the victorious empress, with no less contempt than all the others which Stephen's queen had ventured to prefer, although her suit in this instance was backed by the powerful mediation of Henry de Blois. This prelate, who appears to have thought more of peace than of brotherhood, was not only desirous of settling public order on such easy terms for his new sovereign, but willing to secure to his nephew the natural inheritance of his parents, of which the empress's party had obtained possession. So blind, however, was this obdurate princess, in pursuing the headlong impulse of her vindictive nature, that nothing could induce her to perceive how much it was her interest to grant the prayer of her unhappy cousin; and she repulsed the suit of Henry de Blois so rudely, that, when next summoned to her presence, he refused to come. Queen

---

[1] Malmsbury. Speed.   [2] Ypodigma Neustria. Speed. Rapin.

Matilda improved this difference between her haughty rival and her brother-in-law, to her own advantage; and, having obtained a private interview with him, she prevailed on him, by the eloquence of her tears and entreaties, to absolve all her husband's party, whom, as pope's legate, he had a few days before excommunicated, and to enter into a negotiation with her for the deliverance of his brother.[1]

Nor did the queen Matilda rest here. In the name of her son, prince Eustace, aided by William of Ypres, Stephen's able but unpopular minister of state, she raised the standard of her captive lord, in Kent and Surrey, where a strong party was presently organized in his favour; and finding that there was nothing to be hoped for from her obdurate kinswoman, the empress Matilda, on any other terms but the unreasonable one of giving up her own fair inheritance, she, like a true daughter of the heroic house of Boulogne, and the niece of the illustrious Godfrey and Baldwin, prepared herself for a struggle, with such courageous energy of mind and promptitude of action, that many a recreant baron was shamed into quitting the inglorious shelter of his castle, and leading forth his vassals to strengthen the muster of the royal heroine.

In the pages of superficially written histories, much is said of the prowess and military skill displayed by prince Eustace at this period; but Eustace was scarcely seven years old, at the time when these efforts were made for the deliverance of his royal sire. It is, therefore, plain to those who reflect on the evidence of dates, that it was the high-minded and prudent queen, his mother, who avoided all Amazonian display, by acting under the name of her son.

Her feminine virtues, endearing qualities, and conjugal devotion, had already created the most powerful interest in her favour; while reports of the pride and hardness of heart of her stern relative and namesake, the new domina, began to be industriously circulated through the land, by the offended legate, Henry de Blois.[2]

William of Malmsbury mentions expressly, that the empress Matilda never bore or received the title of regina, or queen of England, but that of domina, or lady of England. On her broad seal, which she caused to be made for her royal use at Winchester, she entitles herself, " Romanorum Regina Macthildis;" and in a charter granted by her, just after the death of her brother and champion, Robert earl of Gloucester, she styles herself " Regina Romanorum, et Domina Anglorum."

The seal to which we have just alluded bears the figure of the grand-daughter of the Norman conqueror, crowned and seated on the King's Bench, with a sceptre in her right hand, but bearing neither orb nor dove, the symbols of sovereign power and mercy. She was not an anointed queen, neither had the crown-royal ever been placed on her brow.[3] The garland of fleur de lis, by which the folds of her matronly

[1] Speed. Tyrrell.   [2] Tyrrell.
[3] We are indebted to our kind friend, Mr. Howard, of Corby Castle, for a drawing of the impression of another seal pertaining to Matilda the empress, delineated by Miss Mary Aglionby from a deed belonging to her family. The headdress of the empress is simpler than that above-mentioned, the veil being confined by a mere twisted fillet, such as we see beneath helmets and crests in

wimple are confined, is of a simpler form than the royal diadems of the Anglo-Norman sovereigns, as shown on the broad seals of William Rufus, Henry I., and Stephen. Probably an alteration would have been made, if the coronation of Matilda, as sovereign of England, had ever taken place. But the consent of the city of London was an indispensable preliminary to her inauguration; and to London she proceeded in person, to obtain this important recognition. Though the majority of the city authorities were disposed to favour the cause of Stephen, for the sake of his popular consort, Matilda of Boulogne, the Saxon citizens, when they heard, "that the daughter of Molde, their good queen," claimed their homage, looked with reverence on her elder claim, and threw open their gates to receive her with every manifestation of affection.

The first sentence addressed to them by this haughty claimant of the crown of St. Edward, was the demand of an enormous subsidy.

The citizens of London replied, by inquiring after the great charter granted by her father.

" Ye are very impudent to mention privileges and charters to me, when ye have just been supporting my enemies," was the gracious rejoinder.[1]

Her prudent and gallant brother, Robert of Gloucester, who stood by her side, immediately perceiving that the citizens of London stood aghast, at this intimation, of their new sovereign's intention, to treat them as a conquered people, endeavoured to divert the public rage, by a most discreet speech, beginning with this complimentary address :—

" Ye citizens of London, who of olden time were called barons——"

Although the valiant Robert was a most complete and graceful orator, we have no space for his speeches, so carefully preserved by the contemporary historians, nor could all his conciliatory eloquence draw the attention of the Londoners from the harshness of their new liege lady.

Her uncle, king David, was present at this scene, and earnestly persuaded the empress to adopt a more popular line of conduct, but in vain.[2]

The Londoners craved leave to retire to their hall of common council, in order to provide the subsidy.

The empress-domina was waiting in full security at the new palace at Westminster, built by her uncle William, the Red King, till the deputies from the city of London should approach, to offer on their knees the bags of gold she had demanded; when suddenly the bells of London rang out an alarum, and from every house in London and its vicinity issued a man with a sword in his hand. "Just," says the old chronicler, "like bees swarming round the hive when it is attacked." A formidable army soon gathered in the streets, ready to defend themselves from de-

---

heraldic blazonry. The inscription, in Roman letters, is S·MATHIDIS·DEI·GRATIA·ROMANORUM·REGINA. The manner of sitting, and the arrangement of the drapery on the knees, resemble the portrait of the mother of the empress described in her memoir.

[1] J. P. Andrews.   [2] Carruthers' Hist. of Scotland, p. 341.

mands of subsidies and all other grievances. The empress-domina, with her Norman and Angevin chevaliers, by no means liked the idea of charging this possé in their own crooked and narrow streets, where chivalric evolutions could avail but little. They therefore mounted their steeds, and fled. Scarcely had they cleared the suburbs, when a troop of citizens broke open the doors of the palace, and finding no one there, plundered the effects left behind.

The empress, with her barons and chevaliers, galloped on the road to Oxford; and when they had arrived there, her train had become so small with numerous desertions, that, with the exception of Robert of Gloucester, she entered it alone.

Her uncle, king David, who left London with her, would have lost either his life or liberty, but for the fidelity of his godson, David Oliphaunt. Thoroughly disgusted with the obstinacy and haughtiness of his niece, he made the best of his way to his own borders. It is said that he held her ever after in low estimation.

A strong reaction of popular feeling in favour of Stephen, or rather of Stephen's queen, followed this event. The counties of Kent and Surrey were already her own, and prepared to support her by force of arms; and the citizens of London joyfully received her within their walls once more. Henry de Blois had been induced, more than once, to meet his royal sister-in-law secretly, at Guildford. Thither she brought the young prince, her son,[1] to assist her in moving his powerful uncle to lend his aid, in replacing her husband on the throne. Henry de Blois, touched by the tears and entreaties of these interesting supplicants, and burning with rage at the insolent treatment he had received from the imperial virago, whom Camden quaintly styles "a *niggish* old wife," solemnly promised the queen to forsake the cause of her rival.

Immediately on his return to Winchester, the prelate fortified his castle, and having prepared all things for declaring himself in favour of his brother, he sent messengers to the queen, begging her to put herself at the head of the Kentishmen and Londoners, and march with her son, prince Eustace, to Winchester.[2]

The empress Matilda, and the earl of Gloucester, having some intelligence of Henry de Blois' proceedings, advanced from Oxford, accompanied by David, king of Scotland, at the head of an army, to overawe him. When they approached the walls of Winchester, the empress sent a herald to the legate, requesting a conference, as she had something of importance to communicate; but to this requisition Henry de Blois only replied, "*Parabo me*,"[3] that is, " I will prepare myself;" and finding that the Norman party in Winchester were at present too strong for him, he left the city, and retired to his strong castle in the suburbs; causing, at the same time, so unexpected an attack to be made on the empress, that she had a hard race to gain the shelter of the royal citadel.[4]

Queen Matilda, with her son and sir William Ypres, at the head of the Londoners and the Kentishmen, were soon after at the gates of Winchester; and the empress was now so closely blockaded in her palace,

[1] Tyrrell.   [2] Malmsbury. Gervase.   [3] Malmsbury.   [4] Ibid.

that she had ample cause to repent of her vindictive folly, in driving her gentle cousin to desperate measures, by repulsing the humble boon she had craved with such earnest prayers. For nearly two months the most destructive warfare, of famine, fire, and sword, was carried on in the streets of Winchester; till the empress Matilda, dreading the balls of fire which were nightly thrown from the legate's castle, and which had already destroyed upwards of twenty stately churches and several monasteries, prevailed on her gallant brother to provide for her retreat. This he and her uncle David, king of Scotland, did, by forcing their way through the besiegers at swords' points; but it was at the cost of the noble earl's liberty. While the empress and the king of Scotland, by dint of hard riding, escaped to Lutgershall, the earl of Gloucester arrested the pursuit, by facing about and battling on the way, till almost all his followers were slain, and he was compelled to surrender, after a desperate defence. This skirmish took place on the 14th of September, 1141. The earl of Gloucester was conducted to queen Matilda at Winchester, and she with great joy committed him to the charge of William of Ypres, as a sure hostage for the safety of the king her husband.

The wife of king Stephen obtained the praise and admiration of all parties, by her generous conduct to her illustrious captive; for, instead of loading him with chains, and subjecting him to the same cruel treatment under which her beloved lord was suffering, the confinement of the earl of Gloucester, at Rochester Castle, was alleviated by every indulgence consistent with the safe custody of his person.[1]

The empress and her party, with some difficulty, fled from Lutgershall to Devizes, where she was so closely pursued by the queen's troops, that she only escaped their vigilance by personating a corpse, wrapped in grave-clothes, and being placed in a coffin, which was bound with cords, and borne on the shoulders of some of her trusty partisans[2] to Gloucester, the stronghold of her valiant brother, where she arrived, faint and weary, with long fasting and mortal terror.

Her party was so dispirited by the loss of her approved counsellor and trusty champion, the earl of Gloucester, that she was compelled to make some overtures to the queen, her cousin, for his release; but Matilda would hear of no other terms than the restoration of her captive husband, king Stephen, in exchange for him. This the empress peremptorily refused in the first instance, though she offered a large sum of gold, and twelve captive earls of Stephen's party, as her brother's ransom. Queen Matilda was inflexible in her determination, never to resign her illustrious prisoner, on any other condition than the release of her royal husband. Although she had treated the captive earl most humanely, she now had recourse to threats; and she caused the countess of Gloucester to be informed, that unless the king were speedily exchanged for the earl, she should cause him to be transported to one of her strong castles in Boulogne,[3] there to be kept as rigorously as Stephen had been by the orders of the empress and her party. Not that it

[1] Lingard (from Malmsbury), fourth edition, p. 178.
[2] Brompton. John of Tinemouth. Gervase. Knighton.   [3] Malmsbury.

was in the gentle nature of the queen to have made these harsh reprisals on a gallant gentleman, whom the fortune of war had placed at her disposal; nor did she proceed to the use of threats till she had tried, by eloquent entreaties, to win earl Robert to use his influence with his sister, for the release of her husband. She had even promised that he should be restored to all his possessions and honours, and entrusted with the principal administration of the government, if he would conclude a peace, securing England to Stephen, and Normandy to the empress.[1] Gloucester's high principles, however, would not admit of his entering into any treaty which he considered prejudicial to his sister's interest; and, essential as his presence was to her, the obdurate temper of the empress would never have suffered her to purchase his release, at the price of restoring Stephen to his queen and friends, had it not been for the resolute determination displayed by her sister-in-law, Aimabel, countess of Gloucester. Fortunately, the person of Stephen happened to be in the possession of this lady, who was the castellaine of Bristol during the captivity of Gloucester, her redoubted lord. Her anxiety for his restoration being no less than that of the queen for the liberation of Stephen, these two ladies contrived to arrange a sort of amicable treaty, which ended in the exchange of their illustrious prisoners.[2] This memorable event took place in the month of November. 1141.

Queen Matilda was not long permitted to enjoy the re-union which took place between her and her beloved consort, after she had succeeded in procuring his deliverance from the fetters of her vindictive rival; for nothing could induce the empress to listen to any terms of pacification, and the year 1142 commenced with a mutual renewal of hostilities between the belligerent parties.

While Stephen was pursuing the war at York, with the fury of a newly enfranchised lion, he was seized with a dangerous malady. His affectionate queen hastened to him on the first news of his sickness, which was so sore, that for some hours he was supposed to be dead, and was only restored to life by the indefatigable care of his faithful consort. In all probability his illness was a return of the lethargic complaint with which he had once or twice been afflicted, at the commencement of the internal troubles of his realm.

Through the tender attentions of his queen, Stephen was, however, soon after able to take the field again; which he did with such success, that the empress's party thought it high time to claim the assistance of Geoffrey, count of Anjou, who was now exercising the functions of duke of Normandy. Geoffrey, who had certainly been treated by his imperial spouse, her late father king Henry, and her English partisans, as " a fellow of no reckoning," thought proper to stand on ceremony, and required the formality of an invitation, preferred by the earl of Gloucester in person, before he would either come himself, or part with the precious heir of England and Normandy, prince Henry. The empress, impatient to embrace her first-born son, and to obtain the Angevin and Norman

---

[1] Malmsbury.		[2] Malmsbury. Speed.

succours to strengthen her party, prevailed upon her brother to undertake this mission, to which he was also urged by all the empress's adherents.

Gloucester left her, as he thought, safe in the almost impregnable castle of Oxford, and embarked for Normandy. As soon as he was gone, the memorable siege of Oxford took place, which was pushed by Stephen with the greatest ardour, in the hope of capturing the empress. But when the besieged were reduced to such distress for want of provision, that a surrender was inevitable, the haughty domina, by a shrewd exercise of female ingenuity, eluded the vengeance of her exasperated rival. One night she, with only four attendants, clothed in white garments, stole through a postern that opened upon the river Thames, which at that time was thickly frozen over and covered with snow.[1] The white draperies in which the empress and her little train were enveloped from head to foot, prevented the sentinels from distinguishing their persons, as they crept along with noiseless steps under the snowbanks, till they were at a sufficient distance from the castle to exert their speed. They then fled with headlong haste, through the blinding storms that drifted full in their faces, as they scampered over hedges and ditches, and heaps of snow and ice, till they reached Abington, a distance of six miles, where they took horse, and arrived safely at Wallingford the same night.[2] The Saxon annals aver, that the empress was let down from one of the towers of Oxford Castle, by a long rope, and that she fled on foot all the long weary miles to Wallingford.

At Wallingford the empress was welcomed by her faithful brother, Robert of Gloucester, who had just returned from Normandy with her son prince Henry; "at the sight of whom," says the chroniclers, "she was so greatly comforted, that she forgot all her troubles and mortifications, for the joy she had of his presence."[3] Thus we see that the sternest natures are accessible to the tender influences of maternal love, powerful in the heart of an empress as in that of a peasant.

Geoffrey count of Anjou, having no great predilection for the company of his Juno, thought proper to remain in Normandy with his son, the younger Geoffrey of Anjou.

After three years of civil strife, during which the youthful Henry learned the science of arms under the auspices of his redoubted uncle, the earl of Gloucester, the count of Anjou sent a splendid train of Norman and Angevin nobles to England, to reclaim his heir. Earl Robert of Gloucester accompanied his princely élève to Warham, where they parted,[4] never to meet again; for the brave earl died of a fever at Gloucester, October 31, 1147, and was interred at Bristol. With this great man, and true-hearted brother, died the hopes of the empress Matilda's party for the present, and she soon after quitted England, having alienated all her friends, by the ungovernable violence of her temper, and her overweening haughtiness. The great secret of government consists mainly in an accurate knowledge of the human heart, by which princes

[1] M. Paris. W. Malmsbury. Sim. Dunelm. Ypodigma Neustria.
[2] Ypodigma Neustria. Malmsbury. Speed. Rapin.
[3] Gervase.　　　　　　　　[4] Chronicle of Chester, as cited by Tyrrell.

acquire the art of conciliating the affections of those around them, and, by graceful condescensions, win the regard of the lower orders, of whom the great body of the nation, emphatically called " the people," is composed. The German education, and the self-sufficiency, of the empress, prevented her from considering the importance of these things, and, as a matter of course, she failed in obtaining the great object for which she contended.

" Away with her !" was the cry of the English population; " we will not have this Norman woman to reign over us." [1]

Yet this unpopular claimant of the throne was the only surviving child and representative of their adored queen Matilda, the daughter of a Saxon princess, the descendant of the great Alfred. But the virtues of Matilda of Scotland, her holy spirit, and her graces of mind and manners, had been inherited, not by her daughter, (who had been removed in her tender childhood from under the maternal influence,) but by her niece and name-child, Matilda of Boulogne, who was undoubtedly educated under her wise superintendence, and exhibited all the excellence of her prototype. The younger queen Matilda was, however, not only one of the best, but one of the greatest, women of the age in which she lived. That she was perfect in that which we have shown to be the most important of all royal accomplishments — the art of pleasing — that art in which her haughty cousin the empress was so little skilled — was acknowledged even by that diplomatic statesman-priest, Henry de Blois; and she was of more effectual service in her husband's cause, than the swords of the foreign army which Stephen had rashly called to the support of his tottering throne.

Stephen and Matilda kept their Christmas this year, 1147, at Lincoln, with uncommon splendour, for joy of the departure of their unwelcome kinswoman the empress Matilda, and the re-establishment of the public peace; and so completely did Stephen consider himself a king again, that, in defiance of certain oracular denouncements of evil, to any monarch of England who should venture to wear his crown in that city on Christmas-day, he attended mass in his royal robes and diadem, against the advice of his sagest counsellors, both temporal and spiritual.[2] While at Lincoln, prince Eustace, the son of Stephen and Matilda, (then in his thirteenth year,) received the oath of fealty from such of the barons as could be prevailed upon to acknowledge him as heir-apparent to the throne. Stephen and Matilda were desirous of his being crowned at Lincoln, in hopes of securing to him the right of succession; but the nobles would not consent.

The mind of queen Matilda appears, during the year 1148, to have been chiefly directed to devotional matters. It was in this year that she carried into execution her long-cherished design, of founding and endowing the hospital and church of St. Katherine, by the Tower,[3] for the repose of the souls of her deceased children, Baldwin and Maud.

[1] Thierry's Anglo-Norman History.　　　　　　[2] Gervase. Speed.
[3] This royal institution, which, under the fostering protection of the queens of England, has survived the fall of every other monastic foundation of the olden times, has been transplanted to the Regent's Park, and affords a delightful asy

The same year queen Matilda, jointly with Stephen, founded the royal abbey of Feversham in Kent, and personally superintended its erection. For many months she resided in the nunnery of St. Austin's, Canterbury, to watch the progress of the work,[1] it being her desire to be interred within that stately church, which she had planned with such noble taste. There is great probability that she was at this time in declining health, having gone through many sore trials and fatigues, both of mind and body, during the long protracted years of civil war. The repose of cloistered seclusion, and heavenward employment in works of piety and benevolence, whereby the royal Matilda sought to charm away the excitement of the late fierce struggle, in which she had been forced to take so active a part, were succeeded by fresh anxieties, of a political nature, caused by the return of the young Henry Fitz-Empress in the following year (1149), and by the evident intention of her uncle, David of Scotland, to support his claims. The king her husband, apprehending that an attack on the city of York was meditated, flew to arms once more; on which David, after conferring knighthood on his youthful kinsman, retired into Scotland, and prince Henry returned to Normandy, not feeling himself strong enough to bide the event of a battle with Stephen at that period.[2]

A brief interval of tranquillity succeeded the departure of these invading kinsmen; but queen Matilda lived not long to enjoy it. Worn out with cares and anxieties, this amiable princess closed her earthly pilgrimage at Heningham Castle in Essex, the mansion of Alberic de Vere, where she died of a fever, May 3d, 1151, in the fifteenth year of her husband's reign. Stephen was forty-seven years old at the time of this his irreparable loss; Matilda was probably about the same age, or a little younger.

This lamented queen was interred in the newly erected abbey of Feversham, of which she had been so munificent a patroness, having endowed it with her own royal manor of Lillechurch, which she gave to William of Ypres for his demesne of Feversham, the spot chosen by her as the site of this noble monastic establishment, which was dedicated to St. Saviour, and filled with black monks of Cluni.

The most valued of all the gifts presented by queen Matilda to her favourite abbey, was a portion of the holy cross, which had been sent by her illustrious uncle, Godfrey of Boulogne, from Jerusalem, and was, therefore, regarded as doubly precious, none but heretics presuming to doubt of its being "*vera crux.*"[3]

"Here," says that indefatigable antiquary, Weever, "lies interred Maud, wife of king Stephen, the daughter of Eustace earl of Boulogne (brother of Godfrey and Baldwin, kings of Jerusalem), by Mary Atheling (sister to Matilda Atheling, wife to Henry, her husband's predeces-

---

lum and ample maintenance for a limited number of those favoured ladies who, preferring a life of maiden meditation and independence to the care-worn paths of matrimony, are fortunate enough to obtain sisterships. A nun of St. Katherine may truly be considered in a state of single-blessedness.

[1] Stowe.   [2] Roger Hoveden.   [3] Robert of Gloucester.

sor).　She died at Heningham Castle in Essex, the 3d of May, 1151; whose epitaph I found in a nameless manuscript."

"Anno milleno C. quinquagenoque primo,
　　Quo sua non minuit, sed sibi nostra tulit,
Mathildis felix conjux Stephani quoque Regis
　　Occidit, insignis moribus et titulis;
Cultrix vera Dei, cultrix et pauperiei.
　　Hic subnixa Deo, quo frueretur eo.
Femina si qua Polos conscendere queque meretur,
　　Angelicis manibus diva hæc Regina tenetur."

The monastic Latin of this inscription may be thus rendered:—" In the year one thousand one hundred and fifty-one, not to her own, but to our great loss, the happy Matilda, the wife of king Stephen, died, ennobled by her virtues as by her titles.　She was a true worshipper of God, and a real patroness of the poor.　She lived submissive to God, that she might afterwards enjoy his presence.　If ever woman deserved to be carried by the hands of angels to heaven, it was this holy queen."

Queen Matilda left three surviving children, by her marriage with Stephen: Eustace, William, and Mary.

The eldest, prince Eustace, was, after her death, despatched by Stephen to the court of his royal brother-in-law, Louis VII., to solicit his assistance in recovering the duchy of Normandy, which, on the death of Geoffrey of Anjou, had reverted to Henry Fitz-Empress, the rightful heir.　Louis, who had good reason for displeasure against Henry, re-invested Eustace with the duchy, and received his homage once more. Stephen then, in the hope of securing this beloved son's succession to the English throne, endeavoured to prevail on the archbishop of Canterbury to crown him, as the acknowledged heir of England.　But neither the archbishop, nor any other prelate, could be induced to perform this ceremony, lest, as they said, " they should be the means of involving the kingdom once more in the horrors of civil war."[1]

According to some historians, Stephen was so exasperated at this refusal, that he shut all the bishops up in one house, declaring his intention to keep them in ward, till one or other of them yielded obedience to his will.　The archbishop of Canterbury, however, succeeded in making his escape to Normandy, and persuaded Henry Plantagenet, who, by his marriage with Eleanor duchess of Aquitaine, the divorced queen of France, had become a powerful prince, to try his fortune once more in England.

Henry, who had now assumed the titles of duke of Normandy and Aquitaine, and count of Anjou, landed in England, January 1153, before preparations were made to oppose his victorious progress.　He marched directly to the relief of his mother's friends, at Wallingford, and arrived at a time when Eustace was carrying on operations, in the absence of the king his father, who had gone to London, to procure fresh supplies of men and money.　Eustace maintained his position till the return of Stephen, when the hostile armies drew up in battle-array, with the in-

---

[1] Rapin.

tention of deciding the question between the rival claimants of the crown, at swords' points. An accidental circumstance prevented the deadly effusion of kindred blood, that seemed as if doomed to stain the snows of the wintry plain of Egilaw. "That day Stephen's horse," says Matthew Paris, " reared furiously thrice, as he advanced to the front to array his battle, and thrice fell with his fore-feet flat to the earth, and threw his royal rider. The nobles exclaimed it was a portent of evil, and the men murmured among themselves;[1] on which the great William de Albini, the widower of the late dowager queen Adelicia, took advantage of the pause, which this superstitious panic on the part of Stephen's adherents had created, to address the king on the horrors of civil war, and reminding him of the weakness of his cause, and the justice of that of his opponent, implored him to avoid the effusion of his subjects' blood, by entering into an amicable arrangement with Henry Plantagenet."

Stephen and Henry, accordingly, met for a personal conference, in a meadow at Wallingford, with the river Thames flowing between their armies, and there settled the terms of pacification, whereby Stephen was to enjoy the crown during his life, on condition of solemnly guaranteeing the succession to Henry Plantagenet, to the exclusion of his own children.[2] Henry, on his part, swore to confirm to them the earldom of Boulogne, the inheritance of their mother, the late queen Matilda, and all the personal property and possessions enjoyed by Stephen, during the reign of his uncle, Henry I. After the treaty was ratified, William de Albini first affixing his sign manual, as the head of the barons, by the style and title of William earl of Chichester,[3] Stephen unbraced his armour, in token of peace, and Henry saluted him as " king," adding the endearing name of " father;" and if Polydore Vergil, and other chroniclers who relate this incident, are to be believed, not without good reason.

Of a more romantic character, however, is the circumstantial account of the cause of this pacification, as related by that courtly historian, Matthew Paris, which, though he only mentions it as a report, is of too remarkable a nature to be omitted here. We give the passage in his own words :—

" The empress, they say, who had rather have been Stephen's paramour than his foe, when she saw him and her son arrayed against each other, and their armies ready to engage on Egilaw Heath, caused king Stephen to be called aside, and coming boldly up to him, she said,—

" ' What mischievous and unnatural thing go ye about to do? Is it meet the father should destroy the son, or the son kill the sire? For the love of the most high God, fling down your weapons from your hands, sith that (as thou well knowest) he is indeed thine own son: for you well know how we twain were acquaint before I wedded Geoffrey!' The king knew her words to be sooth, and so came the peace."[4]

The most doubtful part of this story is, that the empress is represented as making this communication personally to Stephen, yet no other historian mentions that she was in England at this period, much less that

[1] Henry of Huntingdon. Lord Lyttleton. Speed. Tierney's Arundel.
[2] Tierney's Arundel. Matthew Paris. Speed.   [3] Tierney's Arundel.
[4] Matthew Paris.

she was the author of the pacification.   Lord Lyttleton, however, in his
history of Henry II., says, " that at one of his interviews with Stephen,
previous to the settlement of the succession on Henry, that prince is
stated by an old author to have claimed the king for his father, on the
confession of the empress, when she supposed herself to be on a death-
bed."   Rapin also mentions the report.   That which lends most colour
to the tale, is the fact, that the empress Matilda's second son Geoffrey,
on the death of his father, set up a claim to the earldom of Anjou,
grounded on the supposed illegitimacy of prince Henry.   This ungracious youth even went so far as to obtain the testimony of the Angevin
barons, who witnessed the last moments of the count his father, to the
assertion " that the expiring Geoffrey named him as the successor to his
dominions, because he suspected his elder brother to be the son of
Stephen."[1]

Prince Eustace was so much enraged at the manner in which his
interests had been compromised by the treaty of Wallingford, that he
withdrew, in a transport of indignation, from the field, and gathering
together a sort of free company, of the malcontent adherents of his
father's party, he marched towards Bury St. Edmund's, ravaging and
laying under contribution all the country through which he passed.
The monks of Bury received him honourably, and offered to refresh his
men, but he sternly replied, " That he came not for meat but money,"
and demanded a subsidy, which being denied by the brethren of St. Edmund—" they being unwilling," they said, " to be the means of raising
fresh civil wars, which fell heavily on all peacefully disposed men, but
heaviest of all on the clergy"—Eustace, reckless of all moral restraints,
instantly plundered the monastery, and ordered all the corn and other
provisions belonging to these civil and hospitable ecclesiastics to be
carried to his own castle, near the town; and " then sitting down to
dinner in a frenzy of rage, the first morsel of meat he essayed to swal-
low choked him," says the chronicler, who relates this act of wrong and
violence.   According to some historians, Eustace died of a brain fever,
on the 10th of August, 1153.[2]   His body was conveyed to Feversham
Abbey, and was interred by the side of his mother, queen Matilda.
Eustace left no children by his wife, Constance of France.

William, the third son of Stephen and Matilda, inherited his mother's
earldom of Boulogne, which, together with that of Mortagne, and all his
father's private property, were secured to him by the treaty of Wallingford.   He is mentioned in that treaty by name, as having done homage
to Henry of Anjou and Normandy.   Shortly afterwards, however, this
prince, though of tender age, entered into a conspiracy with some of the
Flemish mercenaries, to surprise the person of prince Henry on Barham
Downs, as he was riding from Dover, in company with the king.   Stephen himself is not wholly clear from a suspicion of being concerned in
this plot, which failed through an accident which befell prince William,
for just before the assault should have taken place, he was thrown by his
mettlesome steed, and had the ill luck to break his leg.   Henry, on re-

[1] Vita Gaufredi de Normandi.   [2] Speed.

ceiving a secret hint of what was in agitation, took the opportunity of the confusion created by William's fall, to ride off at full speed to Canterbury, and soon after sailed for Normandy.

It does not appear that he bore any ill-will against William de Blois for this treacherous design, as he afterwards knighted him, and confirmed to him his mother's earldom, and whatever was possessed by Stephen before his accession to the throne. This prince died in the year 1160, while attending Henry II. on his return home from the siege of Thoulouse.

The lady Marie de Blois, the only surviving daughter of Stephen and Matilda, took the veil, and was abbess of the royal nunnery of Rumsey, in which her grandmother, Mary of Scotland, and her great aunt, Matilda, the good queen, were educated. When her brother William, count of Boulogne, died without issue, the people of Boulogne, desiring to have her for their countess, Matthew, the brother of Philip, count of Flanders, stole her from her convent, and, marrying her, became in her right count of Boulogne. She was his wife ten years, when, by sentence of the pope, she was divorced from him, and forced to return to her monastery. She had two daughters by this marriage, who were allowed to be legitimate; and Ida, the eldest, inherited the earldom of Boulogne, in right of her grandmother, Matilda, Stephen's queen.

Stephen died at Dover, of the iliac passion, October 25th, 1154, in the fifty-first year of his age, and the nineteenth of his reign.

He was buried by the side of his beloved queen Matilda, and their unfortunate son Eustace, in the abbey of Feversham. "His body rested here in quietness," says Stowe, "till the dissolution, when, for the trifling gain of the lead in which it was lapped, it was taken up, uncoffined, and plunged into the river:—so uncertain is man, yea, the greatest princes, of any rest in this world, even in the matter of burial." Honest old Speed, by way of conclusion to this quotation from his brother chronicler, adds this anathema: "And restless may their bodies be also, who, for filthy lucre, thus deny the dead the quiet of their graves!"

ELEANORA OF AQUITAINE,

QUEEN OF HENRY II.

CHAPTER I.

Provençal queens—Country of Eleanora of Aquitaine—Her grandfather—Death of her father—Her great inheritance—Marriage—Becomes queen of France—Beauty—She becomes a crusader—Her guard of Amazons—Eleanora and ladies encumber the army—Occasion defeat—Refuge with queen's uncle—Eleanora's coquetries—Returns to France—Her disgusts—Taunts—Henry Plantagenet—Scandals—Birth of infant princess—Eleanora falls in love with Henry—Jealousies—She applies for divorce—Her marriage dissolved—Returns to Aquitaine—Adventures on journey—Marries Henry Plantagenet—Birth of her son—Enables Henry to gain England—Henry's love for Rosamond—Returns to Eleanora—Succeeds to the English throne—Eleanora crowned at Westminster—Costume—Birth of prince Henry—Queen presents her infants to the barons—Death of eldest son—Her court—Tragedy played before her—Her husband—His character—Rosamond discovered by the queen—Eleanora's children—Birth of prince Geoffrey—Eleanora regent of England—Goes to Normandy—Conclusion of empress Matilda's memoir—Matilda regent of Normandy—Mediates peace—Dies—Tomb—Eleanora Norman regent—She goes to Aquitaine.

THE life of the consort of Henry II. commences the biographies of a series of Provençal princesses, with whom the earlier monarchs of our royal house of Plantagenet allied themselves, for upwards of a century. Important effects, not only on the domestic history of the court of England, but on its commerce and statistics, may be traced to its union, by means of this queen, with the most polished and civilized people on the face of the earth, as the Provençals of the twelfth and thirteenth centuries indisputably were. With the arts, the idealities, and the refinements of life, Eleanora brought acquisitions of more importance to the Anglo-Norman people, than even that "great Provence dower" on which Dante dwells with such earnestness.

But before the sweet provinces of the south were united to England, by the marriage of their heiress with the heir of the Conqueror, a varied tissue of incidents had chequered the life of the duchess of Aquitaine, and it is necessary to trace them, before we can describe her conduct as queen of England.

It would be in vain to search on a map for the dominions of Eleanora, under the title of dukedom of Aquitaine. In the eleventh century, the counties of Guienne and Gascony were erected into this dukedom, after the ancient kingdom of Provence, established by a diet of Charlemagne,[1] had been dismembered. Julius Cæsar calls the south of Gaul, Aquitaine, from the numerous rivers and fine ports belonging to it; and the poetical population of this district adopted the name for their dukedom, from the classics.

The language which prevailed all over the south of France was called Provençal, from the kingdom of Provence; and it formed a bond of national union among the numerous independent sovereigns under whose feudal sway this beautiful country was divided. Throughout the whole tract of country, from Navarre to the dominions of the dauphin of Auvergne, and from sea to sea, the Provençal language was spoken—a language which combined the best points of French and Italian, and presented peculiar facilities for poetical composition. It was called the *langue d'oc*, sometimes *langue d'oc et no*, the tongue of "yes" and "no," because, instead of the "*oui*" and "*non*" of the rest of France, the affirmative and negative were "*oc*" and "*no*." The ancestors of Eleanora were called *par excellence* the lords of "*Oc*" and "*No*." William IX., her grandfather, was one of the earliest professors and most liberal patrons of the art. His poems were models of imitation for all the succeeding troubadours.[2]

The descendants of this minstrel hero were Eleanora, and her sister Petronilla. They were the daughters of his son, William count de Poitou, by one of the daughters of Raymond of Thoulouse.[3] William of Poitou was a pious prince; which, together with his death in the Holy Land, caused his father's subjects to call him St. William. The mother of this prince was the great heiress Philippa of Thoulouse, duchess of Guienne and Gascony, and countess of Thoulouse in her own right. Before Philippa married, her husband was William, the seventh count of Poitou and Saintonge; afterwards he called himself William the fourth duke of Aquitaine. He invested his eldest son with the county of Poitou, who is termed William the tenth of Poitou. He did not live to inherit the united provinces of Poitou and Aquitaine, which comprised nearly the whole of the south of France. The rich inheritance of Thoulouse, part of the dower of the duchess Philippa, was pawned for a sum of money, to the count of St. Gilles, her cousin, which enabled her husband to undertake the expense of the crusade led by Robert of Normandy. The count St. Gilles took possession of Thoulouse, and withheld it, as a forfeited mortgage, from Eleanora, who finally inherited her grandmother's rights to this lovely province.

The father of Eleanora left Aquitaine in 1132, with his younger brother, Raymond of Poitou, who was chosen by the princes of the crusade that year to receive the hand of the heiress of Conrad prince of Antioch, and maintain that bulwark of the Holy Land against the assaults of pagans and infidels. William fell, aiding his brother in this arduous contest; but Raymond succeeded in establishing himself as prince of Antioch.

---

[1] Atlas Géographique.   [2] Sismondi's Literature of the South.
[3] Rer. Script. de Franc.; likewise Suger.

The grandfather of Eleonora had been gay and even licentious in his youth; and now, at the age of sixty-eight, he wished to devote some time, before his death, to meditation and penitence, for the sins of his early life. When his grand-daughter had attained her fourteenth year, he commenced his career of self-denial, by summoning the baronage of Aquitaine, and communicating his intention of abdicating in favour of his grand-daughter, to whom they all took the oath of allegiance.[1] He then opened his great project of uniting Aquitaine with France, by giving Eleonora in marriage to the heir of Louis le Gros.[2] The barons agreed to this proposal, on condition that the laws and customs of Aquitaine should be held inviolate; and that the consent of the young princess should be obtained. Eleonora had an interview with her suitor, and professed herself pleased with the arrangement.

Louis and Eleanora were immediately married with great pomp, at Bourdeaux; and, on the solemn resignation of duke William, the youthful pair were crowned duke and duchess of Aquitaine, August 1, 1137.

On the conclusion of this grand ceremony, duke William,[3] grandsire of the bride, laid down his robes and insignia of sovereignty, and took up the hermit's cowl and staff. He departed on a pilgrimage to St. James's of Compostenella, in Spain, and died soon after, very penitent, in one of the cells of that rocky wilderness.[4]

At the time when duke William resigned the dominions of the south to his grand-daughter, he was the most powerful prince in Europe. His rich ports of Bourdeaux and Saintonge supplied him with commercial wealth; his maritime power was immense; his court was the focus of learning and luxury; and it must be owned, that at the accession of the fair Eleanora, this court had become not a little licentious.

Louis and his bride obtained immediate possession of Poitou, Gascony, Biscay, and a large territory extending beyond the Pyrenees. They repaired afterwards to Poictiers, where Louis was solemnly crowned duke of Guienne.[5] Scarcely was this ceremony concluded,

---

[1] Suger. Ordericus Vitalis.

[2] Called Le Jeune, to distinguish him from his father Louis VI., who caused his son to be crowned in his lifetime.

[3] Montaigne, who speaks from his own local traditions of the south, asserts that duke William lived in his hermitage, at Montserrat, ten or twelve years, wearing, as a penance for his youthful sins, his armour under his hermit's weeds. It is said by others, that he died as a hermit, in a grotto at Florence, after having macerated his body by tremendous penances, and established the severe Order of the Guillemines.

[4] To this great prince, the ancestor, through Eleanora of Aquitaine, of our royal line, may be traced armorial bearings, and a war-cry, whose origin has not a little perplexed the readers of English history. The patron saint of England, St. George, was adopted from the Aquitaine dukes, as we find, from the MS. of the French herald, Gilles de Bonnier, that the duke of Aquitaine's *mot*, or war-cry, was, " St. George for the puissant duke." His crest was a leopard: and his descendants in England bore leopards on their shields till after the time of Edward I. Edward III. is called " valiant pard" in his epitaphs; and the emperor of Germany sent Henry III. a present of three leopards, expressly saying they were in compliment and allusion to his armorial bearings.

[5] Suger, cited by Gifford.

when Eleanora and her husband were summoned to the death-bed of Louis VI., that admirable king and lawgiver of France. His dying words were,

"Remember, royalty is a public trust, for the exercise of which a rigorous account will be exacted by Him who has the sole disposal of crowns and sceptres."

So spoke the great legislator of France, to the youthful pair whose wedlock had united the north and south of France. On the conscientious mind of Louis VII. the words of his dying father were strongly impressed, but it was late in life before his thoughtless partner profited by them.

Eleanora was very beautiful; she had been reared in all the accomplishments of the south; she was a fine musician, and composed and sang the *chansons* and *tensons* of Provençal poetry. Her native troubadours expressly inform us that she could both read and write. The government of her dominions was in her own hands, and she frequently resided in her native capital of Bourdeaux. She was perfectly adored by her southern subjects, who always welcomed her with joy, and they bitterly mourned her absence, when she was obliged to return to her court at Paris; a court whose morals were severe; where the rigid rule of St. Bernard was observed by the king her husband, as if his palace had been a convent. Far different was the rule of Eleanora, in the cities of the south.

The political sovereignty of her native dominions, was not the only authority exercised by Eleanora in "gay Guienne." She was, by hereditary right, chief reviewer and critic of the poets of Provence. At certain festivals held by her, after the custom of her ancestors,[1] called Courts of Love, all new *sirventes* and *chansons* were sung or recited before her, by the troubadours. She then, assisted by a conclave of her ladies, sat in judgment, and pronounced sentence on their literary merits. She was herself a popular troubadour poet. Her *chansons* were remembered, long after death had raised a barrier against flattery, and she is reckoned among the authors of France.[2]

The amusements of the young queen of France seemed little suited to the austere habits of Louis VII.; yet she had the power of influencing him to commit the only act of wilful injustice which stains the annals of his reign.

The sister of the queen, the young Petronilla, whose beauty equalled that of her sister, and whose levity far surpassed it, could find no single man, in all France, to bewitch with the spell of her fascinations, but chose to seduce Rodolf, count of Vermandois, from his wife. This prince, who was cousin and prime minister to Louis VII., had married a sister of the count of Champagne, whom he divorced for some frivolous pretext, and married the fair Petronilla, by the connivance of Eleanora. The count of Champagne laid his sister's wrongs before the pope, who commanded Vermandois to put away Petronilla, and to take back the injured sister of Champagne. Queen Eleanora, enraged at the dishonour

---

[1] Sismondi.   [2] Nostradamus's History of Provence, and Du Chesne.

of Petronilla, prevailed on her husband to punish the count of Champagne for his interference. Louis, who already had cause of offence against the count, invaded Champagne at the head of a large army, and began a devastating war, in the course of which a most dreadful occurrence happened, at the storming of Vitry: the cathedral, wherein thirteen hundred persons had taken refuge, was burnt, and the poor people perished miserably.

It was at this juncture that St. Bernard preached the crusade at Vezalai, in Burgundy. King Louis and queen Eleanora, with all their court, came to hear the eloquent saint; and such crowds attended the royal auditors, that St. Bernard was forced to preach in the market-place, for no cathedral, however large, could contain them. St. Bernard touched with so much eloquence on the murderous conflagration at Vitry, that the heart of the pious king Louis, full of penitence for the sad effects of his destructiveness on his own subjects, resolved to atone for it to the God of mercy, by carrying sword and fire, to destroy thousands of his fellow-creatures, who had neither offended him, nor even heard of him. His queen, whose influence had led to the misdeed at Vitry, likewise became penitent, and as sovereign of Aquitaine, vowed to accompany her lord to the Holy Land, and lead the forces of the South to the relief of the Christian kingdom of Jerusalem.

The wise and excellent abbot, Suger, the chancellor of Louis VII., endeavoured to prevail on his royal master to relinquish his mad expedition to Syria, assuring him that it would bring ruin on his country; but the fanaticism of the king was proof against such persuasions. Moreover, the romantic idea, of becoming a female crusader, had got into the light head of Eleanora his queen; and, being at this time in the very flower of her youth and beauty, she swayed the king of France according to her will and pleasure. Suger gives us the description of the preparations Eleanora made for this campaign, which were absurd enough to raise the idea, that the good statesman was romancing, if contemporary historians had not confirmed his evidence. When queen Eleanora received the cross from St. Bernard, at Vezalai, she directly put on the dress of an Amazon; and her ladies, all actuated by the same frenzy, mounted on horseback, and forming a lightly armed squadron, surrounded the queen when she appeared in public, calling themselves queen Eleanora's body-guard. They practised Amazonian exercises, and performed a thousand follies in public, to animate their zeal as practical crusaders. By the suggestion of their young queen, this band of madwomen sent their useless distaffs, as presents, to all the knights and nobles who had the good sense to keep out of this insane expedition. This ingenious taunt had the effect of shaming many wise men out of their better resolutions; and to such a degree was this mania of the crusade carried, that, as St. Bernard himself owns, whole villages were deserted by their male inhabitants, and the land left to be tilled by women and children.

Such fellow soldiers as queen Eleanora and her Amazons, would have been quite sufficient to disconcert the plans, and impede the projects, of Hannibal himself; and though king Louis conducted himself with great ability and courage in his difficult enterprise, no prudence could counteract the misfortune of being encumbered with an army of fantastic women. King Louis, following the course of the emperor Conrad, whose army, roused by the eloquence of St. Bernard, had just preceded them, sailed up the Bosphorus, and landed in Thrace.

The freaks of queen Eleanora and her female warriors, were the cause of all the misfortunes that befell king Louis and his army, especially in the defeat at Laodicea.[1] The king had sent forward the queen and her ladies, escorted by his choicest troops, under the guard of count Maurienne. He charged them to choose for their camp, the arid but commanding ground which gave them a view over the defiles of the valley of Laodicea. While this detachment was encamping, he, at the distance of five miles, brought up the rear and baggage, ever and anon turning to battle bravely with the skirmishing Arab cavalry who were harassing his march.

Queen Eleanora acted in direct opposition to his rational directions. She insisted on her detachment of the army halting, in a lovely romantic valley, full of verdant grass and gushing fountains. The king was encumbered by the immense baggage which, William of Tyre declares, the female warriors of queen Eleanora insisted on retaining in the camp, at all risks. Darkness began to fall as the king of France approached the entrance of the valley; and to his consternation, he found the heights above it unoccupied by the advanced body of his troops. Finding the queen was not encamped there, he was forced to enter the valley in search of her, and was soon after attacked from the heights by swarms of Arabs, who engaged him in the passes among the rocks, close to the fatal spot where the emperor Conrad and his heavy horse had been discomfited but a few weeks before. King Louis, sorely pressed in one part of this murderous engagement, only saved his life by climbing a tree, whence he defended himself with the most desperate valour.[2] At length, by efforts of personal heroism, he succeeded in placing himself between the detachment of his ladies and the Saracens. But it was not till the dawn of day that he discovered his advanced troops, encamped in the romantic valley chosen by his poetical queen. Seven thousand of the flower of French chivalry paid with their lives the penalty of their queen's inexperience in warlike tactics; all the provision was cut off; the baggage, containing the fine array of the lady-warriors, which had proved such an encumbrance to the king, was plundered by the Arabs and Saracens, and the whole army was reduced to great distress. Fortunately Antioch was near, whose prince was the uncle of the crusading queen of France. Prince Raymond opened his friendly gates to the distressed warriors of the cross, and by the beautiful streams of the Orontes the defeated French army rested and refreshed themselves, after their recent disasters.

Raymond of Poitou was brother to the queen's father, the saintly William of Poitou. There was, however, nothing of the saint in the disposition of Raymond, who was still young, and was the handsomest

---

[1] William of Tyre, Odo, and Suger.   [2] William of Tyre.

man of his time. The uncle and niece, who had never met before, were much charmed with each other. It seems strange that the man who first awakened the jealousy of king Louis, should stand in such very near relationship to his wife; yet it is certain, that as soon as queen Eleanora had recovered her beauty, somewhat sullied by the hardships she endured in the camp, she commenced such a series of coquetries with her handsome uncle, that king Louis, greatly scandalized and incensed, hurried her out of Antioch one night, and decamped to Jerusalem, with slight leave-taking of Raymond, or none at all.

It is true, many authorities say that Raymond's intrigues with his niece were wholly political, and that he was persuading his niece to employ her power, as duchess of Aquitaine, for the extension of his dominions, and his own private advantage.

Eleanora was enraged at her sudden removal from Antioch, and entered the Holy City in a most indignant mood. Jerusalem, the object of the ardent enthusiasm of every other crusader, raised no religious ardour in her breast; she was burning with resentment, at the unaccustomed harshness king Louis exercised towards her. In Jerusalem, king Baldwin received Eleanora, with the honours due both to her rank as queen of France, and her power as a sovereign ally of the crusading league; but nothing could please her. It is not certain whether her uneasiness proceeded from a consciousness of guilt, or indignation at being the object of unfounded suspicions; but it is indisputable that, after her forced departure from Antioch, all affection between Eleanora and her husband was at an end. While the emperor of Germany and the king of France laid an unsuccessful siege to Damascus, Eleanora was detained at Jerusalem, in something like personal restraint.

The great abilities of Sultan Noureddin rendered this siege unavailing, and Louis was glad to withdraw, with the wreck of his army, from Asia. After many perils at Constantinople, and detention at Sicily, the king and queen of France arrived safely in their own dominions, 1148. There are letters [1] still extant from Suger, abbot of St. Denis, the minister and confidant of king Louis, by which it appears that the king had made complaints, of the criminal attachment of his queen to a young Saracen emir, of great beauty, named Sal-Addin. For this misconduct the king of France expressed his intention of obtaining a divorce immediately, but was dissuaded from this resolution by the suggestions of his sagacious minister, who pointed out to him the troubles which would accrue to France, by the relinquishment of the " great Provence dower," and that his daughter, the princess Marie, would be deprived, in all probability, of her mother's rich inheritance, if the queen were at liberty to marry again.

This remonstrance so far prevailed on Louis, that from the unfortunate crusade, Eleanora resided at Paris, with all her usual state and dignity, as long as Suger lived, about four years. She was, however, closely watched, and not permitted to visit her southern dominions — a

[1] In the collection of Du Chesne, which has furnished much of the information in this narrative.

prohibition which greatly disquieted her. She made many complaints, of the gloom of the northern Gallic capital, and the monkish manners of her devout husband. She was particularly indignant at the plain and unostentatious clothing of king Louis, who had likewise displeased her by sacrificing, at the suggestion of the clergy, all his long curls, besides shaving off his beard and moustachios. The giddy queen made a constant mockery of her husband's appearance, and vowed that his smooth face made him look more like a cloistered priest than a valiant king.

Thus two years passed away in mutual discontent, till, in the year 1150, Geoffrey [1] Plantagenet, count of Anjou, appeared at the court of Louis VII. Geoffrey did homage for Normandy, and presented to Louis his son, young Henry Plantagenet, surnamed Fitz-Empress. This youth was about seventeen, and was then first seen by queen Eleanora. But the scandalous chroniclers of the day declare, the queen was much taken by the fine person and literary attainments of Geoffrey, who was considered the most accomplished knight of his time. Geoffrey was a married man; but queen Eleanora as little regarded the marriage engagements of the persons on whom she bestowed her attention, as she did her own conjugal ties.

About eighteen months after the departure of the Angevin princes, the queen of France gave birth to another princess, named Alice. Soon after this event, Henry Plantagenet once more visited Paris, to do homage for Normandy and Anjou, a pleuritic fever having suddenly carried off his father. Queen Eleanora now transferred her former partiality for the father, to the son, who had become a noble, martial-looking prince, full of energy, learned, valiant, and enterprising, and ready to undertake any conquest, whether of the heart of the gay queen of the south, or of the kingdom from which he had been unjustly disinherited.

Eleanora acted with her usual disgusting levity, in the advances she made to this youth. Her beauty was still unimpaired, though her character was in low esteem with the world. Motives of interest induced Henry to feign a return to the passion of queen Eleanora; his mother's cause was hopeless in England, and Eleanora assured him that if she could effect a divorce from Louis, her ships and treasures should be at his command, for the subjugation of king Stephen.

The intimacy between Henry and Eleanora soon awakened the displeasure of the king of France, and the prince departed for Anjou. Queen Eleanora immediately made an application for a divorce, under the plea that king Louis was her fourth cousin. It does not appear that he opposed this separation, though it certainly originated from the queen. Notwithstanding the advice of Suger, Louis seems to have accorded heartily with the proposition, and the divorce was finally pronounced, by a council of the church, at Baugenci,[2] March 18, 1152; where the marriage was not dissolved on account of the queen's adultery, as is commonly asserted, but declared invalid because of consanguinity.

[1] Vie de Gaufred, Duc de Normand.
[2] Sir Harris Nicolas' Chronology of History.

15 *

Eleanora and Louis, with most of their relations, met at Baugenci, and were present when the divorce was pronounced.[1]

When the divorce was first agitated, Louis VII. tried the experiment of seizing several of the strongholds in Guienne, but found the power of the south was too strong for him. It is useless for modern historians either to blame or praise Louis VII. for his scrupulous honesty, in restoring to Eleanora her patrimonial dominions; he restored nothing that he was able to keep, excepting her person. Gifford, who never wrote a line without the guide of contemporary chronicles, has made it fully apparent that the queen of the south was a stronger potentate than the king of the north. If the lady of *Oc* and *No*, and the lord of *Oui* and *Non*, had tried for the mastery, by force of arms, the civilized, the warlike, and maritime Provençal would certainly have raised the banner of St. George and the golden leopards far above the oriflamme of France, and rejoiced at having such fair cause of quarrel with their suzerain, as the rescue of their princess. Moreover, Louis could not detain Eleanora, without defying the decree of the pope.

On her way southward to her own country,[2] Eleanora stayed some time at Blois. The count of this province was Thibaut, elder brother to king Stephen, one of the handsomest and bravest men of his time. Much captivated with the splendour of "the great Provence dower," Thibaut offered his hand to his fair guest. He met with a refusal, which by no means turned him from his purpose, as he resolved to detain the lady, a prisoner in his fortress, till she complied with his proposal. Eleanora suspected his design, and departed by night, without the ceremony of leave-taking. She embarked on the Loire, and went down the stream to Tours, which was then belonging to the dominions of Anjou.

Here her good luck, or dexterous management, brought her off clear from another mal-adventure. Young Geoffrey Plantagenet, the next brother to the man she intended to marry, had likewise a great inclination to be sovereign of the south. He placed himself in ambush, at a part of the Loire called the Port of Piles, with the intention of seizing the duchess and her train, and carrying her off, and marrying her. "But," says the chronicler, "Eleanora was pre-warned by her good angel, and she suddenly turned down a branch of the stream southwards, towards her own country."

Thither Henry Plantagenet, the elder brother of Geoffrey, repaired, to claim the hand which had been promised him months before the divorce.

The celerity with which the marriage of Eleanora followed her divorce, astonished all Europe; for she gave her hand to Henry Plantagenet, duke of Normandy and count of Anjou, only six weeks after the divorce was pronounced. Eleanora is supposed to have been in her thirty-second year, and the bridegroom in his twentieth—a disparity somewhat ominous, in regard to their future matrimonial felicity.

The duchess of Aquitaine and the duke of Normandy were married at Bourdeaux,[3] on May-day, with all the pomp that the luxurious taste

[1] Bouquet des Histoires.   [2] Script. Rer. Franc.   [3] See Gervase. Brompton.

of Eleanora, aided by Provençal wealth, could effect. If Henry and Eleanora could have been married a few months earlier, it would have been better for the reputation of the bride, since all chroniclers are very positive in fixing the birth of her eldest son, William,[1] on the 17th of August, 1152, little more than four months after their union, on the first of May. The birth of this boy accounts for the haste with which Eleanora was divorced. Had king Louis detained his unfaithful wife, a dispute might have arisen, respecting the succession to the crown of France.

This child was born in Normandy, whither Henry conveyed Eleanora directly after their marriage, leaving the garrisons of Aquitaine commanded by Norman officers faithful to his interest; a step which was the commencement of his unpopularity, in his wife's dominions.

Louis VII. was much displeased at the marriage of his divorced queen with Henry of Anjou. He viewed with uneasiness, the union of the fair provinces of the south with Anjou and Normandy; and, in order to invalidate it, he actually forbade Henry to marry without his permission, claiming that authority as his feudal lord. His measures, we think, ought to acquit king Louis of the charge of too much righteousness in his political dealings, for which he is blamed by the superficial Voltaire. However, the hostility of Louis, who entered into a league with king Stephen, roused young Henry from the pleasures in which he was spending the first year of his nuptials; and, breaking from his wedded Circe, he obtained, from her fondness, a fleet, for the enforcement of his claims to his rightful inheritance. Eleanora was sovereign of a wealthy maritime country, whose ships were equally used for war and commerce. Leaving his wife and son in Normandy, Henry embarked from Harfleur with thirty-six ships, May, 1153. Without the aid of this Provençal fleet, England would never have reckoned the name of Plantagenet among her royal dynasties.

These circumstances are alluded to, with some dry humour, in the following lines, by Robert of Gloucester:

> "In eleven hundred years of grace and forty-one,
> Died Geoffrey of Plantagenet, the earl of Anjou.
> Henry his son and heir, earl was made thorough
> All Anjou, and duke of Normand—much it was his mind
> To come and win England, for he was next of kind (kin),
> And to help his moder, who was oft in feeble chance.
> But he was much acquaint with the queen of France,
> *Some deal too much, as me weened;* so that in some thing
> The queen loved him, as me trowed, more than her lord the king;
> So that it was forth put that the king and she
> So sibbe were, that they must no longer together be.
> The kindred was proved so near, that king Louis there
> And Eleanor his queen by the pope departed were.

[1] Toone's Chronological History gives this date: it is supported by Sandford and Speed from chronicles, and the assertion of Robert of Gloucester in the following words:—Henry was acquaint with the queen of France *some deal too much, as me weened.*"

Some were glad enow, as might be truly seen,
For Henry the empress' son forthwith espoused the queen.
The queen riches enow had under her hand,
Which helped Henry then to war on England.
In the eleventh hundred year and fifty-two
After God on earth came, this spousing was ado ;
The next year after that, Henry his power nom (took),
And with six-and-thirty ships to England com."

There is reason to believe that, at this period, Henry seduced the
heart, and won the affections, of the beautiful Rosamond Clifford, under
the promise of marriage, as the birth of her eldest son corresponds with
Henry's visit to England at this time; for he left England the year before Stephen's death, 1153.[1]   Henry was busy, laying siege to the castle
of one of his rebels in Normandy, when the news of Stephen's death
reached him.   Six weeks elapsed before he sailed to take possession of
his kingdom.   His queen and infant son accompanied him.   They waited
a month at Barfleur, for a favourable wind,[2] and after all they had a dangerous passage, but landed safely at Osterham, Dec. 8.   The king and
queen waited at the port for some days, while the fleet, dispersed by the
wind, collected.   They then went to Winchester,[3] where they received
the homage of the southern barons.

Theobald archbishop of Canterbury, and some of the chief nobles,
came to hasten their appearance in London, "where Henry was," say
the Saxon chroniclers, "received with great honour and worship, and
blessed to king the Sunday before Midwinter-day."

Eleanor and Henry were crowned in Westminster Abbey, December
19, 1154, "after England," to use the words of Henry of Huntingdon,
"had been without a king for six weeks."   Henry's security, during this
interval, was owing to the powerful fleet of his queen, which commanded
the seas between Normandy and England, and kept all rebels in awe.

The coronation of the king of England, and the luxurious lady of
the south, was without parallel for magnificence.   Here were seen in
profusion mantles of silk and brocade, of a new fashion and splendid
texture, brought by queen Eleanora[4] from Constantinople.   In the illuminated portraits of this queen, she wears a wimple, or close coif, with
a circlet of gems put over it; her kirtle, or close gown, has tight sleeves,
and fastens with full gathers, just below the throat, confined with a rich
collar of gems.   Over this is worn the elegant pelisson, or outer robe,
bordered with fur; with very full loose sleeves, lined with ermine,
showing gracefully the tight kirtle sleeves beneath.   The elegant taste
of Eleanora, or, perhaps, her visit to the Greek capital, revived the beautiful costume of the wife of the Conqueror.   In some portraits, the
queen is seen with her hair braided, and closely wound round the head
with jewelled bands.   Over all was thrown a square of fine lawn or

---

[1] His proceedings in England have been detailed in the preceding biography.
[2] Brompton.   [3] Sir Harris Nicolas' Chronology of History.
[4] It is said she introduced the growth of silk in her southern dominions, a benefit attributed to Henry the Great; but in the murderous civil wars of France
this art might have been lost.

gauze, which supplied the place of a veil, and was worn precisely like the *faziola*, still the national costume of the lower orders of Venice. Sometimes this coverchief, or kerchief was drawn over the features, down below the chin; it thus supplied the place of veil and bonnet, when abroad; sometimes it descended but to the brow; just as the wearer was disposed to show or conceal her face. Frequently the coverchief was confined, by the bandeau, or circlet, being placed on the head, over it. Girls before marriage wore their hair in ringlets or tresses on their shoulders. The church was very earnest in preaching against the public display of ladies' hair after marriage.

The long hair of the men likewise drew down the constant fulminations of the church; but after Henry I. had cut off his curls, and forbidden long hair at court, his courtiers adopted periwigs; indeed, if we may judge by the queer effigy on his coins, the handsome Stephen himself wore a wig. Be this as it may, the thunder of the pulpit was instantly levelled at wigs, which were forbidden by a sumptuary law of king Henry.

Henry II. made his appearance, at his coronation, with short hair, mustachios, and shaven chin; he wore a doublet, and short Angevin cloak, which immediately gained for him from his subjects, Norman and English, the sobriquet of Court-mantle. His dalmatica was of the richest brocade, bordered with gold embroidery. At this coronation, ecclesiastics were first seen in England dressed in sumptuous robes of silk and velvet, worked with gold. This was in imitation of the luxury of the Greek church : the splendour of the dresses seen by the queen at Constantinople, occasioned the introduction of this corruption in the western church.

Such was the costume of the court of Eleanora of Aquitaine, queen of England, in the year of her coronation, 1154.

The Christmas festivities were celebrated that year with great pomp, at Westminster Palace; but directly the coronation was over, the king conducted his queen to the palace of Bermondsey, where, after remaining some weeks in retirement, she gave birth to her second son, the last day of February, 1155.

Bermondsey, the first place of Eleanora's residence in England, was, as delineated in its ancient plans, a pastoral village, nearly opposite to London, of a character decidedly Flemish. Rich in well-cultivated gardens, and wealthy velvet meads, it possessed, likewise, an ancient Saxon palace, and a priory then newly built.

Assuredly the metropolis must have presented itself to the view of its foreign queen, from the palace of Bermondsey, with much more picturesque grandeur than it does at present, when its unwieldy size and smoky atmosphere prevent an entire *coup d'œil*. But at one glance from the opposite bank of the river, the eyes of the fair Provençal could then behold London, her royal city, situated on rising ground from the Thames. It was at that time girdled with an embattled wall, which was studded with gateways, both by water[1] and land. The new Tower of London kept guard on the eastern extremity of the city, and the lofty

[1] Dowgate and Billingsgate.

M

spire of the ancient cathedral presided over the western side, just behind the antique gateway of Ludgate. This gate led to the pleasant road of the river's Strand, ornamented with the Old Temple, its fair gardens and wharf, and interspersed with a few *inns*,[1] or metropolitan dwellings of the nobility, the cultivated grounds of which sloped down to their water-stairs and boat-houses, the Thames being then the highway of London.

The Strand road terminated in the majestic palace and abbey of West-minster; the Old Palace, with its yard and gardens, once belonging to St. Edward; and the New Palace, its noble hall and water-stairs, which owed their origin to the Norman dynasty.

Such was the metropolis when Henry II. succeeded to the English crown.

If the example and conduct of the first Provençal queen was neither edifying nor pleasing to her subjects, yet, in a commercial point of view, the connexion of the merchants of England with her Aquitanian domi-nions was highly advantageous. The wine trade with Bourdeaux became considerable.[2] In a few months after the accession of Eleanora, as queen-consort of England, large fortunes were made by the London traders, who imported the wines of Gascony from the port of Bourdeaux;[3] and above all (by the example of the maritime cities of Guienne) the shipping of England was governed by the ancient code of laws, called the code of Oleron.

In compliment to his consort Eleanora, Henry II. adopted for his plate-mark the cross of Aquitaine, with the addition of his initial letter ℔. An instance of this curious fact is still to be seen, in the grace-cup of Thomas à Becket.[4]

The English chose to regard Henry II. solely as the descendant of their ancient Saxon line. "Thou art son,"[5] said they, "to the most glorious empress Matilda, whose mother was Matilda Atheling, daughter to Margaret, saint and queen, whose father was Edward, son to king Edmund Ironside, who was great-grandson to king Alfred."

Such were the expressions of the English, when Henry convened a great meeting of the nobility and chief people, at Wallingford, in March 1155; where, by the advice of his mother, the empress Matilda, (who

[1] Inn was not, in early times, a word used for a house of public entertainment. Its original signification was a temporary abode in London, used by abbot, bishop, or peer.   [2] Anderson's History of Commerce.

[3] "The land," says one of the malcontent Saxon chroniclers, "became full of drink and drunkards." Claret was 4*d*. per gallon at this time. Gascon wine in general sold at 20*s*. per tun.

[4] This cup formerly belonged to the Arundel Collection, and was given by Bernard Edward, the late duke of Norfolk, to H. Howard, Esq., of Corby Castle, who thus became the possessor of this highly-prized relic of Eleanora's era. The cross of Aquitaine somewhat resembles the Maltese cross; the cup is of ivory mounted with silver, which is studded on the summit and base with pearls and precious stones. The inscription round the cup is, *Vinum tuum bibe cum gaudio*, —"Drink thy wine with joy;" but round the lid, deeply engraved, is the restrain-ing injunction, *Sobrii estote*, with the initials T. B. interlaced with a mitre, the peculiarly low form of which stamps the antiquity of the whole.

[5] Ailred Chronicle.

had learned wisdom from adversity,) he swore to confirm to the English the laws of Alfred and Edward the Confessor, as set forth in the great charter of Henry I. At this grand convocation queen Eleanora appeared, with her eldest son, then in his fourth year, and the infant Henry. The baronage of England kissed the hands of the infants, and vowed to recognise them as the heirs of the English monarchy. A few weeks after this recognition, the queen lost her eldest son, who was buried at Reading, at the feet of his great-grandfather, Henry I.

The principal residences of the court were Winchester Palace, Westminster Palace, and the country palace of Woodstock. The amusements most favoured by queen Eleanora were of a dramatic kind. Besides the Mysteries and Miracles played by the parish clerks and students of divinity, the classic taste of the accomplished Eleanora patronized representations nearly allied to the regular drama; since we find that Peter of Blois,[1] in his epistles, congratulates his brother William on his tragedy of Flaura and Marcus, played before the queen. This William was an abbot, but was master of the revels or amusements at court; he composed all the Mysteries and Miracles performed before the queen, at Westminster and Winchester.

It is to Peter of Blois we owe a graphic description of king Henry's person and manners; likewise the picture of his court setting out in progress.

"When king Henry sets out of a morning, you see multitudes of people running up and down as if they were distracted, horses rushing against horses, carriages overturning carriages, players, gamesters, cooks, confectioners, morrice-dancers, barbers, courtesans, and parasites, making so much noise, and, in a word, such an intolerable tumultuous jumble of horse and foot, that you imagine the great abyss hath opened, and that hell hath poured forth all its inhabitants."

We think this disorderly crew must have belonged to the queen's court, for the sketch given us by the same most amusing author, of king Henry himself, would lead us to suppose that he countenanced no such riotous doings. The chaplain Peter[2] thus minutely describes king Henry, the husband of Eleanora of Aquitaine, in his letter to the archbishop of Panormitan.

"In praising David the king, it is read that he was ruddy, but you must understand that my lord the king is sub-rufus, or pale-red; his harness (armour) hath somewhat changed his colour. Of middle stature he is, so that among little men seemeth he not much, nor among long men seemeth he over little. His head is round, as in token of great wit, and of special high caunsel the treasury."

---

[1] Or Petrus Blesensis, who was born 1120, at the city of Blois, of a noble family. This person was the very first who ever used the word *transubstantiation*. He was preceptor to William II. of Sicily, 1157; was invited to England by Henry II., and made his chaplain, and archdeacon of Bath, likewise private secretary to the king. He spent some years at the court of England, and died about the end of the twelfth century. He wrote about one hundred and thirty letters, in the most lively and individualizing style. These he collected and perpetuated, by making many copies, at the express desire of his royal master, Henry II.

[2] As edited by Hearne.

Our readers would scarcely expect phrenological observations in an epistle of the twelfth century, but we faithfully write what we find therein.

"His head is of such quantity, that to the neck, and to all the body, it accordeth by even proportion. His een pykeled (fine), and clear as to colour, while he is of pleased will, but through disturbance of heart, like sparkling fire or lightning with hastiness. His head of curly hair, when clipped square in the forehead, sheweth a lyonous visage, the nostrils even and comely, according to all the other features. High vaulted feet, legs able to riding, broad bust, and long champion arms, which telleth him to be strong, light, and hardy. In a toe of his foot the nail groweth into the flesh, and in harm to the foot over waxeth. His hands through their greatness sheweth negligence, for he utterly leaveth the keeping of them; never, but when he beareth hawks, weareth he gloves. Each day at mass and council, and other open needs of the realm, throughout the whole morning he standeth a foot, and yet when he eateth he never sitteth down. In one day he will, if need be, ride two or three journeys, and thus hath he oft circumvented the plots of his enemies. A huge lover of woods is he, so that when he ceaseth of war he haunteth places of hawking and hunting. He useth boots without folding caps, and homely and short clothes weareth he. His flesh would have charged him with fatness, but with travel and fasting he adaunteth, (keeps it down,) and in riding and going travaileth he mightily his youth. Not as other kings lieth he in his palace, but travelling about by his provinces espieth he the doings of all men. He doometh those that he judges when they do wrong, and punisheth them by stronger judgment than other men. No man more wise in counsel, ne more dreadful in prosperity, ne stedfaster in adversity. When once he loveth, scarcely will he ever hate; when once he hateth, scarcely ever receiveth he into grace. Oft holdeth he in hand swords, bows, and hunting gear, excepting he be at council or at book. When he may rest from worldly business, privily he occupieth himself about learning and reading, and among his clerks asketh he questions. For though your king[1] be well y-lettered, (learned,) our king by far is more y-lettered. I, forsooth, in science of letters, know the cunning of them both, ye wotting well that my lord the king of Sicily a whole year was my disciple, and though by you he had the beginning of teaching, yet by me he had the benefit of more full science.[2] And as soon as I went out of Sicily, your king cast away his books, and gave himself up to palatine[3] idleness. But, forsooth, our lord the king of England has each day a school for right well lettered men; hence his conversation, that he hath with them, is busy discussing of question. None is more honest than our king in speaking; ne in alms largess. Therefore, as holy writ saith, we may say of him, 'his name is a precious ointment, and the alms of him all the church shall take.'"

[1] The king of Sicily, William the Good, afterwards Henry the Second's son-in-law.

[2] By this passage it appears that Peter Blois had been the tutor to Henry II. and the king of Sicily. [3] The idleness and luxuries of the palace.

Such is the picture of the first of our great Plantagenet monarchs, drawn in minute pencilling, by the man who had known him from his childhood.

It is not a very easy task to reduce to anything like perspicuity the various traditions which float through the chronicles, regarding queen Eleanora's unfortunate rival, the celebrated Rosamond Clifford. No one who studies history ought to despise tradition, for we shall find that tradition is generally founded on fact, even when defective, or regardless of chronology. The learned and accurate Carte has not thought it beneath him, to examine carefully the testimony that exists regarding Rosamond; and we find, from him, that we must confine her connexion with Henry to the two years succeeding his marriage. He has proved that the birth of her youngest son, and her profession as a nun at Godstow, took place within that space of time, and he has proved it from the irrefragable witness of existing charters, of endowments of lands given by the Clifford family to benefit the convent of Godstow, of provision made by Henry II. for her son William Long Espee and his brother, and of benefactions he bestowed on the nunnery of Godstow, because Rosamond had become a votaress therein. It appears that the acquaintance between Rosamond and Henry commenced in early youth, about the time of his knighthood by his uncle the king of Scotland; that it was renewed at the time of his successful invasion of England, when he entered privately into marriage contract[1] with the unsuspecting girl; and before he left England, to return to his wife, his noble boy William, surnamed Long Espee, was born. His own words afterwards confirmed this report: "Thou art my legitimate son," said he to one of the sons of Rosamond, who met him at the head of an armed force, at a time when the rebellion of the princes had distressed him; "and," continued he, "the rest are bastards."[2] Perhaps these words afford the truest explanation of the mysterious dissensions which perpetually distracted the royal family.

How king Henry excused his perjury, both to Rosamond and the queen, is not explained by chronicle; he seems to have endeavoured, by futile expedients, to keep them both in ignorance of his perfidy.

As Rosamond was retained by him as a prisoner, though not an unwilling one, it was easy to conceal from her the facts, that he had wedded a queen, and brought her to England; but his chief difficulty was to conceal Rosamond's existence from Eleanora, and yet to indulge himself with frequent visits to the real object of his love.

Brompton says, "That one day queen Eleanora saw the king walking in the pleasance of Woodstock, with the end of a ball of floss silk attached to his spur; coming near him unperceived, she took up the ball, and the king walking on, the silk unwound, and thus the queen traced him to a thicket in the labyrinth or maze of the park, where he disappeared. She kept the matter secret, often revolving in her own mind in what company he could meet with balls of silk. Soon after, the king left Woodstock for a distant journey; then queen Eleanora,

[1] Carte. Brompton. Boswell's Antiquities. [2] Lingard.
VOL. I.—16

bearing this discovery in mind, searched the thicket in the park, and discovered a low door cunningly concealed; this door she had forced, and found it was the entrance to a winding subterranean path, which led out at a distance to a sylvan lodge in the most retired part of the adjacent forest." Here the queen found, in a bower, a young lady of incomparable beauty, busily engaged in embroidery.

Queen Eleanora then easily guessed how balls of silk attached themselves to king Henry's spurs. Whatever was the result of the interview between Eleanora and Rosamond, it is certain that the queen did not destroy her rival either by sword or poison, though in her rage it is possible that she might threaten both. That Rosamond was not killed, may be ascertained by the charters before named, which plainly show that she lived twenty years, in great penitence, after her retirement from the king. It is extremely probable that her interview with Eleanora led to her first knowledge that Henry was a married man, and consequently to her profession at Godstow, which took place the second year of Henry's reign. The grand error in the statements regarding Rosamond is the assertion, that she was a young girl seduced and concealed by the king, when he was in advanced life. Now the charters collated by Carte, prove that the acquaintance of Rosamond and Henry commenced in early youth; that they were nearly of the same age, and that their connexion terminated soon after queen Eleanora came to England.

Twenty years afterwards, when Rosamond's death really occurred in her convent, it happened to coincide with Eleanora's imprisonment and disgrace. This coincidence revived the memory of the romantic incidents connected with Henry's love for Rosamond Clifford. The high rank of the real object of the queen's jealousy, at that time, and the circumstances of horror regarding Henry's profligacy, as the seducer of his son's wife, occasioned a mystery at court which no one dared to define. The common people, in their endeavours to guess this state secret, combined the death of the poor penitent at Godstow with Eleanora's imprisonment, and thus the report was raised that Eleanora had killed Rosamond. To these causes we trace the disarrangement of the chronology in the story of Rosamond, which has cast doubts on the truth of her adventures. In Brompton's narrative we find the labyrinth [1]

[1] As to the labyrinth or maze at Woodstock, it most likely existed before the time of Rosamond, and remained after her death, since all pleasances or gardens in the middle age were contrived with this adjunct. Traces of them exist to this day, in the names of places near defunct royal palaces; witness Mazehill at Greenwich, (near the site of the maze or labyrinth of Greenwich Palace,) and the Maze in Southwark, once part of the garden of the princess Mary Tudor's palace. We have evidence that Edward III. (between whom and the death of Rosamond little more than a century intervened) familiarly called a structure pertaining to Woodstock Palace, Rosamond's Chamber, the locality of which he minutely describes in a letter preserved in the Fœdera, vol. iv. p. 629. In this document he directs William de Montacute to order various repairs at his manor of Woodstock, and that the house *beyond the gate in the new wall* be built again, and that same chamber, called Rosamond's Chamber, to be restored as before, and crystal plates, and marble, and lead to be provided for it. Here is indisputable proof that there was a structure called Rosamond's Chamber,

at Woodstock, and the clue of silk, famous in the romance and ballad. His chronology of the incidents is decidedly wrong, but the actual events are confirmed by the most ancient authorities.

Queen Eleanora brought her husband a princess in the year 1156; this was the eldest daughter, the princess Matilda.

The next year the queen spent in England. Her celebrated son, Richard Cœur de Lion, was born September 1157, at a palace considered one of the finest in the kingdom, called the Beau Monte, in Oxford. Thus, that renowned University claims the honour of being the birth-place of this great warrior. This palace was afterwards turned into the White Friar's church, and then to a workhouse. The chamber in which Richard was born still remains, a roofless ruin, with some vestiges of a fireplace;[1] but such as it is, this fragment is deeply interesting to the English, as the birth-place of a hero of whom they are proud.

Eleanora of Aquitaine, in some passages of her life, appears as one of the most prominent characters of her age: she was very actively employed, either as sovereign of her own dominions, or regent of Normandy, during the period from 1157 to 1172.

Eleanora was crowned a second time at Worcester, with the king, in 1159. When the royal pair came to the oblation, they both took off their crowns, and, laying them on the altar, vowed never to wear them more.

A son was born to Henry and Eleanora, September 23d, after the Worcester coronation: this prince bore the name of the king's father, Geoffrey Plantagenet.

The same year the king betrothed this boy to Constance, the heiress of Conan, duke of Bretagne. The infant Constance was about eighteen months older than the little prince Geoffrey. Henry had made most unjust seizure of Bretagne, by way of conquest; he, however, soothed the independent Bretons, by marrying their infant duchess to his son. His ambitious thirst for extension of empire was not sated by the acquisition of this dukedom; he immediately laid siege to Thoulouse, and, in the name of queen Eleanora, claimed that sovereignty of earl Raymond, who was in possession, and the ally of the king of France. A year was occupied with skirmishing and negotiation, during which time Eleanora acted as queen-regent in England.

Henry sent for his queen to Normandy, in 1160; she went in great state, taking with her prince Henry and her eldest daughter, to meet their father. The occasion of her presence being required, was the marriage of Marguerite, the daughter of her former husband Louis VII. by his second wife, with her young son Henry. Chancellor Becket went, with a magnificent retinue, to Paris, and brought the little bride, aged three years, to the queen at Rouen. Both bride and bridegroom were

_____

distinct from Woodstock Palace, yet belonging to its domain, being a building situated beyond the park wall. Edward III. passed the first years of his marriage principally at Woodstock, therefore he well knew the localities of the place; which will agree with the old chroniclers, if we suppose Rosamond's residence was approached by a tunnel under the park wall.

[1] Boswell's Antiquities.

given, after their marriage, to Becket[1] for education; and this extraordinary person inspired, in their young bosoms, an attachment to him, that ended but with their lives.

Queen Eleanora kept her Christmas at Mans, with the king, in great state and splendour, the year of this betrothment.

After a sharp dispute, between Henry II. and Louis VII., relative to the portion of the princess Marguerite, the king of France compromised the matter, by giving the city of Gisors, as a portion, with another infant princess of France, named Alice, in 1162.[2] This child was in her third year when wedded to prince Richard, who was then seven years old. The little princess was unfortunately consigned to the king of England for education. Two marriages were thus contracted between the daughters of Louis VII., and the sons of his divorced queen; connexions which must seem most extraordinary, when we consider that the father of the brides, and the mother of the bridegrooms, had been married, and were the parents of children, who were sisters to both.

Louis VII. gave his eldest daughter, by queen Eleanora, in marriage to Henry the Large, count of Champagne. It was in this year that king Henry's troubles began with Thomas à Becket, who had, hitherto, been his favourite, his friend, and prime minister.

The contest between the king and Becket, which fills so many folio pages of modern history, must be briefly glanced at here. It was the same quarrel which had agitated England, between Henry I. and Anselm. But England no longer possessed a virtuous daughter of her royal race for a queen, who, keenly feeling the cry of the poor deprived of their lawful provision, mediated between these haughty spirits. The gay, luxurious daughter of the South was occupied with her own pleasures, and heeded not the miseries which the king's sequestrations of benefices brought on the destitute part of the population. Becket appealed to the empress Matilda, the king's mother, who haughtily repulsed his suit. Becket was the son of a London citizen, who had followed Edgar Atheling, on his crusading expedition, and was made prisoner in Syria; he obtained his liberty through the affection of a Syrian lady, an emir's daughter, who followed her lover after his departure, and succeeded in finding him in London, although she knew but two European words, "London" and "Gilbert," the place of abode, and Christian name, of her lover. The pagan maiden was baptized, by the favourite Norman name of Matilda, and from this romantic union sprang Thomas à Becket, who was remarkable for his learning and brilliant talents, and his fine stature and beauty. The love which Gilbert Becket bore to the race and blood of Alfred, which had sent him crusading with prince Edgar, rendered him the firm partisan of his niece, the empress Matilda.

Young Becket had taken the only road to distinction open to an Anglo-

---

[1] The secular education and support of the little princess, was consigned to Robert de Newburgh, one of Henry the Second's barons, who engaged to guard her person, and bring up the princess Marguerite in a manner befitting her royal birth.

[2] Louis had two daughters of that name,—one by Eleanora, and this child by his second queen, Alice of Champagne.

Saxon; yet he was *of* the church, but not in it; for he was neither priest, nor monk, being rather a church-lawyer than a clergyman. Henry II. had distinguished this Anglo-Saxon with peculiar favour, to the indignation of his wife and mother, who warned him against feeling friendship for an Anglo-Saxon serf, with the loathing that the daughters of rajahs might feel for a pariah.

The see of Canterbury having remained vacant a year and a half, Henry urged his favourite to accept it, in hopes that he would connive at his plans, of diverting the revenues of the church, to enrich those of the crown; for this was simply the whole cause of the perpetual contest, between the Anglo-Norman kings, and the archbishops of Canterbury, since the conquest; but as the church supported the destitute poor, it is not difficult to decide which had the moral right. Archdeacon Becket protested that, if he were once a bishop, he must uphold the rights of the church; but the king still insisted on investing him with the archbishopric. The night before his consecration, at supper, he told the king that this archbishopric would place an eternal barrier between their friendship. Henry would not believe it. Becket was consecrated priest one day, and was invested as archbishop of Canterbury the next. To the annoyance of the king, he instantly resigned his chancellorship, and became a firm champion for the rights of his see.

For seven years, the contest between Becket and Henry continued, during which time we have several events to note; and to conclude the history of the empress Matilda.

She was left[1] regent of Normandy by her son, which country she governed with great wisdom, and kept in a peaceful state; but she never returned to England.

In the year 1165, king Louis VII. gave the princess Alice, his youngest daughter, by queen Eleanora, in marriage to the count of Blois, but, at the same time, endowed him with the office of high-seneschal of France, which was the feudal right to Henry II., as count of Anjou. Henry violently resented this disposal of his office; and the empress his mother, who foresaw the rising storm, and who had been thoroughly satiated with the horrors of war in her youth, wrote to pope Alexander, begging him to meet her, to mediate between the angry kings.

The pope obeyed the summons of the royal matron, and the kings met Matilda, and the pontiff at Gisors. The differences between Becket and Henry II. had then risen to a fearful height. It appears that Matilda was charged, by the pope, with a commission of peace-making, between Becket and his royal master. Emboldened by the mandate of the pope, Becket once more referred to the empress Matilda, as the mediator between the church and her son, and no more met with repulse.

We have seen the disgust, with which Matilda recoiled from any communication with Becket, as the son of a Saxon villein; nevertheless, this great man, by means of his eloquent epistles, was beginning to exercise the same dominion over the mind of the haughty empress, that he did over every living creature with whom he communicated. Henry II.,

---

[1] Hoveden. Gervase. Newbury.

16 *

alarmed at his progress, sent to his mother a priest named John of Oxford, who was charged to inform her of many particulars derogatory to
Becket's moral character—events probably that happened during his gay
and magnificent career, as chancellor and archdeacon.

The death of the duke of Bretagne had called Henry II. to take possession of that duchy, in the name of the infant duchess Constance, and
her betrothed lord, his son Geoffrey, when the news arrived of the death
of the empress Matilda, which occurred September 10, 1167. The mother of Henry II. was deeply regretted in Normandy, where she was
called " the lady of the English." She governed Normandy with discretion and moderation, applying her revenues wholly to the benefit of
the common weal, and many public works.[1] Her partiality for bridge-
building is the only point of resemblance between her actions and those
of her mother. While regent of Normandy, she applied her private
revenues to building the magnificent stone bridge, of thirteen arches,
over the Seine, called Le Grand Pont. The construction of this bridge
was one of the wonders of the age, being built with curved piers, to
humour the rapid current of the river. The empress built and endowed
three monasteries; among these was the magnificent structure of St.
Ouen. She resided chiefly at the palace of Rouen, with occasional visits
to the abbey of Bec.

Matilda was interred, with royal honours, in the abbey of Bec, before
the altar of the Virgin. Her son left his critical affairs in Bretagne to
attend her funeral. He raised a stately marble tomb to her memory;
upon it was the following epitaph, whose climax tends rather to advance
the glory of the surviving son, than the defunct mother :—

> " Great born, great married, greater brought to bed,
>   Here Henry's daughter, wife, and mother's laid." [2]

Here her body remained till the year 1282, when the abbey church
of Bec being rebuilt, the workmen discovered it, wrapped up in an ox-
hide. The coffin was taken up, and, with great solemnity, re-interred
in the middle of the chancel, before the high altar. The ancient tomb
was removed to the same place, and, with the attention the church of
Rome ever showed to the memory of a foundress, erected over the new
grave. This structure falling to decay, in the seventeenth century, its
place was supplied by a fine monument of brass, with a pompous
inscription.

The character of this celebrated ancestress of our royal line was as
much revered by the Normans, as disliked by the English. Besides
Henry II., she was the mother of two sons, Geoffrey and William, who
both preceded her to the grave.

Queen Eleanora was resident, during these events, at the palace of
Woodstock, where prince John was born, in the year 1166.

Henry completed the noble hall of the palace of Rouen,[3] begun by

---

[1] Ducarel's Normandy.
[2] " Ortu magna, viro major, sed maxima partu,
      Hic jacet Henrici filia, sponsa, parens."
[3] Thierry.

Henry I., and nearly finished by the empress Matilda. He sent for queen Eleanora, from England, to bring her daughter, the princess Matilda, that she might be married to her affianced lord, Henry the Lion, duke of Saxony. The nuptial feast was celebrated in the newly-finished hall of Rouen Palace, first opened for this stately banquet, 1167.

Queen Eleanora was left regent of Normandy by her royal lord; but the people, discontented at the loss of the empress Matilda, rebelled against her authority; which insurrection obliged Henry to come to the aid of his wife.

Guienne and Poitou became in a state of revolt soon after.[1] The people, who earnestly desired Eleanora, their native princess, to govern them, would not be pacified till Henry brought his queen, and left her at Bourdeaux, with her son Richard. Henry, the heir of England, was entitled the duke of Guienne; but for Eleanora's favourite son, Richard, was intended the county of Poitou, subject to vassalage to his brother and father. This arrangement quieted the discontents of Aquitaine. The princess Marguerite, the young wife of prince Henry, was left in Guienne, with her mother-in-law, while Henry II. and his heir proceeded to England, then convulsed with the disputes between church and state, carried on by Becket. Queen Eleanora and prince Richard remained at Bourdeaux, to the satisfaction of the people of the South, who were delighted with the presence of their reigning family, although the Norman deputies of king Henry still continued to exercise all the real power of the government.

The heart of Henry's son and heir still yearned to his old tutor, Becket—an affection which the king beheld with jealousy. In order to wean his son from this attachment, in which the young princess Marguerite fully shared, Henry II. resolved, in imitation of the Capetian royal family, to have his son crowned king at Westminster Abbey, and to associate him in the government.

"Be glad, my son,"[2] said Henry II. to his son, at this coronation, when he set the first dish on the table, at the coronation banquet; "there is no prince in Europe has such a sewer[3] at his table!"

"No great condescension for the son of an earl to wait on the son of a king," replied the young prince, aside to the earl of Leicester.

The princess Marguerite was not crowned at the same time with her husband;[4] she remained in Aquitaine, with her mother-in-law, queen Eleanora. Her father, the king of France, was enraged at this slight offered to his daughter, and flew to arms to avenge the affront. Yet it was no fault of king Henry, who had made every preparation for the coronation of the princess, even to ordering her royal robes to be in readiness. But when Marguerite found that Becket, the guardian of her youth, was not to crown her, she perversely refused to share the coronation of her husband.

[1] Tyrrell.   [2] Hoveden.
[3] This being one of the functions of the grand seneschal of France, which Henry had to perform, as his feudal service, at the coronation of a king of France, as count of Anjou, led to his performing the same office at his son's banquet.
[4] Peter of Blois.

The character of Henry II., during the long strife that subsisted between him and his former friend, had changed from the calm heroism portrayed by Peter of Blois; he had given way to fits of violence, agonizing to himself, and dangerous to his health. It was said, that when any tidings came, of the contradiction of his will by Becket, he would tear his hair, and roll on the ground with rage, grasping handsful of rushes, in the paroxysms of his passion.[1]

It was soon after one of these frenzies of rage, that, in 1170, he fell ill,[2] at Domfront, in Maine: he then made his will, believing his end approaching. To his son Henry, he left England, Normandy, Maine, and Anjou; to Richard he left the Aquitanian dominions; Geoffrey had Bretagne, in right of his wife, while John was left dependent on his brothers. From this order of affairs John obtained the nickname of Lackland, first given him by Henry himself, in jest, after his recovery.

During a fit of penitence, when he thought himself near death, Henry sought reconciliation with Becket; but when fresh contradictions arose, between the archbishop and the king, in one of those violent accessions of fury described above, Henry unfortunately demanded, in his rage, before the knights who attended in his bedchamber,[3] " Whether no man loved him enough to revenge the affronts he perpetually received from an insolent priest?"

On this hint, Fitz-Urse, Tracey, Britton, and Morville, slaughtered Becket, before the altar in his cathedral, the last day of the year 1171.

ELEANORA OF AQUITAINE,

QUEEN OF HENRY II.

CHAPTER II.

Eleanora in Aquitaine—Controlled by Normans—Conspires with her sons—Jealousy—Escapes, in man's attire—Means to visit her former husband—Seized—Carried prisoner to Bourdeaux—Queen Marguerite, her daughter-in-law—The two queens in captivity—Henry defeats his sons—Eleanora imprisoned in Winchester palace—Death of Rosamond—Turbulent sons of Henry, and Eleanora—Troubadour agitators—Death of the younger king—Temporary reconciliation of king and queen—Prince Richard's wrongs—Princess Alice—Reports of divorce—Eleanor again imprisoned—Songs concerning her—Her subjects' love—Death of prince Geoffrey—Grief of Eleanora—Eleanora brought to Poitou—Claims her dominions of prince Richard—King Henry's disquiets—Death—Burial—Queen in captivity—King Richard releases her—Appoints her queen regent—Her justice—Treasure-vault at Winchester—Queen mother's dower—Eleanora sets out for Navarre—Berengaria—Eleanora arrives at Messina, with Richard's bride—Departs—Mediates a dispute at Rome—Eleanora's regency—Her toilsome age.

[1] Hoveden.   [2] Brompton. Gervase. Hoveden.
[3] Fitz-Stephen calls the four who murdered the archbishop, the barons or servants of the king's bedchamber.

FROM the time of the marriage of her daughter Matilda to the Lion of Saxony, Eleanora had not visited England. The coronation of her eldest son, and the murder of Becket, had occurred while she resided in her native province. She had seen her son Richard, in 1170, crowned count of Poitou, with all the ceremonies pertaining to the inauguration of her ancestors. But king Henry only meant his sons to superintend the state and pageantry of a court; he did not intend that they should exercise independent authority; and Richard's will was curbed, by the faithful Norman veterans pertaining to his father. These castellans were the real governors of Guienne; an order of affairs equally disapproved of by prince Richard, queen Eleanora, and their Aquitanian subjects. The queen told her sons[1] Richard and Geoffrey, that Guienne and Poitou owed no obedience to a king of England, or to his Normans; if they owed homage to any one, it was to the sovereign of France; and Richard and Geoffrey resolved to act as their Provençal forefathers of old, and pay no homage to a king of England.

All these fermentations were approaching a violent crisis, when Henry II., in the summer of 1173, arrived, with his son, the young king, in Guienne, to receive the long-delayed homage of count Raymond of Thoulouse, and to inquire into the meaning of some revolts in the south, against his Norman castellans, evidently encouraged by his wife and prince Richard.

It was part of the duty of a feudal vassal to give his sovereign advice in time of need; and when Raymond of Thoulouse[2] came to this part of his oath of homage, as he knelt before Henry II., he interpolated it with these emphatic words:—

"Then I advise you, king, to beware of your wife and sons."

That very night the young king, although he always slept in his father's bedroom, escaped to the protection of his father-in-law, Louis VII. From Paris he made all manner of undutiful demands on his father.

Simultaneously with the flight of young Henry, his brothers, Richard and Geoffrey, decamped for Paris. Richard's grievance was, that his wife, the princess Alice of France, was withheld from him; while Geoffrey insisted, as he had arrived at the mature age of sixteen, that the duchy of Bretagne, and his wife Constance, whose dower it was, should be given to his sole control.

Reports had been brought to Eleanora, that her husband meditated a divorce; for some lady had been installed, with almost regal honours, in her apartments at Woodstock. Court scandal pointed at her daughter-in-law, the princess Alice, whose youthful charms, it was said, had captivated her father-in-law, and for that reason the damsel was detained from her affianced lord, prince Richard. Enraged at these rumours, Eleanora resolved to seek the protection of the king of France; but as she was surrounded by Henry's Norman garrisons, she possessed so little power in her own domains as to be reduced to quit them in disguise. She assumed male attire, and had travelled part of her way in this dress, when Henry's Norman agents followed, and seized her, before

[1] Script. Rer. Franc.   [2] Ibid.   [3] Gervase.

she could reach the territories of her divorced husband. They brought her back very rudely, in the disguise she had adopted, and kept her prisoner in Bourdeaux, till the arrival of her husband. Her sons pursued their flight safely, to the court of the king of France.

Now commenced that long, dolorous, and mysterious imprisonment, which may be considered the third era in the life of Eleanora of Aquitaine. But the imprisonment of queen Eleanora was not stationary; we trace her carried, with her royal husband, in a state of restraint, to Barfleur, where he embarked for England. He had another prisoner, in company with Eleanora; this was his daughter-in-law, the young Marguerite, who had contumaciously defied him, left the royal robes, he had made for her coronation, unworn upon his hands, and scorned the crown he had offered to place on her brow, if not consecrated by Becket. With these royal captives, Henry II. landed at Southampton, some time in July, 1173.[1]

Henry II. proceeded directly to Canterbury, carrying the captive queens in his train. Here he performed the celebrated penance so often described, at the tomb of Becket. We have no new light to throw on this well-known occurrence, except the extreme satisfaction that his daughter-in-law Marguerite (who was in the city of Canterbury at the time) must have felt at the sufferings and humiliation of the man who had caused the death of her tutor and friend.

Scarcely had king Henry completed his penance, when tidings were brought him that his high constable had defeated prince Richard and the earl of Leicester, near Bury;[2] and this news was followed by a messenger announcing the capture of king William the Lion, at Alnwick, and that the royal prisoner was approaching, with his legs tied beneath his horse —the most approved method of showing contumely to a captive, in the middle ages. All this manifested very clearly, to the Anglo-Saxons, that St. Thomas had forgiven his royal friend, and was now exerting himself very actively in his behalf; but when, within a very few hours, intelligence came that the fleet of young king Henry, which had set sail to invade England, had been entirely demolished by a storm, public enthusiasm for the saint knew no bounds. The king went to return thanks to St. Thomas, at the shrine before which he had done penance, and the peace of the kingdom was wholly restored.

Then was queen Eleanora consigned to confinement, which lasted, with but short intervals, for sixteen years. Her prison was no worse place than her own royal palace at Winchester,[3] where she was well guarded by her husband's great justiciary and general, Ranulph de Glanville, who likewise had the charge of the royal treasury, at the same place. That Glanville treated her with respect, is evident from some subsequent events.

The poor penitent at Godstow expired in the midst of these troubles, —not cut off in her brilliant youth by queen Eleanora, but " from slow

[1] Diceto. Dr. Henry has likewise traced the progress of Henry with two queens, from the contemporary chroniclers.　　　　[2] Brompton and Hoveden.

[3] Benedict Abbas, and many chronicles. Benedict was her prime minister, during her long regency, in the succeeding reign; therefore he must have known where his royal mistress resided, during so long a period of her life.

decay by pining." She was nearly forty, and was the mother of two sons, both of age. She died practising the severest penances, in the high odour of sanctity, and may be considered the Magdalen of the middle ages. Tradition says she declared on her death-bed, that when a certain tree[1] she named, in the convent garden, was turned to stone, they would know the time she was received into glory.[2] She died deeply venerated by the simple-hearted nuns of Godstow, who would have been infinitely scandalized had she received visits from Henry. Nor does one of the many church manifestoes, fulminated against Henry, charge him with such an aggravation of his offences as the seduction of a nun; an indubitable proof that the conventual vows had effectually estranged Henry and Rosamond.

As the princess Alice was still the betrothed of prince Richard, no one dared to hint at anything so deeply heinous as her seduction by her father-in-law; for the vengeance of the victorious Henry would have severely visited the promulgators of such scandal. The public, finding that the queen was imprisoned on account of her restless jealousy, compared the circumstance with the death of Rosamond, and revived the old story of Henry's passion for the penitent of Godstow. From this accidental coincidence, of Eleanora's imprisonment and Rosamond's death, the memory of the queen has been unjustly burdened with the murder of her former rival.

Henry II. seems to have indulged his eldest and his youngest son,

---

[1] The body of Rosamond was buried at Godstow, near Oxford, a little nunnery among the rich meadows of Evenlod. (Camden.) According to the peculiar custom of the times, the grave was not closed, but a sort of temporary tabernacle, called in chronicle a hearse, (of which the modern hatchment is a relic,) was erected over the coffin; this was raised before the high altar, covered with a pall of fair white silk, tapers burnt around it, and banners with emblazonment waved over it. Thus lying in state, it awaited the time for the erection of a monument. Twenty years after, the stern moralist, St. Hugh, bishop of Lincoln, in a course of visitation of convents, came to Godstow, and demanded, "Who laid there in such state under that rich hearse?" And when the simple nuns replied, "It was the corpse of their penitent sister, Rosamond Clifford," the reformer, perhaps remembering she was the mother of his superior, the archbishop, declared "that the hearse of a harlot was not a fit spectacle for a quire of virgins to contemplate, nor was the front of God's altar a proper station for it." He then gave orders for the expulsion of the coffin into the churchyard. The sisters of Godstow were forced to obey at the time; but after the death of St. Hugh, they gathered the bones of Rosamond into a perfumed bag of leather, which they enclosed in a leaden case, and, with all the pertinacity of woman's affection, deposited them in their original place of interment, pretending that the transformation of the tree had taken place, according to Rosamond's prophecy. Southey records a visit to the ruins of Godstow. The principal remnant serves for a cowhouse. A nut-tree grows out of the penitent's grave, which bears every year a profusion of nuts without kernels. King John thought proper to raise a tomb to the memory of Rosamond; it was embossed with fair brass, having an inscription about its edges, in Latin, to this effect:—

"This tomb doth here enclose | Rose passing sweet erewhile,
The world's most beauteous rose— | Now nought but odour vile."

[2] Boswell's Antiquities.

with the most ruinous fondness; he always kept them near him, if possible, while prince Richard and prince Geoffrey, equally beloved by their mother, were chiefly resident with her, on the continent.   Prince John had entirely an English education, having for his tutor that learned ecclesiastic, allied to the Welsh royal family, well known to historians, as the chronicler Giraldus Cambriénsis.   But small profit, either to his country or to himself, accrued from the English education of prince John.

Through the mediation of the king of France, his father-in-law, the young king Henry was reconciled to Henry II. for a time, and his young queen Marguerite was restored to him.   King Louis himself visited England in 1178, for the purpose of praying for his son's health at the shrine of St. Thomas à Becket.

Notwithstanding the singular relationship in which the kings of England and France stood to each other, as the former and present husband of the same queen, they appear to have frequently met in friendly intercourse.   Henry received Louis with much respect, and rode all night, August 18, with his train, to meet Louis VII. at Dover, where the chroniclers relate that Henry made many curious observations, on a total eclipse of the moon, which happened during his nocturnal journey,— a fact reminding us of his fondness for scientific questions, as recorded in his character by Peter of Blois.

Henry II. afterwards took his royal guest to his Winchester Palace, where he showed him his treasure-vault, and invited him to take anything he chose.   Queen Eleanora was then at Winchester, but whether she met her divorced lord, is not recorded.

In the course of a few months Louis VII. died, of a cold caught at his vigils near the tomb of St. Thomas à Becket.   Such was the end of the first husband of Eleanora of Aquitaine.

To enter into a minute detail of all the rebellions and insurrections undertaken by the insurgent sons of Eleanora, during their mother's imprisonment, were an endless, and indeed an impracticable task.   It must suffice to hold up a picture of the manners and temper of the people over whom she was the hereditary sovereign, and who disdained the rule of any stranger, however nearly connected with the heiress of their country.

All the elements of strife were kept in a perpetual state of activity, by the combativeness of the troubadours, whose *tensons*, or war-songs, perpetually urged the sons of Eleanora to battle, when they were inclined to repose.   Such, among many of inferior genius, was Bertrand de Born, viscount de Hauteforte, whom Dante has introduced with such terrific grandeur, in his Inferno, as the mischief-maker between Henry II. and prince John.   But he began this work with Henry's eldest and best beloved son.   Bertrand, and all the other troubadours, hated Henry II., whom they considered as an interloper, and a persecutor of their rightful princess, the duchess of Aquitaine, his wife.   It is said that Bertrand was in love with queen Eleanora, for he addresses many covert declarations to a "royal Eleanora" in his *chansons*, adding exultingly, that " they were not unknown to her, for she can *read !*"[1] But there is a mistake of the mother for the daughter, since prince Richard, who was a brother troubadour, encouraged Bertrand in a passion for his beautiful sister Eleanora;[2] and to the daughter of the queen of England, not to herself, these passionate declarations were addressed.

In the midst of insurrection against his sire, the mainspring of which was the incessant struggle to obtain an independent sovereignty, young Henry Plantagenet died, at the castle of Martel in Guienne, in his twenty-eighth year. When he found his illness mortal, he was seized with deep remorse, for his frequent rebellions against his ever-indulgent father. He sent to king Henry, to implore his pardon for his transgressions. Before he expired, he had the satisfaction of receiving a ring from his sire, as a token of forgiveness. On the receipt of this pledge of affection, the penitence of the dying prince became passionate; when expiring, he caused himself to be taken out of bed, and died on sackcloth and ashes, as an atonement for his sins.

The death of their heir for a short time reconciled queen Eleanora and her royal husband. Henry mourned for the loss of this son, with the deep grief of David over Absalom. The contemporary chroniclers agree, that from the year 1183 to the year 1184, when the princess Matilda, with her husband Henry the Lion of Saxony, sought refuge in England, the captive queen was restored to her rank at the English court.[3]

Prince Richard, now become the heir of Henry and Eleanora, remained some time quiet, in order to see how his father would conduct himself towards him. Although he had arrived at the age of twenty-seven, and the princess to whom he was half-married was twenty-three, she was still detained from him. Richard had formed, at Guienne,[4] an attachment to a virtuous and beautiful princess, the daughter of a neighbouring potentate, and he was anxious that his mysterious entanglement with the princess Alice should be brought to a termination.

Richard seems to have met with nought but injury from his father; nor was his brother Geoffrey much better treated. The continual urgency of prince Richard, in regard to the princess Alice, was met with constant evasion. Reports were renewed, of the king's intention to divorce queen Eleanora; and the legate resident in England, cardinal Hugo, was consulted on the practicability of this divorce, and likewise on the possibility of obtaining a dispensation for the king's marriage with some person nearly allied to him.[5]

The consequence was, that prince Richard flew to arms, and got possession of his mother's inheritance, while queen Eleanora was again committed to some restraint in Winchester Palace.

---

[1] Count Thierry.
[2] The royal family considered the love of the noble troubadour as a mere poetical passion, and the young princess was married very passively to Alphonso king of Castille. It was no trifle in the eyes of Bertrand, and the cause, doubtless, of the fierce restlessness with which he disturbed the royal family during the life of Henry II.—Sismondi.
[3] Benedict Abbas.   [4] Hoveden and Dr. Henry.   [5] Gervase.

The lengthened imprisonment of queen Eleanora infuriated her subjects in Aquitaine. The troubadours roused the national spirit in favour
of their native princess, by such strains as these, which were the war-
songs that animated the contest maintained by Richard in the name of
his mother.

"Daughter of Aquitania,[1] fair fruitful vine, thou hast been torn from
thy country, and led into a strange land. Thy harp is changed into the
voice of mourning, and thy songs into sounds of lamentation. Brought
up in delicacy and abundance, thou enjoyedst a royal liberty, living in
the bosom of wealth, delighting thyself with the sports of thy women,
with their songs, to the sound of the lute and tabor: and now thou
mournest, thou weepest, thou consumest thyself with sorrow. Return,
poor prisoner—return to thy cities, if thou canst; and if thou canst not,
weep and say, 'Alas! how long is my exile!' Weep, weep, and say,
'My tears are my bread both day and night.'"

"Where are thy guards, thy royal escort?—where thy maiden train,
thy counsellors of state? Some of them, dragged far from thy country,
have suffered an ignominious death; others have been deprived of sight;
others banished and wandering in divers places. Thou criest, but no
one hears thee!—for the king of the north keeps thee shut up like a
town that is besieged. Cry, then—cease not to cry! Raise thy voice
like a trumpet, that thy sons may hear it; for the day is approaching
when thy sons shall deliver thee, and then shalt thou see again thy native
land!"

These expressions of tenderness for the daughter of the old national
chiefs of Aquitaine, are followed by a cry of malediction against the
towns which, either from force or necessity, still adhered to the king of
the foreign race.

"Woe to the traitors which are in Aquitaine, for the day of their chastisement is at hand! La Rochelle dreads that day. She doubles her
trenches, she girds herself all round with the sea, and the noise of her
great works is heard beyond the mountains. Fly before Richard, duke
of Aquitaine, ye who inhabit the coast! for he shall overthrow the glorious of the land—he shall annihilate, from the greatest to the least, all
who deny him entrance into Saintonge!"

For nearly two years, the Angevin subjects of Henry II., and the Aquitanian subjects of his captive queen, gave battle to each other; and from
Rochelle to Bayonne, the dominions of queen Eleanora were in a state
of insurrection.

The contemporary chroniclers who beheld this contest of husband
against wife, and sons against father, instead of looking upon it as the
natural consequence of a divided rule in an extended empire, swayed by
persons of great talents, who had received a corrupt education, considered it as the influence of an evil destiny presiding over the race of
Plantagenet, and as the punishment of some great crime.

Many sinister stories, relating to the royal family, were current. Queen
Eleanora, when pursuing, in her early days, her guilty career as queen

---

[1] Chronic. Ricardi Pictaviensis ap. Script. Rer. Franc.

of France,[1] it was whispered, had been too intimate with Geoffrey Plantagenet, her husband's father. Then the story of Fulk the Red,[2] the first that took the name of Plantagenet, was revived, and the murder of his brother discussed. Likewise, the wonderful tale was remembered of the witch-countess of Anjou, Henry II.'s great-grandmother, wife to Foulke le Rechin (or the Quarreller). This count, having observed that his wife seldom went to church, (and when she did, quitted it always at the elevation of the host,) thought proper not only to force her to mass, but made four of his esquires hold her forcibly by the mantle when she was there; when, lo! at the moment of consecration, the countess, untying the mantle by which she was held, left it in the hands of the esquires, and, flying through the window of the chapel, was never heard of more. A great thunder-storm happened at the moment of her departure; a dreadful smell of brimstone remained, which " no singing of the monks could allay."

The truth of this marvellous tale probably is, that the countess was killed by lightning, in a church injured by a thunder-storm.

Her ungracious descendant, Richard Cœur de Lion, used to tell this tale with great glee, to his knights at Poitou, and added, " Is it to be wondered, that having sprung from such a stock, we live on bad terms with each other? From Satan we sprang, and to Satan we must go."

Geoffrey held out Limoges, in his mother's name, with great pertinacity. Among other envoys came a Norman clerk, holding the cross in his hand, and supplicated Geoffrey not to imitate the crime of Absalom.

" What!" said Geoffrey, " wouldst thou have me deprive myself of mine inheritance? It is the fate of our family that none shall love the rest. Hatred is our rightful heritage," added he, bitterly, " and none will ever succeed in depriving us of it."

During a conference which prince Geoffrey soon after had with his father, in the market-place at Limoges, for the purpose of discussing peace, the Aquitanian soldiers and supporters of Geoffrey, full of rage at the sight of the monarch who kept their duchess imprisoned, broke the truce, by aiming from the castle a shower of cross-bow shafts at the person of the king, one of which came so close as to shoot his horse through the ear. The king presented the arrow to Geoffrey, saying, with tears, " Tell me, Geoffrey, what has thy unhappy father done to thee, to deserve that thou, his son, shouldst make him a mark for thine archers?"

Geoffrey was greatly shocked at this accident, of which he declared he was wholly innocent. It was the outbreak of popular fury in his mother's subjects.

When prince Richard and prince Geoffrey were not combating with their father's subjects, they employed themselves in making war on each other. Just before the death of Geoffrey, his brother Richard invaded his dominions in Bretagne, with fire and sword, on some unaccountable affront, blown into a blaze by the *sirventes* of the troubadours. After this faction was pacified, Geoffrey went to assist at a grand tournament

[1] Brompton.   [2] Script. Rer. Franc.

at Paris, where he was flung from his steed in the midst of the *melée*, and was trodden to death beneath the feet of the coursers. He was buried at Notre Dame.

This was the second son queen Eleanora had lost since her imprisonment, in the very flower of his youth and strength. Like his brother Henry, this prince was remarkable for his manly beauty, and the agile grace of his martial figure. His death afflicted his mother equally with that of her first-born; for Geoffrey had been brought up a Provençal, and had shown far more resentment for his mother's imprisonment than the young king Henry. That Eleanora loved both with all a mother's passionate tenderness, we have the evidence of her own most eloquent words. In one of her letters to the pope, preserved in the collection of Peter Blois, she says,—

" The younger king and the count of Bretagne both sleep in dust, while their most wretched mother is compelled to live on, though tortured by the irremediable recollections of the dead."[1]

The dislike that queen Eleanora manifested for the widow of her son Geoffrey, is one of the circumstances that float like straws on the stream of common history, without any one defining from whence it came. A passage in the " Newbury Chronicle," hitherto little noticed, casts some light on this aversion, which certainly did not commence, on the queen's part, till after the death of Geoffrey. From it we find that the misfortunes of prince Arthur began before his birth, and were strengthened by his baptism, on the 29th of March, 1187. The duchess Constance brought this heir of misfortune into the world a few months after the death of his father. Eleanora, the eldest child of Constance, had been proclaimed heiress of Bretagne, but was disinherited on the birth of her brother. " It was the pleasure of king Henry and queen Eleanora that the infant should be named Henry; but the Bretons chose to indulge their natural prejudices in favour of king Arthur, whom they claim as their countryman; and as they looked forward to the boy as the possible heir of England, they insisted on giving the last descendant of the Armorican princes that favourite name. This was the first public displeasure given by Constance to the parents of her husband; their enmity increased with years."

" Great scandal arose after the death of Geoffrey, regarding the duchess Constance and her brother-in-law John: till his marriage with Isabella of Angoulême, he was constantly ' haunting her;' and on this account, it is supposed, Henry II., after the birth of her posthumous son Arthur, forced the duchess to marry the earl of Chester, as prince John's attentions to his sister-in-law caused considerable comment."[2]

Prince Richard having got possession of the whole of Aquitaine, his father commanded him to surrender it to his mother, queen Eleanora, whom he had brought as far as Normandy, to claim her right.[3] The

---

[1] Rex junior et comes Britanniæ in pulvere dormiunt, et eorum mater infelicissima vivere cogitur, ut irremediabiliter de mortuorum memoriâ torqueatur.— Second Letter from Eleanora to Pope Celestine.—Fœdera, vol. i. p. 74.
[2] Carte.   [3] Benedict Abbas.

moment the prince received this mandate, he gave up the territory, and hastened to Normandy to welcome the queen, and congratulate her on her restoration to freedom.

This release is recorded by the friend of the queen, abbot Benedict. From him we learn, that, during the year 1186, Eleanora exercised sovereign power at Bourdeaux, and then resigned it to her son Richard, who, in the meantime, had made his peace with his father.

Henry II. was with his queen during this period; for Benedict declares that, the following April, they sailed from Barfleur to England. Eleanora was again put under some restraint at Winchester Palace, which she quitted no more till the death of King Henry, three years afterwards.

The commission of moral wrong had involved Henry, great and powerful as he was, in a net, within whose inextricable folds he either vainly struggled, or awaited the possibility of deliverance by the death of the queen. If Eleanora had preceded him to the grave, as in the common course of nature might have been expected, he would have sued instantly for a dispensation to marry the affianced bride of his son. While the queen lived, this could not be done without an explosion of scandal, which would have dishonoured him in the eyes of all Europe. Henry had only two alternatives; either to permit his heir to marry the princess Alice, or to shorten the life of the queen Eleanora by violent means. Although his principles were not sufficiently firm to resist indulgence in guilt, he was not depraved enough to commit deliberately either atrocity. So time wore uneasily on, till prince Richard attained the age of thirty-four, and Alice that of thirty; while the king still invented futile excuses, to keep his son in this miserable state of entanglement, wherein Richard could neither free himself from Alice, nor give his hand to any other bride. Yet Richard, to further his own ends, made the brother of Alice believe that he was willing to complete his engagement.

"It was the wish of Henry II. to crown his son John king of England during his lifetime, and to give Richard all his dominions that lay beyond the English sea. Richard was not content: he came to the king of France, and cried for aid, saying, 'Sire, for God's sake suffer me not to be disinherited thus by my sire. I am engaged to your sister Alice, who ought by right to be my wife. Help me to maintain my rights and hers.' "[1]

The king of France, after vainly seeking for explanation of the reason why his sister was not married to her betrothed, made, with prince Richard, an appeal to arms. King Philip contrived to induce prince John to join in the rebellion. When Henry heard that this idolized child of his old age had followed the insurgent example of his brethren, he threw himself into a paroxysm of rage, and invoked the bitterest curses on his head, and that of prince Richard; he cursed the day of his own birth; and, after giving orders to his painter at Windsor, to paint a device, of a young eaglet pecking out the eyes of an eagle, as a reproach to prince John, he set out for the continent in an agonized state of mind.

After waging, for the first time in his life, an unsuccessful war, king

---

[1] Bernard le Tresorier. Guizot's Chron.

Henry agreed to meet his son Richard and the king of France at Ve-zalai.

As the king was on his progress to this congress, he fell ill at Chinon, after indulging in one of his fits of violent passion.[1] Finding that his life was departing, he caused himself to be carried before the high altar of the cathedral, where he expired in the supporting arms of Geoffrey, the youngest son of Rosamond, who was the only one of his children from whom he received filial attention in his last moments. Before he died, he spoke earnestly to his son, and gave him a ring of great value; then laying his head on the bosom of Geoffrey,[2] his spirit departed, leaving his features still convulsed with the agony of rage, which had hastened his end.

When the news was brought to Richard, that the crown of England had devolved upon him by the sudden death of his father, he was torn with remorse and regret. He went to meet the royal corpse at Fonte-vraud, the place of interment pointed out by the will of the deceased monarch.

King Henry, when he was carried forth to be buried, was first appa-reled in his princely robes, having his crown on his head, gloves on his hands, and shoes on his feet, wrought with gold; spurs on his heels, a ring of gold on his finger, a sceptre in his hand, his sword by his side, and his face uncovered. But this regalia was of a strange nature; for the corpse of Henry, like that of the Conqueror, had been stripped and plundered; and when those who were charged with the funeral de-manded the ornaments in which Henry was to lie in state, the treasurer, as a favour, sent a ring of little value, and an old sceptre. As for the crown with which the warlike brow of Henry was encircled, it was but the gold fringe from a lady's petticoat, torn off for the occasion; and in this odd attire, the greatest monarch in the world went down to his last abode.[3]

Thus he was conveyed to the abbey of Fontevraud, where he lay with his face uncovered, showing, by the contraction of his features, the violent rage in which he departed. When Richard entered the abbey he shuddered, and prayed some moments before the altar, when the nose and mouth of his father began to bleed so profusely, that the monk in attendance kept incessantly wiping the blood from his face. Richard testified the most poignant remorse at this sight. He wept bitterly; and, prostrating himself, prayed earnestly, under the mingled stimulus of grief and superstition, and then, rising, he departed, and looked on the face of his sire no more.[4]

Henry died July 6th, 1189.

The first step taken by Richard I., on his accession to the English crown, was to order his mother's release from her constrained retirement at Winchester Palace. From a captive, queen Eleanora in one moment became a sovereign; for the reins of the English government were placed in her hands, at the time of her release. She made a noble use of her authority, according to a manuscript cited by Tyrrell.

[1] Which Brompton declares was the immediate cause of death.
[2] Lord Lyttleton. [3] Roger Wendover.
[4] Count Thierry, from Norman Chronicles.

"Eleanora of Guienne, directly she was liberated from her restraint at Winchester, was invested with full powers as regent, which she most beneficially exercised, going in person from city to city, setting free all those confined under the Norman game-laws, which in the latter part of Henry's life were cruelly enforced. When she released prisoners, it was on condition that they prayed for the soul of her late husband. She likewise declared she took this measure for the benefit of his soul."

Her son had given her full power, but, to her great honour, she did not use it, against those who had been her gaolers or enemies. Her regency was entirely spent in acts of mercy and wisdom, and her discriminating acumen in the prisoners she liberated may be judged by the following list.

She liberated fully —"All confined for breach of forest laws, who were accused of no further crime. All who were outlawed for the same, she invited back to their homes and families. All who had been seized by the king's arbitrary commands, and were not accused by their hundred or county, she set free."

"But all malefactors accused on good and lawful evidence were to be kept in prison, without bail."

When we consider Eleanora going from city to city, examining thus into the wrongs of a government that had become arbitrary, and seeing justice done to the lowest, we are apt to think that her imprisonment had improved her disposition.

The queen-regent next ordained that "every freeman of the whole kingdom should swear that he would bear faith to his lord, Richard, son of king Henry and queen Eleanora, for the preservation of life, limbs, and terrene honour, as his liege lord, against all living; and that he would be obedient to his laws, and assist him in the preservation of peace and justice." [1]

Eleanora showed so little distaste to the Winchester Palace, that she returned thither after her justiciary progress, to await the arrival of her son from the coast of Normandy.

It appears that king Richard, when he gave commands for his mother's release, ordered her castellan, the keeper of the treasure-vault at Winchester, Ranulph de Glanville, to be thrown into a dungeon in Winchester Castle, and loaded with fetters weighing a thousand pounds.[2]

Our ancient chroniclers, when labouring to reconcile the prophecies of Merlin with the events of English history, while hunting after the impossible, very often start some particulars which would otherwise have slept shrouded in the dust of the grave. Thus, speaking of the liberation of Eleanora of Aquitaine by her son, Richard I., Matthew Paris says she is designated, by Merlin's sentence, *Aquila rupti fœderis tertiâ nidificatione gaudebit ;* "The destructive eagle shall rejoice in her third nestling." — "Eleanora," pursues Matthew, "is the eagle, for she

---

[1] This is the first oath of allegiance ever taken in England to an uncrowned king.

[2] Tyrrell, to whose most learned and indefatigable research the elucidation o many dark passages of Eleanora's life is owing.

spreads her wings over two nations, England and Aquitaine; also, by reason of her *excessive beauty*, she destroyed or injured nations. She was separated from the king of France by reason of consanguinity, and from the king of England by divorce *upon suspicion*, and kept in close confinement. She rejoiced in her third nestling, since Richard, her third son, honoured her with all reverence after releasing her from prison."

If Matthew would imply that Henry confined Eleanora for impropriety of conduct, he is not supported by other authors.

King Richard 1. landed at Portsmouth, August the 12th, 1189. Three days after, he arrived at his mother's court at Winchester, where his first care was directed to his father's treasure. After he had conferred with his mother, he ordered before him Ranulph de Glanville, who gave him so good an account of the secrets of the Winchester treasure-vault, that he set him at liberty, and ever after treated him with confidence. Either Ranulph de Glanville had behaved to the queen, when his prisoner, with all possible respect, or Eleanora was of a very magnanimous disposition, and forbore prejudicing her son against her late castellan. Glanville gave up to the king the enormous sum of nine hundred thousand pounds, besides valuable jewels. At his first seizure, only 100,000 marks were found in the treasure-vault, which, it seems, possessed some intricacies only known to Glanville.[1]

The king's next care was to settle the revenue of the mother he so passionately loved, and whose wrongs he had so fiercely resented. Her dower was rendered equal to those of the queens Matilda Atheling and Matilda of Boulogne.

The king's coronation took place on the 3d of September, 1189. As the etiquette of the queen-mother's recent widowhood prevented her from sharing in this splendid festival, all women were forbidden to be present at its celebration. The chroniclers declare that Richard issued a proclamation the day before, debarring all women[1] and Jews from entering the precincts of Westminster Abbey, at the time of his inauguration:—a classification of persons greatly impugning the gallantry of the lion-hearted king, when we remember the odium attached to the name of a Jew.

The Provençal alliance had produced a prodigious influx of this usurious race into England: 'As they enjoyed high privileges in the here-

---

[1] Hoveden. Brompton. Tyrrell. Paris. The singular employment of warlike barons as justiciaries, and the combination of the offices of general and of lawyer in one man, are strange features in the Norman and Angevin domination in England. This Ranulph de Glanville is an instance; he was Henry's great general, who defeated and took prisoner William the Lion of Scotland, but he is only known to our gentlemen of the bar as the author of " Glanville's Institutes;" this steel-clad baron being the first who reduced the laws of England to a written code. To make the contrast with modern times still stronger, the great legalist died crusading, having, either to please Cœur de Lion, or to atone for his sins, both as lawyer and general, taken up the cross, for the purpose of battling " Mahoun and Termagaunt."

[2] Hoveden. Brompton. M. Paris. The last says, all women of *bad* character

ditary dominions of queen Eleanora, they supposed they were secure under her son's government. Believing money would buy a place everywhere, they flocked to the abbey, bearing a rich present, but the populace set upon them and slaughtered them, being excited to a religious mania by the preaching of the crusade. The massacre of these unfortunate money-brokers was not perpetrated with the connivance of either king Richard or the queen-mother, since Brompton expressly declares that the ringleaders were, by the king's orders, tried and put to death.

Alice, the long-betrothed bride of Richard, was neither married nor crowned. On the contrary, she was committed to the same species of restraint, by the orders of the queen, in which she herself had been so long held captive. The princess Alice had been twenty-two years without leaving England; and as she was the only person on whom Eleanora retaliated any part of her wrongs, the inference must be drawn, that she considered Alice as the cause of them.

Eleanora departed for Aquitaine as soon as her son had settled her English dower, and Richard embarked at Dover, for Calais, to join the crusade, taking with him but ten ships from the English ports. His troops were disembarked, and he marched across France, to his mother's dominions, where he formally resigned to her the power he had exercised, during his father's lifetime, as her deputy. Richard appointed the rendezvous of the crusade at Messina, and, directing his mother to meet him there, he set sail from Marseilles, for Sicily; while Eleanora undertook a journey to Navarre, to claim for him the hand of Berengaria, the daughter of king Sancho.

Richard had much to effect at Messina, before he commenced the crusade. Before he struck a blow for Christendom, he was obliged to right the wrongs of his sister Joanna, queen of Sicily, the youngest daughter of Eleanora and Henry II. William the Good, through the recommendations of Peter of Blois, (who had formerly been his tutor,) asked the hand of Joanna Plantagenet of her father. The Sicilian ambassador granted Joanna an immense dower; but when the aged bridegroom found that his young queen was still more beautiful and sweet-tempered than her father's chaplain, Peter, had set forth, he greatly augmented her dower. The king of Sicily died childless, leaving his young widow great legacies in his will.

King Tancred robbed her of these, and of her dower: and, to prevent her complaints, enclosed her in prison at Messina. It was this outrage Richard hastened there to redress. But the list of goods the fair widow directed her brother to claim of Tancred, could surely have only existed in a catalogue of Aladdin's household furniture:—an arm chair of solid gold;[1] footstools of gold; a table of the same with tressels, twelve feet long; besides urns and vases of the same precious metal. These reasonable demands were enforced by the arm of the mighty Richard, who was as obstinate and wilful as Achilles himself.

[1] Hoveden and Vinisauf; likewise Piers of Langtoft, who mentions many other curious articles.

Tancred deserves pity, when we consider the extraordinary nature of the legacy. However, he compounded for dower and legacy at last, with the enormous payment of 40,000 ounces of gold. This treasure, with the royal widow herself, were consigned to Richard forthwith. Thus was a companion provided for Richard's expected bride, the elegant and refined Berengaria, who, under the conduct of Eleanora of Aquitaine, was daily expected.

Richard was so well pleased with the restoration of his sister and her treasures, that he asked Tancred's daughter in marriage for his then acknowledged heir, Arthur of Bretagne.[1]

During this negotiation Eleanora arrived in Messina,[2] bringing with her the long-beloved Berengaria. Although it was long since Eleanora had seen her daughter Joanna, she tarried but four days in her company, and then sailed for Rome. There is reason to suppose that her errand was to settle a dispute which had arisen between king Richard and his half-brother Geoffrey, the son of Rosamond, whom the king had appointed archbishop of York, according to his father's dying request, but had required an enormous sum from the revenues of the archbishopric.[3] Queen Eleanora returned to England,[4] with her friend the archbishop of Rouen; he was soon after appointed its governor, in place of Longchamp, who had convulsed the country by his follies.

We have seen Eleanora taken from captivity by her son Richard, and invested with the high authority of queen-regent: there is no reason to suppose that that authority was revoked; for, in every emergency during the king's absence, she appears as the guiding power. For this purpose she absented herself from Aquitaine, whose government she placed in the hands of a deputy, her grandson Otho of Saxony;[5] and at the end of the reign of Cœur de Lion, we find her, according to the words of Matthew Paris, "governing England with great wisdom and popularity."

Queen Eleanora, when thus arduously engaged in watching over the interests of her best-beloved son, was approaching her seventieth year—an age when rest is imperiously demanded by the human frame. But years of toil still remained before her, ere death closed her weary pilgrimage in 1204; and these years were laden with sorrows, which drew from her that pathetic alteration of the regal style, preserved in her letter to the pope, on occasion of the captivity of Cœur de Lion, where she declares herself—

"Eleanora,[6] by the wrath of God, queen of England."

Not only in this instance, but in several others, traits of the subdued spirit of Eleanora are to be discovered; for the extreme mobility of her spirits diffused itself even over the cold records of state, when in bitter

---

[1] The documents pertaining to this contract prove that Arthur was then considered, by his uncle, as the heir of England.—Fœdera, vol. i.

[2] See the succeeding memoir. [3] Rapin, vol. i. 248. [4] Speed, 518.

[5] Tyrrell. [6] Peter of Blois's Epistles.

grief she subscribes herself, "*in ira* Dei Regina Anglorum," and "Ælie-nora *misera* et *utinam miserabilis* Anglorum Regina." When swayed by calmer feelings, she styles herself "Ælienora, by the grace of God, *humbly* queen of England."[1]

Eleanora of Aquitaine is among the very few women who have atoned for an ill-spent youth, by a wise and benevolent old age. As a sove-reign, she ranks among the greatest of female rulers.[2]

[1] Rymer, vol. i.
[2] To prevent repetition, the rest of her life is comprehended in the memoirs of her daughters-in-law, Berengaria and Isabella.

END OF VOL. I.

CPSIA information can be obtained at www.ICGtesting.com
Printed in the USA
LVOW111601120812

293999LV00014B/127/P